Exploring American History

David H. Montgomery

CHRISTIAN LIBERTY PRESS
ARLINGTON HEIGHTS, ILLINOIS

Originally published as *The Beginners American History*
Copyright © 1892, 1899, 1902, 1915, 1920 by D. H. Montgomery
Published by Ginn and Company, Proprietors, Boston, USA

Revised and Updated Version
Copyright © 1992 by Christian Liberty Press

Second Edition, Copyright © 2009 by Christian Liberty Press
2014 Printing

A publication of

Christian Liberty Press

502 West Euclid Avenue
Arlington Heights, IL 60004
www.christianlibertypress.com

Written by David H. Montgomery
Revised and Updated Version by Michael J. McHugh and Lars Johnson
Second Edition revisions by Lars Johnson and Edward J. Shewan, and
        Contributions by Jeff Dennison
Copyediting by Diane C. Olson
Layout and editing by Edward J. Shewan
Cover design and layout by Bob Fine
Cover image by Keith Neely

ISBN 978–1–932971–45–3
        1–932971–45–9

Photo Credits
Library of Congress: 311, 314, 315 (left), 325, 330, 334, 334, 338

Printed in the United States of America

Table of Contents

Introduction v

Unit 1   *Exploration of the New World* *1*

    Chapter 1   Leif Ericsson 3

    Chapter 2   Christopher Columbus 6

    Chapter 3   John Cabot 13

    Chapter 4   Spain Explores America 16

    Chapter 5   Sir Walter Raleigh 18

    Chapter 6   John Smith 20

    Chapter 7   Henry Hudson 27

Unit 2   *Settlement of a New Land* *33*

    Chapter 8   Miles Standish 35

    Chapter 9   Lord Baltimore 41

    Chapter 10   Roger Williams 46

    Chapter 11   King Philip 49

    Chapter 12   William Penn 55

    Chapter 13   James Oglethorpe 59

    Chapter 14   George Whitefield 62

Unit 3   *Founding of a New Nation* *67*

    Chapter 15   Benjamin Franklin 69

    Chapter 16   John Witherspoon 76

    Chapter 17   George Washington 82

    Chapter 18   George Rogers Clark 96

    Chapter 19   Daniel Boone 100

    Chapter 20   James Madison 104

    Chapter 21   James McGready 112

Unit 4   *Growth of the Nation* *117*

    Chapter 22   America Adds New States 119

    Chapter 23   Eli Whitney 124

    Chapter 24   Thomas Jefferson 128

    Chapter 25   Robert Fulton 131

    Chapter 26   William Henry Harrison 135

    Chapter 27   Andrew Jackson 138

    Chapter 28   Industrial Development 145

    Chapter 29   Expanding to the Pacific 151

    Chapter 30   Abraham Lincoln 158

    Chapter 31   America Grows Again 169

Unit 5   *Maturing of America* *175*

    Chapter 32   Theodore Roosevelt 177

    Chapter 33   America and the Great War 188

    Chapter 34   J. Gresham Machen 196

    Chapter 35   Franklin D. Roosevelt 200

    Chapter 36   Douglas MacArthur 208

    Chapter 37   Dwight D. Eisenhower 216

    Chapter 38   The United States Changes 224

    Chapter 39   Ronald Reagan 233

    Chapter 40   In Recent Years 238

Appendices *249*

    One: The History of Our Presidents 249

    Two: Important Facts on Our Fifty States and Territories 251

Index *255*

Introduction

This textbook seeks to present accurately those facts and principles in the lives of some of the chief founders and builders of America that would be of interest and value to students pursuing the study of our nation's great heritage. The dramatic, personal aspects of these great men appeal powerfully to students, leading them to see the past as a living present, and to think the thoughts and experience the feelings of people who now live only in their words and deeds. Accordingly, the events of American history described in this text are made to center around some hero, and will hopefully inspire each student to search further into the details of the various personalities of our nation's history.

The authors have endeavored to bring out the influence of the Christian faith as it relates to the events and people of America's past. Young people in America today must not be sheltered from the knowledge that our nation has a rich Christian heritage.

In the hope that this text will be a blessing to each student who studies its pages, it is respectfully presented to the public.

Staff of Christian Liberty Press
Arlington Heights, Illinois

The great comprehensive truths written in letters of living light on every page of our history are these: Human happiness has no perfect security but freedom, freedom none but virtue, virtue none but knowledge; and neither freedom nor virtue has any vigor or immortal hope except in the principles of the Christian faith.

President John Quincy Adams

Unit 1
Exploration of the New World

Chapter 1
Leif Ericsson (970–1020)

Captains of the waves we are—
Kings of the seething foam—
Warriors bold from the Norseland cold—
Far o'er the sea we roam.

The Norsemen. Far away in the cold northern countries that we know as Denmark and Norway and Sweden lived a race of men who called themselves Vikings. They are often called Northmen or Norsemen, but I like best their own name for themselves. *Viking* means "son of the bay" or "raiding sailor," and the name helps us to know what kind of people they were—bold and hardy, fond of adventure, and full of love for the great blue ocean that surged into the thousands of bays along their shores. They built many ships and often made daring voyages to almost every part of Europe, where they often brutalized people who opposed their raids.

Would you like to see a Viking ship? It would not look much like one of our ships today, nor would it travel as fast as ships do now. The bow and the stern rose high out of the water, but the middle was lower and had no deck. Each vessel carried from thirty to sixty oarsmen who used oars twenty feet long. A single mast and only one sail, both of which could be taken down when not in use, completed what may seem to us a strange ship. But they were well built, and in them the Vikings traveled many weeks at a time upon the sea.

If we could have followed these Viking sailors, we would have found some of them going to England and to France, some to Ireland and the smaller islands nearby; but perhaps more than to any other place, they went to build up a Viking colony in Iceland. Their settlements there grew rapidly, and we may read about their farms and hay crops, their sheep and cattle, and—as we should expect—about their ships and trade with all the countries nearby.

Artist Conception of Danish Seamen

The Vikings Travel to America. Only two years after Iceland was settled, one of these ships was driven westward by a storm, until it reached the land we now call Greenland, and many years after that a Viking colony was established there. A few years later, a Viking ship sailed even farther into the unknown west than Greenland. The vessel had started on a voyage from Iceland to Greenland, and the captain had set out, steering by the sun and stars, Viking fashion. But a thick fog came, and neither sun nor stars could be seen. Still, on and on sailed the Viking ship, and after a time welcomed land was seen. It was not snowbound Greenland the ship had reached, however, but a low woody shore that looked very strange to the captain. So he turned back, and it was left for another man to land on the newfound shore.

This man was Leif, son of Eric, or Leif Ericsson, as he is often called. In about the year A.D. 1000, Leif set out to search for the new land. After a short voyage, Leif and his thirty-five followers saw the shore and sailed along beside it for some distance. They called one place they saw Helluland because of its large, flat rocks. Another they called Markland because of its wooded land, and another Vinland because of the wild grapes the Vikings found there. In Vinland they spent the winter and, after going home in the spring, told fine stories of the pleasant land they had found.

Where was Vinland? It was in North America somewhere; most likely in Newfoundland—a province of Canada—since a Viking settlement site now called *L'Anse aux Meadows* was discovered there in 1960. We know, however, that the Vikings made no lasting settlements in Vinland. Some voyages were made to its shores to get wood, but battles with the Native Americans kept the Vikings from making homes in the land they had found. In time they stopped sailing to Vinland and deserted even the Greenland colonies, and the New World was left once more to the natives. The New World that the Vikings called Vinland was forgotten for over 400 years. Finally, in the year 1492, a brave explorer named Christopher Columbus rediscovered the land we call America.

The Northmen on the coast of Greenland

Summary. The Norsemen or Vikings were some of the world's greatest sailors. They sailed from what are now the countries of Denmark, Norway, and Sweden on trading and raiding voyages throughout much of the North Atlantic and Mediterranean. They established settlements in England, France, Ireland, and elsewhere. They also discovered and established colonies on the islands of Iceland and Greenland. The Vikings even landed on the New World but were unable to establish any permanent settlements. It was not until the voyages of Columbus that Europe learned again of the new lands across the Atlantic Ocean.

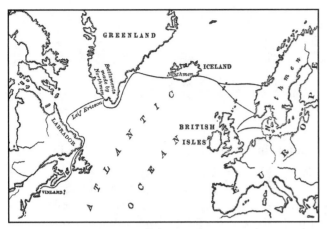

Voyages of the Northmen

Comprehension Questions

1. From where did the Viking people come?

2. What kind of people were they?

3. Describe the kind of ships that they built.

4. List and describe the three places Leif Ericsson found in North America.

5. In 1960, what Viking settlement was discovered in Newfoundland?

6. Why did the Vikings not establish any lasting settlements in America?

Chapter 2
Christopher Columbus (1451–1506)

Christopher Columbus (1451–1506)

A Young Christopher Columbus. Christopher Columbus, the discoverer of America, was born in Genoa, a seaport of Italy, more than 550 years ago. His father was a wool comber, separating fibers for spinning. Christopher did not want to learn that trade, but wanted to become a sailor. Seeing the boy's strong liking for the sea, his father sent him to a school where he could learn geography, map drawing, and whatever else might help him to become, someday, commander of a ship.

When he was fourteen Columbus went to sea. In those days, the Mediterranean Sea swarmed with warships and pirates. Every sailor, no matter if he was but a boy, had to stand ready to fight his way from port to port.

In this exciting life, full of adventure and of danger, Columbus grew to manhood. The rough experiences he then had did much to make him the brave, determined captain and explorer that he afterwards became.

According to some accounts, Columbus once had a desperate battle with a ship off the coast of Portugal. The fight lasted all day. At length, both vessels caught fire. Columbus jumped from his blazing ship into the sea and, catching hold of a floating oar, managed to swim to the shore about six miles away.

"By sailing west, I shall be able to reach the Indies."

He then went to the port of Lisbon. There he married the daughter of a famous sea captain. For a long time after his marriage Columbus earned his living partly by drawing maps, which he sold to commanders of vessels visiting Lisbon, and partly by making voyages to Africa, Iceland, and other lands.

Columbus's Plan for Reaching the Indies. The maps that Columbus made and sold were very different from those we now have. At that time, only half of the world had been discovered. Europe, Asia, and a small part of Africa were the primary places known. The maps that Columbus had might have shown the earth shaped like a ball, but he supposed it to be much smaller than it really is. No one at this time had sailed around the globe. Therefore, no one knew what lands lay west of the broad Atlantic. For this reason we would look in vain on one of the maps drawn by Columbus for the great continents of North and South America or for Australia or the Pacific Ocean.

While living in Lisbon, Columbus made up his mind to try to do what no other man at that time dared try—that was to cross the Atlantic Ocean. He thought that by doing so, he could get directly to Asia and the islands of Southeast Asia called the Indies, which, he believed, were opposite Portugal and Spain. If successful, he could open a very profitable trade with the rich countries of the East, where spices, drugs, and silk were brought to Europe. The people of Europe could not reach those countries directly by ships because they had not yet found their way around the southern point of Africa.

The light-shaded area in the map above shows the known world in the days of Columbus.

Columbus was too poor to buy even a single ship to undertake such a voyage as he had planned. He asked the king of Portugal to provide some money or vessels, but the Portuguese were already trying to get to the East by going around Africa. The king decided not to help Columbus after a Portuguese ship was able to get to India by going around the southern tip of Africa.

Columbus decided, therefore, to see if he could get help from somewhere else. His brother contacted the king of England, and Columbus went back to Italy. The cities of Genoa and Venice did not want to assist Columbus, and Henry VII of England expressed some interest but took too long to decide. Columbus determined, therefore, to go to Spain and see if he could get help there.

On the southern coast of Spain, there is a small port named Palos. Within sight of the village of Palos, and within plain sight of the ocean, there was a convent called the Convent of St. Mary. One morning a tall, fine-looking man, leading a little boy by the hand, knocked at the door of this convent and begged for a piece of bread and a cup of water for the child. The man was Columbus, whose wife was now dead, and the boy was his son.

Isabella I (1451–1504)
Queen of Castile and León

The guardian of the convent noticed Columbus standing at the door. He liked his appearance and, coming up, began to talk with him. Columbus frankly told him what he was trying to do. The guardian of the convent listened with great interest; then he gave him a letter to a friend who, he thought, would help him to lay his plans before Ferdinand and Isabella, the king and queen of Spain.

Columbus left his son at the convent and set out on his journey, full of bright hopes. But Ferdinand and Isabella could not see him. After waiting a long time, the traveler was told that he might go before several learned men and tell them about his proposed voyage across the Atlantic.

People who heard what this captain from Lisbon wanted to do thought he had lost his mind. Boys in the streets laughed at him and called him crazy. Columbus waited for help seven years; he then made up his mind that he would wait no longer. Just as he was about to leave Spain, Queen Isabella, who had always felt interested in the brave sailor, resolved to aid him. Two rich sea captains who lived in Palos also decided to take part in the voyage. With the help that Columbus now received, he could get three small vessels—the *Santa Maria*, the *Pinta*, and the *Niña*. He went in the *Santa Maria*—the largest ship and the only one that had an entire deck—as admiral, or commander of the fleet.

Columbus's Journey Begins. Early on Friday morning, August 3, 1492, Columbus started from Palos to try to cross that ocean which men then called the "Sea of Darkness"—a name that showed how little they knew of it, and how much they feared it. We may be pretty sure that the guardian of the convent was one of those who watched the sailing of the little fleet. From the upper windows of the convent he could plainly see the vessels as they left the harbor of Palos.

Columbus sailed first for the Canary Islands because, from there, he thought it would be a straight line across to Japan and Asia. He was forced to stop at the Canaries from August 12 to September 6—more than three weeks—to make a new rudder for one of his ships and to change the sails of another.

In 1892, replicas of the *Niña, Pinta,* and *Santa Maria* sailed from Spain to the Columbian Exposition in Chicago.

Finally, all was ready, and he again set out on his voyage toward the west. When the ships sailed so far out on the ocean that the sailors could no longer see any of the islands, they became very frightened. They feared they would never be able to get back to Palos again. They were rough men, used to the sea, but now they bowed their heads and cried like children. Columbus had to work hard to quiet their fears and to encourage them to go forward with the voyage that they already wanted to give up.

For more than thirty days, the three ships continued on their way toward the west. To the crew every day seemed like a year. From sunrise to sunset nothing was to be seen but water and sky. Eventually, the men began to think that they were sailing on an ocean that had no end. They whispered among themselves that Columbus had gone mad and that if they continued with him in command they should all be lost.

Twice there was a joyful cry of "Land! Land!" But, when they got nearer they saw that what they had thought was land was nothing but banks of clouds. Then some sailors thought they should go to the admiral and tell him that the ships must turn back. Other sailors wondered what they should do if Columbus would not listen to them. Some thought that they should throw him overboard and explain, when the ships returned to Palos, that Columbus fell into the sea and was drowned.

But, when the crew went to Columbus and told him that they would go no further, he sternly ordered them to their work, declaring that, whatever might happen, he would not now give up the voyage. Columbus had more courage than his crew because he sincerely believed that his voyage had an

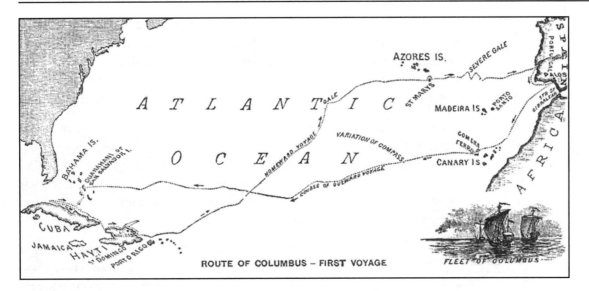

ROUTE OF COLUMBUS – FIRST VOYAGE

important, God-ordained purpose and that God would protect him as he sought to bring Christianity to new lands.

Land Is Discovered. The very next day such certain signs of land were seen that even the most faint-hearted took courage. The men had already noticed great flocks of land birds flying westward, as if to guide them. Now some men on one vessel saw a branch of a thorn bush float by. It was plain that it had not long been broken off the bush, and it was full of red berries.

But a sailor on one of the other vessels found something even better than the thorn branch. He drew out of the water a carved walking stick! Everyone saw that such a stick must have been cut and carved by human hands. These two signs could not be doubted. The men now felt sure that they were approaching the shore, and what was more, there were people living in that foreign land.

That evening Columbus begged his crew to keep a sharp lookout, and he promised a velvet coat to the one who would first see land. All of the men were excited, and no man closed his eyes in sleep that night.

Columbus himself stood on a high part of his ship, looking steadily toward the west. About ten o'clock, he saw a moving light; it seemed like a torch carried in a man's hand. He called to a companion and asked him if he could see anything of the kind. Yes, he, too, plainly saw the moving light, but soon it disappeared.

Two hours after midnight, a cannon was fired from the leading vessel. It was the glad signal that the long-looked-for land was in sight. There it lay directly ahead, about six miles away.

Then Columbus gave the order to furl sails, and the three vessels came to a stop and waited for the dawn. When the sun rose on Friday, October 12, 1492, Columbus saw a beautiful island with many trees growing on it. That was his first sight of the New World.

Attended by the captains of the other two vessels, and by a part of their crews, Columbus set out in a boat for the island. When they landed, all fell on their knees, kissed the ground for joy, and gave thanks to God. Columbus named the island San Salvador (which means "Holy Savior") and took possession of it, by right of discovery, for the king and queen of Spain.

He found that a copper-colored people—who spoke a language he could not understand—inhabited the land. These people had never seen a ship or a white man before. They wore no clothing, but painted their bodies with bright colors. The Spaniards made them presents of strings of glass beads and red caps. In return they gave the Spaniards rolls of cotton yarn, tame parrots, and small ornaments of gold.

Landing of Columbus

After staying here a short time Columbus set sail southward, in search of more land and in the hope of finding out where these people got their gold. Columbus also wanted the opportunity to spread the Christian religion to as many foreign lands as possible.

As Columbus sailed on, he saw many islands in every direction. He thought that they must be part of the Indies he was seeking. Since he had reached them by traveling west from Spain, he called them the West Indies, and to the red men who lived on them, he gave the name of Indians.

During the next six weeks, Columbus discovered the island of Cuba. At first, he thought it must be Japan, but afterward he came to the wrong conclusion that it was not an island at all, but part of the mainland of Asia.

Columbus Returns to Spain. Columbus next came to the large island of Hispaniola (now the Republic of Haiti and the Dominican Republic). Here his ship was wrecked. He took the timber from the wreck and built a fort on the shore. Leaving about forty of his crew in this fort, Columbus set sail for Palos in one of the two remaining vessels.

Columbus's Coat of Arms

When the ship of Columbus was seen entering the harbor of Palos, the whole village was wild with excitement. More that seven months had passed since he sailed away from that port, and as nothing had been heard from him, many thought that the vessels and all on board had been lost. They were happy to see their friends and neighbors coming back home. The bells of the churches rang a merry song of welcome; the people crowded the streets, shouting to each other that Columbus, the great navigator, had crossed the "Sea of Darkness" and had returned in safety.

The king and queen were then in Barcelona, a long distance from Palos. To that city Columbus now went. He entered it on horseback, attended by the proudest and richest noblemen of Spain. He brought with him six Indians from the West Indies. They were gaily painted and wore bright feathers in their hair. Then many men followed, carrying rare birds, plants, and gold and silver ornaments, all found in the New World. These were presents for the king and queen. Ferdinand and Isabella received Columbus with great honor. When he had told them the story of his wonderful voyage, they sank on their knees and gave praise to God; all who were present followed their example.

Columbus's Remaining Days. Columbus made three more voyages across the Atlantic. He discovered more islands near the coast of America, and he touched the coast of Central America and of South America. He never set foot on any part of what is now the mainland of the United States, and he always thought that the land he had reached was part of Asia. He had rediscovered a new world, but he did not know it. All that he knew was how to get to it and how to show others the way.

The King and Queen Receive Columbus with Great Ceremony

The last days of this great man were very sad. The king was disappointed because he brought back no gold to amount to anything. The Spanish governor of San Domingo hated Columbus, and when he landed at that island on one of his voyages, he arrested him and sent him back to Spain in chains. He was immediately set at liberty, but he could not forget the insult. He kept the chains hanging on the wall of his room and asked to have them buried with him.

Columbus was now an old man; his health was broken, he was poor, in debt, and without a home. Once he wrote to the king and queen saying, "I have not a hair upon me that is not gray, my body is weak, and all that was left to me … has been taken away and sold, even the coat which I wore."

Not long after he came back to Spain to stay, the queen died. Then Columbus felt that he had lost his best friend. He gave up hope and said, "I have done all that I could do; I leave the rest to God."

Columbus died full of sadness—maybe it would not be too much to say that he died of a broken heart. He was first buried in Spain; then his body was taken up and carried to San Domingo, where he had wished to be buried. It is hard to say where the body of Columbus found its final resting place. But wherever the grave of the great sailor may be, his memory will live in every heart capable of respecting a brave man; for he first dared to cross the "Sea of Darkness," and he rediscovered the forgotten land of America.

Columbus in Chains

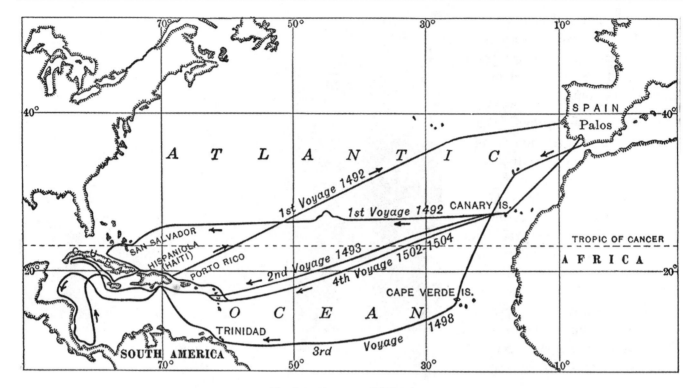

The Four Voyages of Columbus

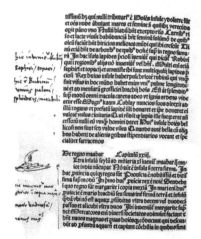

On the left are handwritten notes by Christopher Columbus on the Latin edition of Marco Polo's *Le livre des merveilles* (*The Book of Wonders*).

Summary. In 1492, Christopher Columbus set sail from Spain to find a direct way across the Atlantic to Asia and the Indies. He did not get to Asia, but he did better: he discovered America. He died thinking that the new lands he had found were part of Asia, but by his daring voyage, he first showed the people of Europe how to get to the New World.

Comprehension Questions

1. When and where was Columbus born?

2. What did he do in Lisbon?

3. How much of the world was then known?

4. Why did Columbus go to Spain?

5. How did Columbus finally get help?

6. When did he sail?

7. What happened on the first part of the voyage?

8. Did Columbus think he landed on the Indies?

9. What did Columbus name the island he first landed upon?

10. Did Columbus ever land on any part of what is now the United States?

11. What happened to Columbus in his old age?

Chapter 3
John Cabot (1450–1498)

Spain was not the only country interested in getting to the East by sailing west across the Atlantic Ocean, nor was it the only country to use an Italian sailor to find a way to do so. John Cabot, an Italian merchant, led two voyages of exploration for England in the late 1490s, establishing England's first claims to the New World.

Cabot's early life is something of a mystery, but he is thought to have been born in Naples, Italy. He later moved to Venice, becoming a Venetian citizen in 1476. He was a merchant, trading in the eastern Mediterranean. During Cabot's time in Venice, he married and had three sons, one of whom—Sebastian—also became a famous explorer. He moved to Bristol, England, with his family around 1490.

John Cabot (1450–1498)

John Cabot Discovers the Continent of North America. When Columbus set out on his first voyage across the Atlantic in 1492, John Cabot, an Italian merchant, was living in Bristol, England. When the news reached that city that Columbus had discovered the West Indies, Cabot begged Henry VII, king of England, to let him see if he could find a shorter way to the Indies than that of Columbus. The king gave his consent; and in the spring of 1497 John Cabot, with his son Sebastian, sailed from Bristol. They headed their vessel *Matthew* toward the northwest; by going in that direction they hoped to get to those parts of Asia and the Spice Islands that were known to Europe, which Columbus had failed to reach.

Early one bright morning, near the end of June 1497, they saw land in the west. It was probably Cape Breton Island, a part of Nova Scotia, or Newfoundland. John Cabot named it "The Land First Seen." Cabot thought he had reached an island off of the coast of Asia, never realizing he had actually discovered a new continent. Up to this time, Columbus had discovered only the West Indies, but John Cabot now saw the continent of North America. No English explorer had ever seen it before. There it lay—a great, lonely land, shaggy with forests, with not a house or a human being in sight.

Cabot is thought to have gone ashore at Cape Bonavista, Newfoundland, with his son and some of his crew. In the vast, silent wilderness

Atlantic Ocean

Henry VII (1457–1509)

they set up a large cross. Near to it they planted two flagpoles, and hoisted the English flag on one and the flag of Venice, the city where John Cabot had lived in Italy, on the other. Then they took possession of the land for Henry VII. It was in this way that the English came to consider that the eastern coast of North America was their property, although they did not begin to make settlements there until nearly 100 years later. Cabot also mapped the shore from Nova Scotia to Newfoundland.

After sailing through the Gulf of St. Lawrence without finding the passage to Asia for which they were looking, the sailors returned to England. The Cabots took back to England some Indian traps for catching game and some wild turkeys, an American bird the English had never seen, but whose acquaintance they were not sorry to make. They also brought the rib of a whale, which they had found on the beach in Nova Scotia.

They also brought fish back to England. Cabot had the hold of the *Matthew* filled with cod, a fish prized by many in England. John Cabot reported when he got back to England that the sea near Newfoundland was so thick with fish that they slowed down the passage of his ship. The discovery of the teeming fish in these waters ignited a Newfoundland fishing industry that lasted for hundreds of years. Soon, fishing boats from Portugal, Spain, France, and England were actively catching fish in the New World.

The king was so pleased with what John Cabot had discovered that he made him a handsome present and gave him a yearly pension. When the captain, richly dressed in silk, appeared in the street, the people of Bristol would run after him and cheer for the "Great Admiral," as they called him.

Land First Discovered by John Cabot

Cabot's 1497 voyage helped the English begin to see what a large piece of land they had found beyond the Atlantic. They could not tell, however, whether it was a separate continent or a part of Asia. Like everybody in Europe, they called it the New World, which simply meant the new lands that had been discovered across the Atlantic Ocean.

About a year later, John Cabot set out on a second voyage to the west. He left with five ships from Bristol in May 1498, but he never returned or was heard from again. Only one ship made it back to Bristol, having been damaged in a storm. No one really knows what happened to John Cabot during his last trip to the New World.

CABOT TAKING POSSESSION FOR ENGLAND

America. Columbus and Cabot believed until their deaths that they had found land either on or near Asia. Cabot, for example, hoped with his voyage of 1498 to find a northern route to Japan and Asia. Soon afterwards, however, European explorers began to realize that Columbus had discovered a completely new land. It was not many years later that the New World received the name by which we now call it.

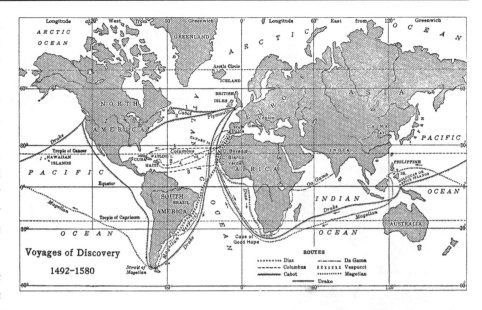

Voyages of Discovery
1492–1580

Another Italian navigator by the name of Amerigo Vespucci made at least two voyages to the New World between 1497 and 1502. He helped explore the coastlines of Central and South America, traveling at least as far south as Brazil. He wrote an account of what he saw and described the new land as a separate continent, rather than just as a part of Asia.

The New World came to be called *America* due to the work of a German geographer and mapmaker, Martin Waldseemüller. In 1507, Waldseemüller published a world map and named the New World *America* after Amerigo Vespucci. Evidently, Waldseemüller considered Amerigo Vespucci to be the true discoverer of America, since he was the first to realize that it was a new land, rather than part of Asia. Others later argued that the New World should be named *Columbia* after Christopher Columbus, but it was too late. *America* had become the accepted name for the New World.

Amerigo Vespucci (1454–1512)

Summary. In 1497 John Cabot and his son, Sebastian, sailed from Bristol, England, and discovered the mainland or continent of North America; they took possession of it for England. The next year they came over and sailed along the eastern coast of what is now the United States. An Italian whose name was Amerigo Vespucci visited the New World and afterward wrote the first published account of the mainland. For this reason, the new land was named after him, *America*.

Comprehension Questions

1. Who was John Cabot?
2. What did John Cabot hope to discover during his first voyage?
3. What land did John Cabot discover on his 1497 voyage?
4. What town in England did the Cabots sail from?
5. What did Cabot bring back from the New World?
6. How did the New World come to be called *America*?

Chapter 4
Spain Explores America (1513–1542)

Juan Ponce de León (1460–1521)

Spanish Explorers. The Indians in the islands of the West Indies believed there was a wonderful fountain in a land to the west of them. They said that if an old man should bathe in its waters, he would become a boy again. Ponce de León, a Spanish soldier who was getting gray and wrinkled, set out to find this magic fountain, for he thought there was more fun in being a boy than in growing old.

He did not find the fountain, and so his hair grew grayer than ever, and his wrinkles grew deeper. But in 1513 he discovered a land bright with flowers, which he named Florida. He took possession of it for Spain.

The same year another Spaniard, named Vasco de Balboa, set out to explore the Isthmus of Panama. One day he climbed to the top of a very high hill and discovered that vast ocean—the greatest of all the oceans of the globe—which we call the Pacific.

Long after Balboa and Ponce de León were dead, a Spaniard named Hernando de Soto landed in Florida and marched through the country in search of gold mines.

Hernando de Soto (1496–1542)

During his long and weary wanderings, he came to a river more than a mile across. The Indians told him it was the Mississippi, or the Great River. In discovering it, de Soto had found the largest river in North America. He had also found his own grave, for he died shortly afterward, and was secretly buried at midnight in its muddy waters.

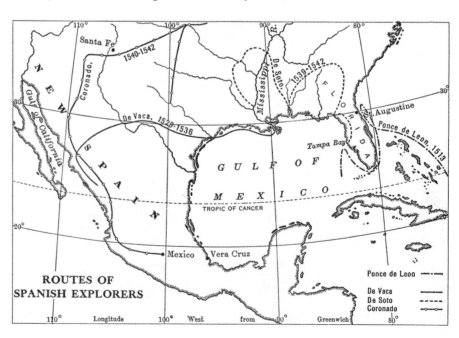

ROUTES OF SPANISH EXPLORERS

Florida. It was some time after Ponce de León first discovered Florida in 1513 and claimed it before the Spanish tried to establish a settlement in the area. The first attempt was at Pensacola in northern Florida. The Spanish settled there in 1559 but abandoned the area in 1561. A Spanish soldier named Pedro Menéndez de Avilés made a second try. In 1565, Menéndez built a fort on the eastern coast, which became the center of a settlement named St. Augustine. It is the oldest continuously occupied city built by European settlers, not only in what is now the United States, but also in all of North America.

Only one other Spanish settlement was ever established in Florida. Pensacola was reoccupied in 1695 to block French expansion east from Mobile along the Gulf of Mexico. Spanish Catholic missionaries established many missions among the Indians of north Florida, beginning in the late 1500s. These missions were initially successful, with about 40 missions and approximately 30,000 native converts by 1635. However, by 1711, the number of converts had declined dramatically as a result of war and disease. The remaining 400 were resettled near St. Augustine.

The Spanish never had firm control over Florida and were often threatened by the French and British. Menéndez conquered a nearby French colony that had been established the year before, killing most of the inhabitants. The British attacked St. Augustine several times during the 1700s and even controlled Florida between 1763 and 1783.

The Spanish regained Florida after the United States won its independence from Great Britain. However, the Spanish did not have any greater control over Florida than they had before. Unrest from American settlers who had moved to Florida and conflict with the United States caused Spain to give up Florida to the United States. Spain agreed in 1819—more than 250 years after St. Augustine was founded—to sell Florida to the United States.

Summary. Ponce de León discovered Florida; another Spaniard, named Balboa, discovered the Pacific; and still another, named de Soto, discovered the Mississippi. In 1565, the Spaniards began to build St. Augustine in Florida. It is the oldest city built by Europeans in the United States or in all of North America.

Pedro Menéndez de Avilés
(1519–1574)

Vasco Núñez de Balboa
(1475–1519)

Comprehension Questions

1. What did Ponce de León think the "magic" fountain could do?
2. What did Ponce de León do?
3. What body of water did Balboa discover?
4. What great river did Hernando de Soto discover?
5. What is the name of the oldest city built by Europeans in North America?

Chapter 5
Sir Walter Raleigh (1552–1618)

The First Virginia Colony. Although John Cabot discovered the continent of North America in 1497 and took possession of the land for England, the English themselves did not try to settle North America until nearly 100 years later.

In 1584, a young man named Walter Raleigh, who was a great favorite of Queen Elizabeth I, sent out two ships to America. The captains of these vessels landed on Roanoke Island, off the coast of

Sir Walter Raleigh (1552–1618)

what is now the state of North Carolina. They found the island covered with tall red cedars and with vines thick with clusters of wild grapes. The Indians called this place the "Good Land." They were pleased to see the Englishmen, and they invited them to a great feast of roast turkey, venison, melons, and nuts.

When the two captains returned to England, Queen Elizabeth I (the "Virgin Queen," as she was called) was delighted with what she heard of the "Good Land." She named it Virginia in honor of herself. She also gave Raleigh a title of honor. From that time he was no longer simply called Mr. Raleigh, but Sir Walter Raleigh.

Sir Walter shipped over English people as emigrants to settle in Virginia during 1585. They sent back to him, as a present, two famous American plants: one called tobacco, the other the potato. The queen had given Sir Walter a fine estate in Ireland, and he set out both plants in his garden. The tobacco plant did not grow very well there, but the potato did; and after a short time thousands of farmers began to raise that vegetable throughout Ireland and England. As far back as that time—or more than 400 years ago—America was beginning to feed the people of the Old World.

Sir Walter spent immense sums of money on his settlement in Virginia, but it did not succeed. One of the settlers, named Dare, had a daughter born there. He named her Virginia Dare. She was the first English child born in America. But the little girl, with her father and mother and all the rest of the settlers, disappeared. It is supposed that the Indians killed them

Queen Elizabeth I
(1533–1603)

or that they wandered away and starved to death; but all that we really know is that not one of them was ever seen again.

The Last Days of Sir Walter Raleigh. After Queen Elizabeth died, King James became ruler of England. He accused Sir Walter of trying to take away his crown in order to make someone else ruler over the country. Sir Walter was sent to prison and kept there for many years. Eventually, King James released him in order to send him to South America to get gold. When Sir Walter returned to London without any gold, the greedy king accused him of having disobeyed him because he had fought with some Spaniards. Raleigh was condemned to death and was beheaded.

But Sir Walter's attempt to settle Virginia led other Englishmen to try. Before he died they built a town, called Jamestown, on the coast. We shall soon read about the history of that town. The English held Virginia from that time until it became part of the United States.

Summary. Sir Walter Raleigh sent over men from England to explore the coast of America. Queen Elizabeth named the country they visited Virginia. Raleigh then shipped emigrants over to make a settlement. These emigrants sent him two American plants, tobacco and the potato; the people of Great Britain and Ireland came to like them both. Sir Walter's settlement failed, but his example led other Englishmen to try to make one. Before he was beheaded, they had succeeded in developing a prosperous settlement in the colony of Virginia.

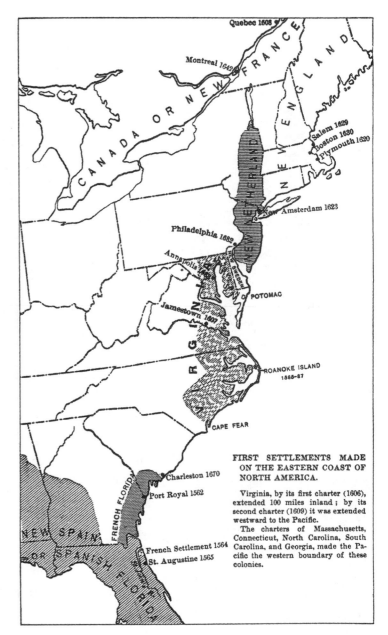

FIRST SETTLEMENTS MADE ON THE EASTERN COAST OF NORTH AMERICA.

Virginia, by its first charter (1606), extended 100 miles inland; by its second charter (1609) it was extended westward to the Pacific.

The charters of Massachusetts, Connecticut, North Carolina, South Carolina, and Georgia, made the Pacific the western boundary of these colonies.

Comprehension Questions

1. Who was Sir Walter Raleigh?
2. What name did Queen Elizabeth give to the country?
3. What American plants did the emigrants send Raleigh?
4. What did he do with those plants?
5. What happened to the Virginia settlement?
6. How did Sir Walter Raleigh die?

Chapter 6
John Smith (1579–1631)

Captain John Smith (1579–1631)

John Smith and a New Settlement in Virginia. One of the leaders in the new expedition, who set out to make a settlement in Virginia while Raleigh was in prison, was Captain John Smith. He began life as a clerk in England. Not liking his work, he ran away and turned soldier. After many strange adventures, he was captured by the Turks and sold as a slave. His master, who was a Turk, placed a heavy iron collar around his neck and forced him to thresh grain with a big wooden club. One day the Turk rode up and struck his slave with his riding whip. This was more than Smith could bear; he rushed at his master, and with one blow of his club he killed the foolish Turk. He then mounted the dead man's horse and escaped. After a time he returned to England, but as England seemed a little dull to Captain Smith, he decided to join some emigrants who were going to Virginia.

On the way to America, Smith was accused of plotting to murder the chief men among the emigrants so that he might make himself "King of Virginia." The accusation was false, but he was put in irons and kept a prisoner for the rest of the voyage.

In the spring of 1607 the emigrants reached Chesapeake Bay and sailed up a river, which they named the James River in honor of King James I of England. When they landed they named the settlement Jamestown for the same reason. Here they built a log fort and placed three or four small cannon on its walls. Most of the men who settled Jamestown came hoping to find mines of gold in Virginia, or else a way through to the Pacific Ocean and the Indies, which they thought could not be very far away. But Captain Smith wanted to help his countrymen to make homes in Virginia for themselves and their children.

As soon as Captain Smith landed, he demanded to be tried by a jury of twelve men. The trial took place. It was the first English court and the first English jury that ever sat in America. The captain proved his innocence and was set free. His chief accuser was required to pay him a large sum of money for damages. Smith kindly gave this money to help the settlement.

As the weather was warm, the emigrants did not begin building log cabins immediately, but slept on the ground, sheltered by boughs of trees. For a church they had an old tent, in which they met on Sunday. They were all members of the Church of England (the Anglican Church).

When the cold weather came, many people became sick. Soon the whole settlement was like a hospital. Sometimes three or four would die in one night. Captain Smith, though not well himself, did everything he could for those who needed his help.

When the sickness was over, some of the settlers were so unhappy that they determined to seize the only vessel there was at Jamestown and go back to England. Captain Smith turned the cannon of the fort against them. The deserters saw that if they tried to leave the harbor he would blast their vessel to pieces, so they came back. One of the leaders of these men was tried and shot; the other was sent to England in disgrace.

The Native Americans of Virginia. When the Indians of America first met Europeans, they were usually friendly to them. This did not last long because the whites often treated the Indians very badly. In fact, the Spaniards made slaves of the Indians and whipped many of them to death. But these were generally the Indians of the West Indies and South America. Some of the Indian tribes of North America, especially those in what is now New York State, were terribly fierce and a match for the Spaniards in cruelty.

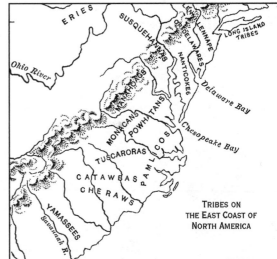

TRIBES ON
THE EAST COAST OF
NORTH AMERICA

The Indians in the East did not build cities, but lived in small villages. These villages were made up of huts, covered with the bark of trees. Such huts were called wigwams. The women did nearly all the work, such as building the wigwams and hoeing corn and tobacco. The men hunted and made war. Instead of guns, the Indians had bows and arrows. With these, they could bring down a deer or a squirrel quite as well as a white man could with a rifle. They had no iron, but made hatchets and knives out of sharp, flat stones.

The Indians never built roads, for they had no wagons, and in the eastern part of America they did not use horses; but they could find their way with ease through the thickest forest. When they came to a river they swam across it, so they had no need of bridges. In small boats, known as canoes, they could go hundreds of miles quickly and silently. Thus every river and stream throughout North America became a roadway to the Indian.

The Native Americans made canoes of birch bark. These canoes were almost as light as paper, yet they were very strong and handsome. The poet Longfellow described the gracefulness of canoes in this passage from his famous epic poem *The Song of Hiawatha*.

> Give me of your bark, O Birch-tree!
> Of your yellow bark, O Birch-tree!
> Growing by the rushing river,
> Tall and stately in the valley!
>
> I a light canoe will build me,
> Build a swift [canoe] for sailing,
> That shall float on the river,
> Like a yellow leaf in Autumn,
> Like a yellow water-lily!

POCKET COMPASS

The tribes in eastern Virginia near Jamestown were part of the Powhatan Confederacy, an alliance of thirty tribes. A chief named Wahunsenacawh, who was also known as Chief Powhatan, ruled this confederacy. Powhatan was initially friendly with the English settlers but came to believe that they were dangerous.

Captain Smith and the Indians. After that first long, hot summer was over, some of the settlers wished to explore the country and see if they could find a short way through to the Pacific Ocean. Captain Smith led the expedition. Indians of the Powhatan Confederacy attacked them, killed three of the men, and took the captain prisoner. To amuse his captors, Smith showed them his pocket compass. When the warriors saw that the needle always pointed toward the north, they were greatly astonished; and instead of killing their prisoner, they decided to take him to their chief. Powhatan had come to hate the settlers at Jamestown because he thought that they had come to steal land from his confederacy.

Smith was dragged before Chief Powhatan. Smith's head was laid on a large, round log, and a tall warrior stood ready to kill him. Just as Powhatan was about to cry "Strike!" his daughter Pocahontas, a girl of twelve or thirteen, ran up and, putting her arms around the prisoner's head, laid her own head on his. Now let the Indian warrior strike with his weapon, if he dare.

Instead of being angry with his daughter, Powhatan promised her that he would spare Smith's life. When an Indian made such a promise, he kept it, so the captain knew that his head was safe. Powhatan released his prisoner and soon sent him back to Jamestown; and Pocahontas, followed by many Indians, carried to the settlers presents of corn and venison.

Some years after this, the Indian maiden married John Rolfe, an Englishman who had come to Virginia. They went to London, and Pocahontas died not far from that city. She left a son, and from that son came some noted Virginians. One of them was John Randolph. He was a famous man in his day, and he always spoke with pride of the Indian princess, as he called her.

The "Father of Virginia." More emigrants came over from England, and Captain Smith was now made governor of Jamestown. Some of the emigrants found some glittering earth, which they thought was gold. Soon nearly everyone was hard at work digging it. Smith laughed at them, but they insisted on loading a ship with the worthless stuff and sending it to London. That was the last that was heard of it.

The people had wasted their time digging this shining dirt when they should have been hoeing their gardens. Soon they began to run out of food. The captain started off with a party of men to buy corn from the Indians. The Indians made up an evil plot to kill the whole party. Fortunately, Smith discovered the plan. Seizing the chief by the hair, he pressed the muzzle of a pistol against his heart and gave him his choice: "Corn, or your life!" He received the corn, and plenty of it.

Captain Smith then ordered part of the men to plant corn, so that they might grow what they needed. The rest of the settlers he took with him into the woods to chop down trees and saw them into boards to send to England. Many tried to escape from this labor, but Smith said, "Men who are able to dig for gold can chop." Then he made this rule: "He who will not work shall not eat." Rather than lose his dinner, the laziest man now took his ax and ran off for the woods.

Although the choppers worked, they grumbled. They liked to see the chips fly and to hear the great trees "thunder as they fell," but the ax handles raised blisters on their fingers. These blisters made the men swear, so that commonly one would hear "a loud oath" at every third stroke of the ax. Smith said the swearing must be stopped. He had each man's oaths numbered. When the day's work was done, every offender was called up. His oaths were counted; then he was told to hold up his right hand, and a can of cold water was poured down his sleeve for each oath. This new style of water cure did wonders. In a short time hardly a single grumble would be heard in a whole week. It was just chop, chop, chop; and the madder the men became, the more the chips would fly.

Captain Smith was not governor for very long. He was actually in Virginia for less than three years; yet in that short time he did a great deal. First, he saved the settlers from starving by making the Indians sell them corn. Next, by his courage, he saved them from the attacks of the Indians. Lastly, he taught them how to work. Had it not been for him, the people of Jamestown would probably have lost all heart and gone back to England. He insisted on staying; and so, through him, the English held their first real foothold in America. But this was not all; he wrote two books on Virginia, describing the soil, the trees, the animals, and the Indians. He also made some excellent maps of Virginia and of New England. These books and maps taught the English people many things about this country, and were a great help to those who wished to travel to America. For these reasons, Captain Smith has rightfully been called the "Father of Virginia."

Smith was forced to leave Jamestown after he met with a terrible accident. He was out in a boat, and a bag of gunpowder he had with him exploded. He was so badly hurt that he had to go back to England to get proper treatment for his wounds. John Smith never came back to Virginia, but he did return to America several years later. He explored the

This statue of Pocahontas (1595–1617) by William Ordway Partridge, was erected in Jamestown, Virginia, in 1922.

"CORN, OR YOUR LIFE!"

Sir William Berkeley (1605–1677)

Sir William Berkeley was governor of Virginia longer than any other man, from 1642 until 1652 and from 1660 until his death in 1677. He advocated economic diversification and promoted trade between the colonists and the Virginia Indians. He allowed the two houses of the General Assembly to develop into a responsible and mature parliamentary body that legislated in the interests of the great planter families who dominated Virginia politics throughout much of the colonial period. Berkeley generally discouraged the persecution of religious minorities and steered a middle course between the factions during the English Civil Wars. His leadership taught Virginians how to settle differences peacefully or to live with differences that could not be settled peacefully. Although Bacon's Rebellion of 1676 almost destroyed Berkeley's legacy, the political culture that Berkeley helped create survived for two centuries.

The Library of Virginia
Richmond, Virginia

coast north of Virginia and gave it the name of New England. He died in England and was buried in the Church of the Holy Sepulchre, a famous Anglican church in the city of London.

The Decline of Jamestown. In 1619, about ten years after Captain Smith left Jamestown, the commander of a Dutch ship brought many African slaves to Virginia and sold them to the settlers. That was the beginning of slavery in what became the United States. Later, when other English settlements had been made, they also bought slaves; and so, after a time, every settlement both north and south owned slaves. The people of Virginia used most of their slaves in raising tobacco. They sold this in England; and as it generally brought a good price, many of the planters became quite rich. It would take almost 250 years and much bloodshed before slavery would be finally ended in America.

Long after Captain Smith was in his grave, Sir William Berkeley was made governor of Virginia by the king of England. Governor Berkeley treated the people very badly. Finally, a young planter named Nathaniel Bacon raised a small army and marched against the governor, who was in Jamestown. The governor, finding that he had few friends to fight for him, moved quickly to get out of the place. Bacon then entered it with his men; but he knew that, if necessary, the king would send soldiers from England to aid the governor in getting it back. So he set fire to the place and burned it.

Jamestown was rebuilt, but the settlement was eventually abandoned. The colonial capitol was moved to the town of Williamsburg in 1699 after the capital building in Jamestown had burned down for the fourth time. The legislature decided that the location of Jamestown was too unhealthy and the capital building too prone to burning. Once Williamsburg had become the colonial capitol, Jamestown lost its importance, and people began to move away from what was actually a low-lying, swampy area. Even the old church building in Jamestown was closed in the 1750s. Only scattered farms were left in the area. Eventually, only a crumbling church tower and a few gravestones were left where Jamestown once stood.

The Old Church Tower in Jamestown

However, Jamestown has not been forgotten. Historic Jamestown is now part of the Colonial National Historic Park. Only a few people, therefore, actually live at Jamestown, but they are always ready to show visitors where Captain Smith and his companions made their settlement. The place is marked by a splendid monument to Captain Smith and by the tower of the old Jamestown church.

The rise of tobacco as a cash crop led to Virginia importing its first slaves in 1619. The painting above shows enslaved Africans working in the tobacco sheds of a colonial tobacco plantation.

Virginia's Importance. Although Jamestown was abandoned, Virginia kept growing in strength and wealth. What was better still, the country grew in the number of its great men. The king of England continued to rule America until 1776, when many of the people of Virginia demanded that independence should be declared. The War for American Independence overthrew the king's power and made us free. The military leader of that war was a Virginia planter named George Washington.

After the United States had gained the victory and peace was made, the people chose presidents to govern the country. Four out of five of our first presidents, beginning with Washington, came from Virginia. For this reason that state has sometimes been called the "Mother of Presidents." One of the most famous men during the War for Independence, Patrick Henry, was a Virginian and ruled faithfully as governor of Virginia for several years.

Tobacco Plant

Summary. In 1607 Captain John Smith, with several other emigrants, made the first lasting settlement built by Englishmen in America. Through Captain Smith's energy and courage, Jamestown, Virginia, took firm root. Virginia was the first state to demand the independence of America; and Washington, who was a Virginian, led the War for American Independence and helped to free the colonies from English rule.

Comprehension Questions

1. What was John Smith accused of doing?
2. Where did the church in Jamestown originally meet?
3. What type of houses did the Indians live in?
4. Did they have guns?
5. Why did the Indians not build roads?
6. What happened to Captain Smith when he went in search of the Pacific?
7. What happened to Jamestown?
8. What did the War for American Independence do?
9. Who was the great military leader of the American army?
10. Why is Virginia sometimes called the "Mother of Presidents"?
11. Who was Patrick Henry?

Chapter 7
Henry Hudson (1570–1611)

Henry Hudson Tries to Find a Northern Route to the East. When Captain John Smith sailed for Virginia, he left in London a friend, named Henry Hudson, who was considered to be one of the best sea captains in England. While Smith was in Jamestown, a company of London merchants sent out Captain Hudson to try to find a passage to China and the Indies. Hudson made two trips to the northeast above Russia in the *Hopewell*—in 1607 and 1608—hoping that he could find a way open to the Pacific across the North Pole or not far below it.

Captain Henry Hudson (1570–1611)

He knew that if he found such a passage, it would be much shorter than a voyage round the globe farther south; because, as anyone can see, it is not so far around the top of an apple, near the stem, as it is around the middle. Hudson discovered various Arctic islands, found abundant whales and walruses, and even thought he saw a mermaid; but he could not find a passage to the East. Instead, Hudson saw mountains of ice. He may have failed in his attempt to find a Northeast Passage to the East, but he went nearer to the North Pole than anyone had ever gone before.

The Dutch in Holland had heard of Hudson's voyage, and a company of merchants in that country hired the brave sailor to see if he could find a passage to Asia by sailing to the northeast. He set out from the port of Amsterdam, in 1609, in a vessel named the *Half Moon*. After he had gone quite a long distance, the sailors got so tired of seeing nothing but fog and ice that they refused to go any further.

Then Captain Hudson turned his ship around and sailed for the coast of North America. He did that because his friend, Captain Smith of Virginia, had sent him a letter, with maps, which made him think that he could find a passage to Asia through North America if he went north of Chesapeake Bay.

Hudson first landed on the coast of Maine and then sailed south as far as Chesapeake Bay, but the weather was so stormy that he thought it would not be safe to enter it. Therefore, he sailed northward along the coast. Hudson sailed into Delaware Bay but soon found it to be too shallow to be a passage to the East. In September 1609, he entered a beautiful bay, formed by the spreading out of a large river that was more than a mile wide. The maps sent by John Smith had labeled the river the "Grande River." On the eastern side of it, not far from its mouth, there is a long, narrow island; the Indians of that day called it Manhattan Island. Hudson claimed all of the land along the river for the Dutch, who later established a colony along the river called New Netherland.

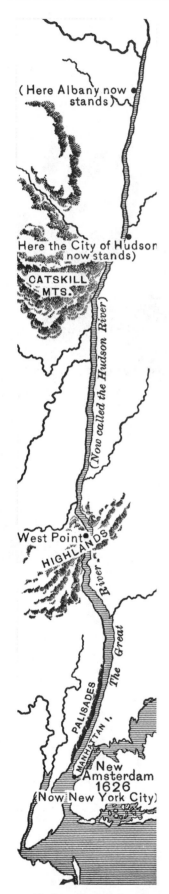

Hudson Explores the "Grande River." One of the remarkable things about the river that Hudson had discovered was that it had hardly any current, and the tide from the ocean moved upstream for more than 150 miles. If no fresh water ran in from the hills, the sea would fill the channel for a long distance, and so make a kind of salt-water river of it. Hudson noticed how salty it was, and that made him think he had finally found a passage that would lead him through from the Atlantic to the Pacific. He was delighted with all he saw, and said, "This is as beautiful a land as one can tread upon." Soon he began to sail up the stream, wondering what he would see and whether he would come out on an ocean that would take him to Asia.

At first the *Half Moon* drifted along, carried by the tide, under the shadow of a great natural wall of rock. That wall, which we now call the Palisades, is from 400 to 600 feet high; it extends for nearly twenty miles along the western shore of the river. Then some distance farther up, Captain Hudson came to a place where the river winds its way through great forest-covered hills, called the Highlands.

Captain Hudson continued up the river until he had reached a point about 150 miles from its mouth. Here the city of Albany now stands. He found that the water was growing shallow, and he feared that if the *Half Moon* went farther she would run aground. It was clear to him, too, that wherever the river might lead, he was unlikely to find it a short way through to China. Early in October the captain set sail for Europe. Ever

Hudson River Valley

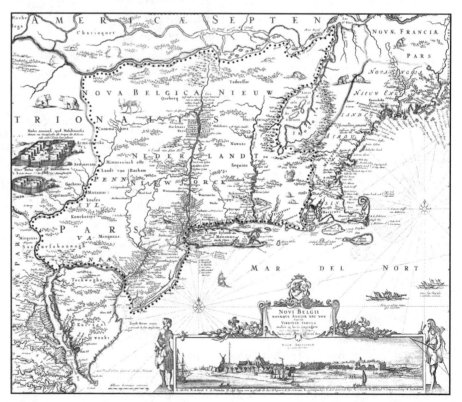

Map of New Netherland, 1650. The dotted border (• • • • •) shows the boundaries of New Amsterdam.

since that time the beautiful river that he explored has been called the Hudson, in his honor.

Relations with the Native Americans. Hudson and his crew often got along very well with the local Indians. The crew frequently traded peacefully with them for food and local products. Sometimes, the natives would give the crew gifts and visit the ship. Hudson was even invited once to a great feast among the Indians.

The *Half Moon* on the Hudson River near the Palisades.

At the end of the fifth day up the "Grande River," at a point on the eastern bank above the Highlands, an old Indian chief invited Hudson to go ashore. Hudson had found the Indians, as he said, "very loving"; so he accepted the invitation. The Indians made a great feast for the captain. They gave him not only roast pigeons, but also a roast dog, which they cooked in his honor. These Indians had never seen a white man before. They thought that the English captain, in his bright scarlet coat trimmed with gold lace, had come down from the sky to visit them. What puzzled them the most, however, was that he had such a pale face.

At the end of the feast Hudson rose to go, but the Indians begged him to stay all night. Then one of them stood up, gathered all the arrows, broke them to pieces, and threw them into the fire, in order to show the captain that he need not be afraid to stay with them.

On the other hand, Hudson and his crew did not fully trust the natives, which sometimes led to unnecessary trouble with local Indians. At times, however, their suspicions were justified. When the *Half Moon* arrived off of the "Grande River," locals killed a crewmember, who was exploring the area. Occasionally, visiting Indians would try to steal something from the ship. On the way down stream a dishonest Indian, who had come out in a canoe, managed to steal something from the ship. One of the crew happened to see the Indian as he was slyly slipping off the ship; picking up a gun, he fired and killed him. After that, Hudson's men had several fights with the Indians.

Hudson's Last Voyage. In April 1610, Hudson began his fourth and final voyage. Hudson sailed again under the English flag, this time on the ship *Discovery*. His crew included his teenage son John as a ship's boy. Henry Hudson was trying once again to find a way to Asia. This time, Hudson was sailing further north to look for what was called the Northwest Passage through North America to the East.

Hudson went north from England to Iceland and then toward Greenland. From Greenland, *Discovery* sailed to the north of Canada through what is now called Hudson Strait. Captain Hudson entered that immense bay in

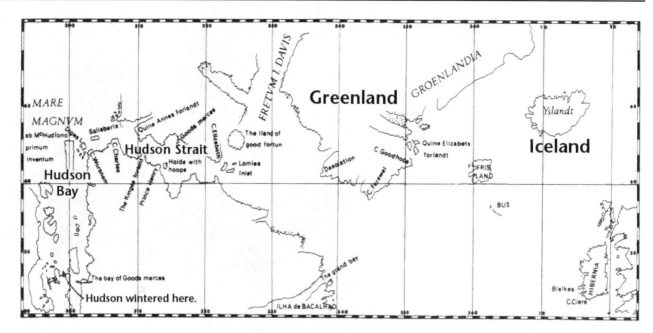

On May 11, 1610, Hudson reached Iceland; and on June 4, he reached south of Greenland, where he sailed around its southern tip. On June 25, Hudson discovered what is now called the Hudson Strait. By following the southern coast of the strait on August 2, Hudson entered what is now called Hudson Bay. By late fall, however, the ship became trapped in the ice in James Bay, where the crew moved ashore for the winter.

the northern part of America, which we now know as Hudson Bay. Hudson explored Hudson Bay for approximately four months, but by November the ship had become stranded in the bay by ice.

The crew survived the winter on shore and, when the ice cleared in the spring of 1611, Hudson wanted to continue exploring the area. However, in June he got into trouble with his men, who wanted to go back to England. Some of them grabbed him and set him adrift in a small boat with his son and a few others. A few crewmembers made it back to England, but nothing more was ever heard of the brave English explorer. The bay that bears his name is probably his grave.

The Dutch Settlement on the Hudson Becomes New York City. When the Dutch in Holland heard that Captain Hudson had found a country where the Indians had plenty of rich furs to sell, they sent out people to trade with them. In 1614, they built their first fort and trading post near what is now Albany, New York, and gave their territory the name of New Netherland after the Netherlands, which is the official name for the country we often call Holland.

In the course of a few years, the Dutch built other forts and settlements in New Netherland. Settlers were first brought to the colony in 1624, and a fort and some log cabins were built on the lower end of Manhattan Island the next year. Peter Minuit, the director of the colony, purchased the island from local Indians in 1626. The fort was named Fort Amsterdam, and after a time the Dutch named this growing little settlement New Amsterdam, in remembrance of the port of Amsterdam in Holland from which Hudson sailed.

After the Dutch had held the colony of New Netherland for about fifty years, the English took it from them in 1664. They changed its name to New York, in honor of the Duke of York, who was brother to the king. The

English also changed the name of New Amsterdam to New York City.

More than a hundred years after this the young men of New York—the "Sons of Liberty," as they called themselves—made ready with the "Sons of Liberty" in other states to do their full part, under the lead of General Washington, in the great War for American Independence—that war by which we gained our freedom from the rule of the king of England, and became the United States of America.

The silent harbor where Henry Hudson saw a few Indian canoes is now one of the busiest seaports in the world. The great Statue of Liberty stands at its entrance. To it fleets of ships are constantly coming from all parts of the globe; from it other fleets of vessels are constantly going. If Captain Hudson could see the river that bears his name, and Manhattan Island now covered with miles of buildings that make the largest and wealthiest city in the United States, he might say: "There is no need of my looking any further for the riches of China and the Indies, for I have found them here."

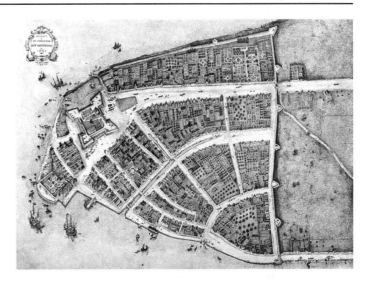

Lower Manhattan in 1660, when it was part of New Amsterdam.

Summary. In 1609 Henry Hudson, an English sea captain, then working for the Dutch, discovered the river now called by his name. The Dutch took possession of the country on the river, named it New Netherland, and built a small settlement on Manhattan Island. Many years later the English seized the colony and named it New York. The settlement on Manhattan Island then became New York City. It is now one of the largest and wealthiest cities in the United States and one of the greatest seaports for shipping and trade in the world.

Comprehension Questions

1. Who was Henry Hudson?
2. What did he try to find?
3. What is the river he discovered called now?
4. What country seized New Netherland?
5. What name did they give it?
6. What would Hudson say if he could see New York City today?

Statue of Liberty

Unit 2

Settlement of a New Land

Chapter 8
Miles Standish (1584–1656)

The English Pilgrims Move to Holland. When the news of Henry Hudson's discovery of the Hudson River reached Holland, many Englishmen were living in the Dutch city of Leyden. These people were mostly farmers who had fled from Scrooby and neighboring villages in the northeast of England. They called themselves Pilgrims, because they were wanderers who were in search of freedom to worship God as the Bible commands. They were known as Separatists because they established a church that was separate from the Church of England, which they believed was corrupt.

The Pilgrims left England because King James I would not let them hold their church meetings in peace. He thought, as most kings then did, that everybody in his kingdom should belong to the same church and worship God in the same way that he did. He was afraid that if people were allowed to go to whatever church they thought best, it would lead to disputes and quarrels, which would end by breaking his kingdom to pieces. Quite a number of Englishmen, seeing that they could not have religious liberty at home, escaped with their wives and children to Holland, for there the Dutch were willing to let them worship God in the way that the Bible commanded.

The Pilgrims Settle in America. The Pilgrims were not happy in Holland. They saw that, if they stayed in that country, their children would grow up to be more Dutch than English. They saw, too, that they could not hope to get land in Holland. They resolved, therefore, to go to America, where they could get farms for nothing, and where their children would never forget the English language or the good old English customs and laws. In the wilderness, they could not only enjoy entire religious freedom but also could build up a settlement that would surely be their own.

On September 16, 1620, a company of Pilgrims sailed for England on their way to America. Captain Miles Standish, an English soldier who had fought in Holland, joined them. He did not belong to the Pilgrim church, but he had become a great friend to those who did.

Captain Miles Standish
(1584–1656)

THE PILGRIMS IN
ENGLAND AND HOLLAND

SCALE OF MILES

0   50   100   150   200   250

In 1620, the *Mayflower* carried the Pilgrims from Southampton, England, to Plymouth, Massachusetts. It was a harrowing two-month journey.

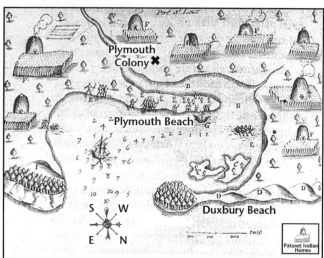

Samuel de Champlain's 1605 map of Plymouth Harbor, showing the Indian village of Patuxet. The approximate location of Plymouth Colony is also shown.

About a hundred of these people sailed from Plymouth, England, for the New World in the ship *Mayflower*. Many of those who went were children and young people. The Pilgrims had a long, rough passage across the Atlantic Ocean. On November 20, they sighted land. It was Cape Cod, that narrow strip of sand more than sixty miles long, which looks on a map like an arm bent at the elbow.

Finding that it would be difficult to go further, the Pilgrims decided to land and explore the cape; so the *Mayflower* entered Cape Cod Harbor, inside the "half-shut fist" of the harbor, and then came to anchor. Before they landed, the Pilgrims held a meeting in the cabin and prepared a written agreement to establish a government for the settlement. They signed the agreement, called the Mayflower Compact, and then chose John Carver as their first governor. This Compact set forth the main purpose for the new colony, to establish a society that would "glorify God and advance the Christian faith...."

On the first Monday after they had reached the cape, all the women went on shore to wash, and so Monday has been kept as washday in New England ever since. Shortly after that, Captain Miles Standish, with several men, started off to see the country. They found some Indian corn buried in the sand; and a little farther on a young man named William Bradford, who afterward became governor, stepped into an Indian deer trap. It jerked him up by the leg in a way that must have made even the soberest Pilgrim smile.

On clear days the people on board the *Mayflower*—which was anchored in Cape Cod Harbor—could see a blue hill on the mainland in the west, about forty miles away. To that blue hill, Standish and some others determined to go. Taking a sailboat, they started off. A few days later they passed the hill, which the Indians called Manomet, and entered a fine harbor. There, on December 21, 1620, the shortest day in the year, they landed on that famous stone that is now known throughout the world as Plymouth Rock. Until now, December 21 is celebrated as Forefathers' Day in Plymouth, Massachusetts.

Standish, with the others, went back to the *Mayflower* with a good report. They had found just what they wanted. The location could be easily defended, had an excellent harbor where ships from England could come in, included a brook with good drinking water, and was nearly free from trees so that nothing would hinder their planting crops early in the spring. Captain John Smith of Virginia had been there before them, and had named the place Plymouth on his map of New England. The Pilgrims liked the name, and so made up their minds to keep it. Soon the *Mayflower* sailed for Plymouth, and the Pilgrims began to build the log cabins of their little settlement.

During that first winter nearly half the Pilgrims died. Captain Standish showed himself to be as good a nurse as he was a soldier. He, with Governor Carver and their minister, Elder Brewster, cooked, washed, waited on the sick, and did everything that kind hearts and willing hands could do to help their suffering friends. But the men who had begun to build houses had to stop that work to dig graves. When these graves were filled, they were smoothed down flat, so that no prowling Indian should count them and see how few Pilgrims there were left.

This is an artist rendering of Elder William Brewster. No known image of him exists.

Over the years, many more settlers came to join Plymouth Colony. From approximately fifty survivors after the first winter, Plymouth Colony had grown to about 7,000 people by the early 1690s.

The Pilgrims and the Native Americans. One day in the spring, the Pilgrims were startled at seeing an Indian walk boldly into their little settlement. He cried out in good English, "Welcome! Welcome!" This visitor was named Samoset. Years before he had met some sailors, who taught him several English words.

The next time Samoset came he brought with him another Indian, whose name was Squanto. Squanto was the only one left of the tribe that had once lived at Plymouth. All the rest had died of a dreadful sickness, or plague. He had been stolen by some sailors and carried to England; there he had learned the English language. After his return, he had joined an Indian tribe known as the Wampanoag that lived about thirty miles farther west. The chief of that tribe was named Massasoit, and Squanto said that he was coming soon to visit the Pilgrims. In about an hour, Massasoit, with some sixty warriors, appeared on a hill just outside the settlement. The Indians had painted their faces in their most carefree style—black, red, and yellow. If paint could make them handsome, they were determined to look their best.

"WELCOME! WELCOME!"

Captain Standish, attended by a guard of honor, went out and brought the chief to Governor Carver. Then Massasoit and the governor made a solemn promise or treaty, in which they agreed that the Indians of his tribe and the Pilgrims should live like friends and brothers, doing all they could to help each other. That promise was kept for more than fifty years; it was never broken until long after the two men who made it were in their graves.

When the Pilgrims had their first Thanksgiving feast to thank God for His blessings, they invited Massasoit and his men to come and share it. The Indians brought venison and other good things; there were plenty of wild turkeys roasted; and so they all

Early Days in Plymouth

The First Thanksgiving took place in Plymouth in 1621.

sat down together to a great dinner and had a merry time in the wilderness.

Squanto was of great help to the Pilgrims. He showed them how to catch eels, where to go fishing, when to plant their corn, and how to put a fish in every hill to make the corn grow faster. After a while, he came to live with the Pilgrims. Squanto liked them so much that, just before he died, he begged Governor Bradford to pray that he might go to the Pilgrim's heaven.

West of where Massasoit lived, the Narragansett tribe controlled the region around Narragansett Bay, in what is now Rhode Island. The chief of the Narragansetts was named Canonicus, and he was no friend to Massasoit or to the Pilgrims. Canonicus thought he could frighten the Pilgrim settlers away; so he sent a bundle of sharp, new arrows, tied round with a rattlesnake skin, to Governor Bradford. That meant that he dared the governor and his men to come out and fight. Governor Bradford threw away the arrows, and then filled the snakeskin to the mouth with powder and ball. This was sent back to Canonicus. When he saw it, he was afraid to touch it, for he knew that Miles Standish's bullets could whistle louder and cut deeper than his Indian arrows.

Although the Pilgrims did not believe that Canonicus would attack them, they thought it best to build a very high, strong fence, called a palisade, around the town. They also built a log fort on one of the hills and used the lower part of the fort for a church. Every Sunday all the people, with Captain Standish at the head, marched to their meetinghouse, where a man stood on guard outside. Each Pilgrim carried his gun, and set it down near him. With one ear, he listened sharply to the preacher; with the other, he listened just as sharply for the cry, "Indians! Indians!" But the Indians never came.

A couple of years later, more emigrants came from England and settled about twenty-five miles north of Plymouth, at a place that is now called Weymouth. The Indians in that neighborhood did not like these new settlers, and they made up their minds to come upon them suddenly and murder them.

Governor Bradford sent Captain Standish, with a few men, to see how great the danger was. He found the Indians very bold. One of them came up to him carrying a long knife. He held it up, to show how sharp it was, and then patting it, he said, "By and by, it shall eat, but not speak." Presently another Indian came up. He was a big fellow, much larger and stronger than Standish. He, too, had a long knife, as keen as a razor. "Ah," said he to Standish, "so this is the mighty captain the white men have sent to destroy us! He is a little man; let him go and work with the women."

Captain Miles Standish and his men

The captain's blood was on fire with rage, but he said not a word. His time had not yet come. The next day the Pilgrims and the Indians met in a log cabin. Standish made a sign to one of his men, and he shut the door fast. Then the captain sprang like a tiger at the big warrior who had laughed at him, and snatching his long knife from him, he plunged it into his heart. A hand-to-hand fight followed between the Pilgrims and the Indians. The Pilgrims gained the victory, and carried back the head of the Indian chief in triumph to Plymouth. Captain Standish's bold action saved both of the English settlements from destruction.

Miles Standish's Final Years. Standish did more things for the Pilgrims than fight for them: he went to England, bought goods for them, and borrowed money to help them.

He lived to be an old man. At his death he left, among other things, three well-worn Bibles and three good guns. In those days, the men who read the Bible most were those who fought the hardest.

Near Plymouth, there is a high hill called Captain's Hill. That was where Standish made his home during the last part of his life. A granite monument, over a hundred feet high, stands on top of the hill. On it is a statue of the brave captain looking toward the sea. He was one of the makers of America.

The English Settlement of New England Grows. Ten years after the Pilgrims landed at Plymouth, a large company of English people under the leadership of Governor John Winthrop came to New England. A fleet of eleven ships—including the governor's ship, the *Arbella*, and a new *Mayflower*—brought about 700 people to establish a new settlement in New England. They were called Puritans; they, too, were seeking that religious freedom which was denied them in the old country.

Governor Winthrop's company named the place where they settled Boston, in grateful remembrance of the beautiful old city of Boston, England, from which some of the chief emigrants came. The new settlement was called the Massachusetts Bay Colony. Massachusetts was the Indian name for the Blue Hills near Boston. The Plymouth Colony was now often called the Old Colony because it had been settled first. After many years, these two colonies were united, and still later they became the state of Massachusetts.

In the late 1880s, a granite monument was erected to the memory of Miles Standish on Captain's Hill in Duxbury, Massachusetts. On top of the 100-foot tower stands a statue of Standish, looking eastward. His right hand, holding the charter of the colony, is extended toward Plymouth, while his left rests upon his sheathed sword.

Governor Winthrop of the
Massachusetts Bay Colony

By the time Governor Winthrop arrived, additional English settlements had been made in Massachusetts, Maine, and New Hampshire. Emigrants who came from the Massachusetts Bay Colony later settled Connecticut and Rhode Island. In 1724, the English established their first permanent settlement in Vermont, which was the last territory in New England that the British settled.

When the War for American Independence broke out, the people throughout New England took up arms in defense of their God-given rights. The first bloody battle of the war was shed on the soil of Massachusetts, near Boston.

Summary. The Pilgrims landed at Plymouth, New England, in 1620. One of the chief men who came with them was Captain Miles Standish. Had it not been for his help, the Indians might have destroyed the settlement. In 1630 Governor John Winthrop, with a large company of Puritan emigrants from England, settled Boston. The first battle of the War for American Independence was fought near Boston.

Comprehension Questions

1. Why did some Englishmen in Holland call themselves Pilgrims?

2. Why had they left England?

3. Why did they now wish to go to America?

4. Who was Miles Standish?

5. From what place in England, and in what ship, did the Pilgrims sail?

6. Why did the Pilgrims hold the first Thanksgiving?

7. What did the Pilgrims build to protect them from the Indians?

8. What else did Miles Standish do besides fight?

9. Who was the first governor of the Boston settlement?

Early New England

Chapter 9
Lord Baltimore (1580–1632)

Lord Baltimore's Settlement in Newfoundland. While Captain Miles Standish was helping build up Plymouth, George Calvert, First Baron of Baltimore, an English nobleman, was trying to make a settlement on the cold, foggy island of Newfoundland.

Lord Baltimore had been brought up a Protestant, but had become a Catholic. At that time, Catholics were treated badly in England. They were ordered by law to attend the Church of England. They did not like that church any better than the Pilgrims did; but if they failed to attend it, they had to take their choice between paying a large sum of money or going to prison.

Lord Baltimore hoped to make a home for himself and for other English Catholics in the wilderness of Newfoundland, where there would be no one to trouble them. The settlers, however, found it difficult to live in Newfoundland because of the cold weather. They had winter a good part of the year, and fog during all of it. They could grow nothing because, as

one man said, the soil was either rock or swamp: the rock was as hard as iron; the swamp was so deep that you could not touch bottom with a ten-foot pole. Baltimore ultimately abandoned the effort in 1629.

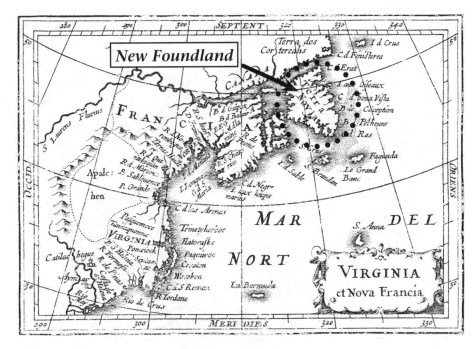

Newfoundland had great potential for a fishing industry. However, war between England and France at the time made it impossible for Lord Baltimore to establish a fishing settlement in Newfoundland. While visiting the settlement in 1628, he found that he had to use his own ships to protect the fishing fleet from French attacks.

The King of England Gives Lord Baltimore Part of Virginia. King Charles I of England was a good friend to Lord Baltimore; and when the settlement in Newfoundland was given up, he made him a present of a large, three-cornered piece of land in America. This piece was cut out of Virginia, north of the Potomac River.

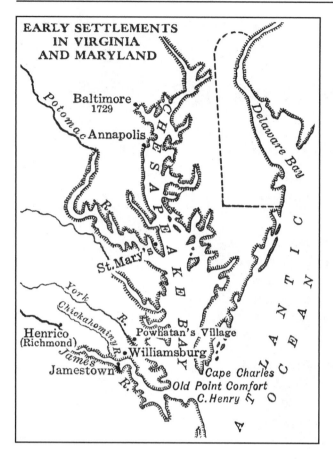

EARLY SETTLEMENTS
IN VIRGINIA
AND MARYLAND

The king's wife, who was Henriette Marie de Bourbon, was a French Catholic. In her honor, Charles named the country he had given Lord Baltimore Marie Land or Maryland. He could not have chosen a better name because Maryland was to be a shelter for many English people who believed in the same religion that the queen did.

All that Lord Baltimore was to pay for Maryland, with its 12,000 square miles of land and water, was two Indian arrows. These he agreed to send every spring to the royal palace of Windsor Castle, near London. The arrows would be worth nothing whatever to the king, but they were sent as a kind of yearly rent. They showed that, though Lord Baltimore was given the use of Maryland as a great noble, and could do pretty much as he pleased with it, still the king did not surrender all control of it. In Virginia and in New England the king had granted all land to groups of persons, and he had been particular to tell them just what they must or must not do; but he gave Maryland to one man only. More than this, he promised to let Lord Baltimore have his own way in everything, so long as he made no laws in Maryland that were contrary to the laws of England. So, Lord Baltimore had greater privileges than any other holder of land in America at that time.

The New Colony Is Established. Lord Baltimore died before he could get ready to come to America. His eldest son, Cecilius (Cecil) Calvert, then became the next Lord Baltimore. He sent over a number of emigrants; many of them were Catholics, and some were Protestants, but all were to have equal rights in Maryland. In the spring of 1634, these people landed on a little island near the mouth of the Potomac River. There they cut down a tree and made a large cross; then, kneeling around that cross, they all joined in prayer to God for their safe journey.

A little later, they landed on the shore of the river. There they met some Indians. Under a huge mulberry tree they bargained with the Indians for a place to build a town, and paid for the land in hatchets, knives, and beads.

The Indians were greatly amazed at the size of the ship in which the white men came. They thought that it was made like their canoes, and that it was simply the trunk of a tree hollowed out. They wondered where the English could have found a tree big enough to make it.

The emigrants named their settlement St. Mary's. The Indians and the settlers lived and worked together, side by side. The Indians showed the emigrants how to hunt in the forest, and the Indian women taught the white women how to make corn meal and to bake Johnnycake before the open fire.

The new Lord Baltimore invited people who had been driven out of the other settlements on account of their religion to come and live in Maryland. He gave a hearty welcome to all, whether they thought as he did or not. Thousands of English Catholics came to live in Maryland, as well as many Protestants. Eventually, there were more Protestants than Catholics in Maryland. Nonetheless, Maryland became one of the few places in the world where religious liberty had a home. In 1649, Maryland passed a religious toleration act, which allowed all Christians to worship God as they thought best. Maryland was different from the other English colonies in America because everyone there, whether Catholic or Protestant, had the right to worship God in his own way.

Saint Mary's Settlement

Maryland Has its Troubles. This happy time of peace did not last long. Maryland had border troubles with the neighboring colonies of Virginia and (later) Pennsylvania. Some of the Virginians were very angry because the king had given Lord Baltimore part of what they thought was their land. They fought with the new settlers and gave them much trouble. The border trouble with Pennsylvania resulted in armed conflicts between Maryland and Pennsylvania in the 1730s. The fighting between Maryland and Pennsylvania ended in 1738, but the border was not settled until the establishment of the Mason-Dixon Line between the two colonies in 1767.

Maryland was also unable to avoid religious conflict. Puritans who had moved to Maryland, many fleeing persecution in Virginia, rebelled against Lord Baltimore's rule of Maryland in 1650. Lord Baltimore had spent a great deal of money in building up the settlement, but his right to the land was taken away from him for a time, and all who dared to defend him were badly treated. He sent an army to Maryland to regain control, but it was defeated. The Puritan government outlawed the Roman Catholic Church and the Church of England during much of the time it controlled Maryland. It was not until 1658 that Lord Baltimore regained control of his colony and reenacted the religious toleration law.

Cecil Calvert died in 1675, and his son Charles became the Third Baron of Baltimore. Charles had already lived in Maryland for several years serving as deputy governor for his father, who had actually never lived in Maryland. Charles Calvert became governor and did much to improve the public services and defenses of the colony. However, he also supported life-

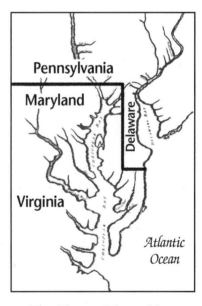

The Mason-Dixon Line

The Mason–Dixon Line was surveyed between 1763 and 1767 by Charles Mason and Jeremiah Dixon, settling border disputes between the colonies of Pennsylvania, Maryland, Delaware, and Virginia (now West Virginia).

In 1688, William III, Prince of Orange, and Mary II became the only joint monarchs in British history.

time slavery in the colony, repressed the rights of Protestants, and restricted the right to vote within the colony. Lord Baltimore was required to return to England to settle the boundary dispute with Pennsylvania and answer questions about his policy toward Protestants, but, while in England, the Catholic King James II of England was overthrown and new Protestant monarchs William and Mary came to the throne of England. Because the Calvert family was Roman Catholic, its control over Maryland was ended, and Maryland became for a time a royal colony.

Maryland Prospers. In spite of its troubles, Maryland became a successful colony. Its wealth, like that of Virginia, became largely based on the cultivation of tobacco. The reestablishment of religious toleration for different Christian denominations in 1658 encouraged a significant population growth as various groups found Maryland to be a hospitable place to live, work, and practice their faith. By 1660, Maryland's population had risen to only 2,500. However, over the next twenty years, Maryland had grown by another 20,000 people, many of whom were religious refugees from other colonies in America.

The initial settlement of St. Mary's never grew to be much of a place. It was the first capitol of the colony, but it was replaced as the seat of government by Annapolis in 1708. In 1729, not quite a hundred years after the English first landed in Maryland, a new and beautiful city near Chesapeake Bay was begun. It was named Baltimore, in honor of Cecil Calvert, Second Lord Baltimore, who sent out the first emigrants. Baltimore has been an important port city almost since its very beginning and has played an important role in American history.

Charles Calvert never returned to Maryland, but his grandson—also named Charles (the Fifth Baron of Baltimore)—regained control over

Maryland. King George I restored the title to Maryland to the Calvert family after Benedict Calvert (the Fourth Baron of Baltimore) renounced Roman Catholicism and joined the Church of England. Charles governed Maryland directly for a time during the period of border dispute with Pennsylvania, but his son Frederick Calvert (the Sixth Baron of Baltimore) never set foot in Maryland, spending much of his life on the continent of Europe. He was more interested in money from the colony than governing the colony. Frederick was the last Lord Baltimore because he and his wife never had any children. By the time a successor to the Calvert family's title to Maryland was established, Maryland was involved in the war against Great Britain and so was lost to the family.

Summary. King Charles I of England gave Lord Baltimore a part of Virginia and named it Maryland, in honor of his wife, Queen Henriette Marie. A company of emigrants came out to Maryland in 1634. It was the first settlement in America in which people had the liberty to worship God in whatever way they thought right. This religious toleration did much to ensure the success of Maryland.

Benedict Leonard Calvert
Fourth Baron Baltimore
(1679–1715)

Comprehension Questions

1. Who was Lord Baltimore, and what did he try to do in the region of Newfoundland?

2. How were Catholics then treated in England?

3. What was Lord Baltimore to pay for Maryland?

4. What wonderful freedom found its home in Maryland?

5. What city was named in honor of the man who sent the first emigrants to Maryland?

Chapter 10
Roger Williams (1600–1684)

Roger Williams (1600–1684)

During his life, Roger Williams was known as a troublemaker. He really caused problems with the Puritans with whom he lived and served as a preacher for many years. As a result of his difficulties with the Puritans, Williams eventually established the colony of Rhode Island. It was as the leader of that colony that history knows Williams not as a troublemaker but rather as the first effective champion of religious liberty in America.

Williams Gets in Trouble. Shortly after Governor John Winthrop and his company settled Boston, Roger Williams came over from England to join them. His purpose in coming over was to be a missionary to the Indians, but his abilities as a preacher caused many Puritan churches to want him as their pastor. Williams did accept a call to a church in Plymouth and then later to a church in Salem. Williams did not have many problems in Plymouth, but he quickly ran into trouble at the Salem church because of its size and importance. In other words, the Puritans believed that Williams could corrupt too many people in Salem, so they forced him out of the colony altogether.

There were a couple of arguments made by Williams that greatly disturbed the Puritans. First, he argued that the Puritans had no right to the Indian lands because they had not bought the lands from the Indians fairly. He rejected the idea that the king of England owned America because John Cabot had discovered it. And even though he never became a missionary to the Indians like he had planned, Williams established friendships with the Indians in both Plymouth and Salem. He made great effort to learn their language and even wrote a book about the Native American languages. Those friendships served him well later in life when he was kicked out of Massachusetts and the Indians helped him survive.

Many people in Massachusetts were afraid to have Williams preach and write about the Indians the way he did. They believed that if they allowed him to continue speaking out so boldly against the king, the English monarch would take Massachusetts away from them and give it to a new group. In that case, those who had settled there would lose everything.

The other, and more serious, problem the Puritans had with Williams was his belief that the state had no business interfering in church matters. For one thing, Williams believed that Massachusetts should have cut all ties to the Church of England because it was so corrupt that it was no longer a true church. The Puritans were committed to "purifying" the Church of England, not separating from it, even though they basically set up their own independent church in America anyways. But Williams did not stop there. He even dared to challenge the key principles of the colony—state-sponsored religion.

The Puritan founders of the Massachusetts Bay Colony sought to develop a holy community. Williams was uncomfortable with the close relationship between church and state that existed in the colony, however. According to Williams, the colony had no business demanding that its citizens go to church since true faith and religion cannot be forced. If the people were genuinely Christian, he continued, they would not need laws to force them to behave like Christians. In fact, requiring church attendance for all the colony's members corrupted the church since it brought people in who were not true Christians. Finally, Williams concluded that people had the right to express their own religious opinions without threat of punishment.

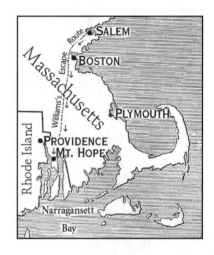

Roger Williams Forms a New Colony. The authorities in Boston tried to make the young minister agree to keep silent on these subjects, but he was not the kind of man to keep silent. So the chief men of Boston agreed to expel Williams from the colony. The influential Puritan leader John Winthrop arranged to have Williams's exit delayed until the spring when the weather was more favorable, but Williams chose to leave immediately.

The story about Williams's surviving the winter he was exiled is the stuff of which legends are made. At the time, to be exiled or banished from a colony was basically a death sentence. It was considered impossible to survive without the support of a large community. Being banished during one of the most severe winters the Puritans had ever seen made Williams's survival even more astounding. There were two keys to his remarkable accomplishment. First, he persevered. In other words, despite the lack of roads, shelter, warmth, and adequate supplies, Williams somehow managed to survive.

Second, Williams would have never made it without help from the Indians. The kindness he had shown to the Indians earlier was proven to be worth it. The friendship he established with an Indian chief named Massasoit proved to be especially significant. After Williams managed an eighty-mile hike from Salem to Massasoit's wigwam near Mount Hope (which is in Rhode Island now), Massasoit welcomed him and allowed Williams to stay with him the remainder of the winter. Williams used the winter to strengthen his friendship with the Indians and to reach out to those he had not yet met. When spring came, Williams was able to use those friendships in his establishing the colony of Rhode Island.

Williams named the first city he founded Providence, believing it was by God's good will and plan that he was able to survive the winter and plant

Roger Williams Fleeing through the Woods.

47

a new colony. Assuming that God was on his side, Williams established as law the right of religious freedom. Thus, Providence was the first place in North America where the freedom to worship as one pleased was defined as a human right.

Even though Williams eventually tried to make laws that restrained some people who came to Rhode Island to take advantage of the freedom being offered, Williams had already anticipated the future. In other words, once people got a taste of religious freedom, they didn't want to give it up. Over one hundred years later, the principle that almost caused Williams's death was the same basic principle that many Americans died for in the War for American Independence. Now the principle is enshrined in American law as the first amendment in the United States Constitution.

Summary. Roger Williams's significance is found in his fight to establish religious freedom in America. His commitment to that principle contributed to his being kicked out of Massachusetts. His amazing survival enabled him to establish that principle as law in Rhode Island, the colony he founded. Now it is a principle that many Americans have fought and died for to protect as a basic human right.

Comprehension Questions

1. Why did Roger Williams come to America?
2. Who did Williams think first owned the land in America?
3. What was the most serious problem the Puritans had with Williams?
4. What are two reasons Williams was able to survive his banishment?
5. What right was given to man for the first time in America at Providence?

Chapter 11
King Philip (1639–1676)

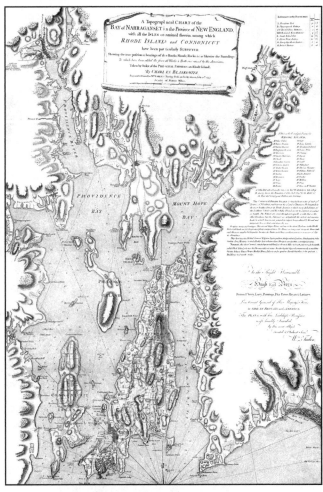

King Philip

Trouble Arises with the Native Americans of New England. When the Indian chief Massasoit died, the people of Plymouth lost one of their best friends. Massasoit left two sons, one named Wamsutta (also called Alexander), who became chief in his father's place, and the other named Metacomet, who was better known as Philip. They both lived near Mount Hope, in Rhode Island.

The governor of Plymouth heard that Wamsutta was stirring up the Indians to make war on the settlers, and he ordered the Indian chief to come to him and give an account of his dealings. Wamsutta went, but on his way back he suddenly fell sick, and soon after he reached home he died. His young wife was a woman who was respected by her tribe, and she told them that she felt sure the settlers had poisoned her husband in order to get rid of him. This was not true, but the Indians believed it.

Philip became chief after his brother's death and became known as "King Philip." His palace was a wigwam made of bark. On great occasions, he wore a bright red blanket and a kind of crown made of a broad belt ornamented with shells. King Philip hated the settlers because he believed they had murdered his brother. He also saw the settlers were growing stronger in numbers every year, while the Indians were becoming weaker.

When the Pilgrims landed at Plymouth, Massasoit, Philip's father, held all the country from Cape Cod back to the eastern shores of Narragansett Bay, a strip of land about thirty miles wide. The European settlers bought a small piece of this land. After a while they were able to buy more because the natives wanted the weapons and iron trade goods that the settlers had to offer. The English settlers continued to buy so much land that, in about fifty years, they owned nearly all of what Massasoit's tribe, the Wampanoag, had once owned. The Indians had nothing left but two little pieces of land, which were nearly surrounded by the waters of Narragansett Bay. Here they felt that they were shut up almost like prisoners, and that the settlers watched everything that they did.

Map of Narragansett Bay

Praying Indians

In 1646, The General Court of Massachusetts passed the "Act for the Propagation of the Gospel amongst the Indians," which brought this great need to the awareness of the English people. Another factor that aroused interest was the preaching of Reverend John Eliot and other missionaries to the Indian tribes of New England. To raise funds for this cause, the Long Parliament passed an act forming "A Corporation for the Promoting and Propagating the Gospel of Jesus Christ in New England." About £12,000 (or US$22,000) was raised to be used primarily in the colonies of Massachusetts and New York. Reverend Eliot received some of these funds to establish schools for the Indian believers.

Also in 1646, Reverend Eliot preached his first sermon to the Nonantum Indians in their own language. Christian Indian villages were eventually established along the coast of Massachusetts and some inland locations.

King Philip was a very proud man; in fact, he was as proud as the king of England. He could not bear to see his people losing power. He thought that if the Indians did not rise and drive out the white men, then the white men would surely drive out the Indians. Most of the Indians now had guns and could use them almost as well as the settlers could; so Philip thought that it was best to fight.

Although many Indians now hated the white settlers, this was not true of all. A minister, named John Eliot, had persuaded some of the Indians near Boston to give up their pagan religion and to try to live like peace-loving Christians. These were called "Praying Indians." One of them, John Sassamon, had even helped King Philip as a translator, since he had attended Harvard College and knew English well. He found out that Philip's warriors were grinding their hatchets sharp for war and sent a warning to the governor of the Plymouth Colony, but he was not believed. Soon afterward this "Praying Indian" was found murdered. The settlers accused three of Philip's men of having killed him. They were tried, found guilty by a jury that included both English settlers and Indians, and hanged.

War Begins. Philip's warriors began the war in June of 1675. King Philip started with an alliance of two tribes—his Wampanoag tribe and the Nipmuck tribe of what is now central Massachusetts—but others joined with him over the next few months. Philip's alliance waged war against all of the English colonies in New England. The English had their own Indian allies, who fought with the settlers, including many of the "Praying Indians." The war took place from Connecticut and Rhode Island in the south to Maine in the north, although most fighting occurred in Massachusetts, Rhode Island, and Connecticut.

The fighting began at Swansea, Massachusetts—a Plymouth colony settlement. Some settlers were going home from church, where they had gone to pray that there might be no fighting. As they walked along, talking together, two guns were fired out of the bushes. One of the Pilgrim men fell dead in the road, and another was badly hurt. Indians had fired the shots. This was the way they always fought when they could. They were not cowards; but they did not come out and fight boldly, but would fire from behind trees and rocks. Frequently a settler would be killed without even seeing who shot him.

At first, the fighting was mainly in those villages near Plymouth Colony that were nearest Narragansett Bay; then it spread to the valley of the Connecticut River. Deerfield, Springfield, Brookfield, Groton, and many other places in Massachusetts were attacked. The Indians would creep up quietly in the night, burn the houses, carry off the women and children as prisoners if they could, kill the men, and take their scalps home and hang them in their wigwams.

Indian Attack on a Village

At Brookfield the settlers left their houses and gathered in one strong house for defense. The Indians burned all the houses but that one, and did their best to burn it, too. They shot blazing arrows into the shingles of the roof. When the Indians saw that the shingles had caught, and were beginning to flame up, they danced for joy, and roared like wild bulls. But the men in the house managed to put out the fire on the roof. Then the warriors got a cart, filled it with hay, set it on fire, and pushed it up against the house. This time they thought that they would surely burn the settlers out; but just then a heavy rain shower came up and extinguished the fire. A little later, some soldiers marched into the village and saved the people in the house.

At Hadley, the people were in the meetinghouse when the terrible Indian war-whoop rang through the village. The warriors drove back those who dared to go out against them, and it seemed as though the village would be destroyed. Suddenly, a white-haired old man, sword in hand, appeared among the settlers. No one knew who he was. But he called them to follow him, as a captain calls his men, and they obeyed him. The astonished Indians turned and ran. When all was over, the townspeople looked for their brave leader, but he was gone; they never saw him again. Many thought that he was an angel who had been sent to save them. But the angel was Colonel William Goffe, an Englishman, one of the judges who, after the Civil War in England, had sentenced King Charles I to death. He had escaped to America after King Charles II—the son of King Charles I—took the throne; and fortunately for the people of Hadley, he was hiding in the house of a friend in that village when the Indians attacked.

Colonel Goffe Leads the Attack

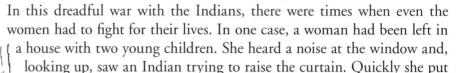

In this dreadful war with the Indians, there were times when even the women had to fight for their lives. In one case, a woman had been left in a house with two young children. She heard a noise at the window and, looking up, saw an Indian trying to raise the curtain. Quickly she put her two little children under two large brass kettles that stood nearby. Then, grabbing a shovelful of red-hot coals from the open fire, she stood ready, and just as the Indian thrust his head into the room, she dashed the coals right into his face and eyes. With a yell of agony, the Indian dropped to the ground as though he had been shot; then he staggered out of the house and ran howling into the woods.

The Great Swamp Fight. During the summer and autumn of 1675 the Narragansett tribe on the west side of Narragansett Bay took no open part in King Philip's War. But the next winter, the settlers found that these Indians were secretly receiving and sheltering the cruel Indians who had been wounded in fighting for their proud chief. For that reason, the settlers determined to raise a large army and attack them. The Indians had gathered in a fort on an island in a swamp. This fort was a very difficult place to reach. It was built from the trunks of trees set upright in the ground. It was so strong that the Indian warriors felt safe.

Starting very early in the morning, a large colonial force, including 150 Mohegan Indian allies, was sent to attack the Narragansett fort. The attacking party waded fifteen miles through deep snow. Many of them had their hands and feet badly frozen. One of the chief men in leading the attack was Captain Benjamin Church of Plymouth. He was a very brave soldier and knew all about Indian life and Indian fighting. In the battle, he was struck by two bullets, and so badly wounded that he could not move a step further; but he made one of his men hold him up and shouted to his soldiers to go ahead. The fight was a very hard one, but finally the fort was taken. More than 250 men in the attacking party were killed or wounded; the Indians lost over 600 killed.

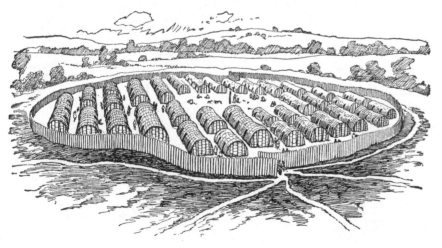

The Indian Village

After the battle was over, Captain Church begged the men not to burn the wigwams inside the fort, for there were a great number of old men and women and little Indian children in the wigwams. But the men were very angry with the Indians and would not listen to him. They set the wigwams on fire and burned many of these poor people to death.

Not all of the Narragansetts were killed, however. Canonchet, the chief of the tribe, escaped and led the rest of his tribe into an alliance with King Philip against the New England settlers. His warriors participated in several battles against the colonists. However, in April 1676, Canonchet was captured by the Mohegan and turned over to the English settlers. The settlers told him they would spare his life if he would try to make peace. "No," said he, "we will all fight to the last man rather than become slaves." He was then told that he must be shot. "I like it well," said he. "I wish to die before my heart becomes soft, or I say anything unworthy of myself."

The End of War. At first, King Philip's Native American alliance was very successful. Several towns in Massachusetts and Rhode Island were abandoned, and several others were fortified against attack. However, by the spring 1676, the war began to turn against King Philip. His supplies began to run low, and he was unable to gain any more allies. The death of Canonchet and defeat of the Narragansetts hurt Philip's war efforts significantly. Indians from his alliance began to surrender to the colonists.

During the summer of 1676, Captain Church, with many "brisk Bridgewater lads," chased King Philip and his men, and took many Indian prisoners. Among those taken captive were King Philip's wife and his little boy. When Philip heard of it he cried out, "My heart breaks; now I am ready to die." He had good reason for saying so. His stubbornness and pride brought misery and death to his own wife and children. King Philip refused to call an end to a war that never should have started.

Not long after that, King Philip himself was shot. He had been hunted like a wild beast from place to place. At last he had returned to see his old home at Mount Hope once more. Shortly after King Philip's return, Captain Church led a team of friendly Indians and colonial soldiers against King Philip's old home. On August 12, 1676, John Alderman, a "Praying Indian" serving with Captain Church, shot the Indian warrior to death.

King Philip's death virtually brought the war to an end, although occasionally raids continued in Maine into 1677. It had lasted a little over a year, from the early summer of 1675 to the latter part of the summer of 1676. It was one of the bloodiest Indian wars in American history. In that short time, over 600 New England settlers died during the war, and Indians burned thirteen villages to ashes, besides partly burning a great many more. The war cost so much money that many people were made poor by it.

On the other hand, with the defeat of King Philip, Indians never dared to trouble the people of southern New England again. The strength of the Indians in the area was broken forever. Approximately 3,000 Native Americans died during the war. Several hundred were executed or were sold as slaves to Bermuda. The tribes in Philip's alliance were largely destroyed, and even the tribes who helped the settlers were greatly weakened.

The Death of King Philip

Summary. In 1675, King Philip began a great Indian war against the people of southern New England. His object was to kill off the English settlers and get back the land for the Indians. He did kill a large number, and he destroyed many villages; but in the end the settlers gained the victory. Philip's wife and child were killed and he was shot. The Indians never again attempted to start a war in this part of the country.

Comprehension Questions

1. Who was Wamsutta?
2. Who was "King Philip"?
3. Who were the "Praying Indians"?
4. Tell how a woman drove off an Indian.
5. What happened to King Philip himself?
6. Who won King Philip's War?

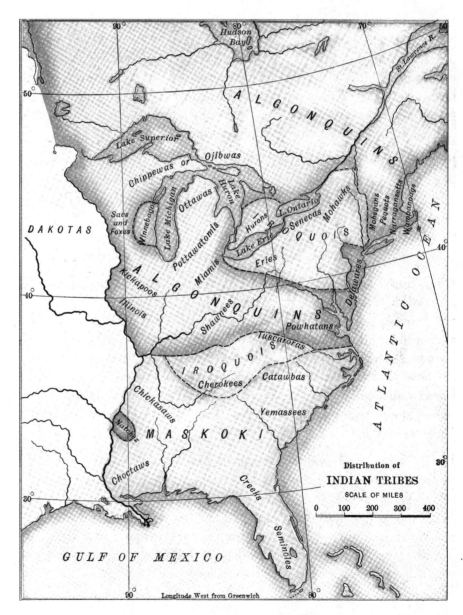

Distribution of
INDIAN TRIBES
SCALE OF MILES
0   100   200   300   400

Chapter 12
William Penn (1644–1718)

America is a land known for its religious tolerance. While many other countries persecute people that believe in different religious traditions than they do, America actually has laws that protect anyone from being harmed for his or her religious beliefs. America was not always so tolerant, however. Most early colonies had laws that limited what someone was allowed to believe or what church someone could attend. Pennsylvania was the one major exception to this rule. Due to his being persecuted in England for his beliefs, William Penn established his colony as one that would celebrate religious freedom.

William Penn's Payment. Basically, William Penn received Pennsylvania because of the fame and fortune of his father, the naval hero Admiral William Penn. King Charles II of England had borrowed a large sum of money from Admiral William Penn in a time of need. The king still owed the debt after the Admiral had died, but he had no cash to settle the debt with the Admiral's son. Penn knew this, so he told His Majesty that if he would give him a piece of wild land in America, he would ask nothing more.

Charles was glad to settle the account so easily, and he gave Penn a great territory north of Maryland and west of the Delaware River. This territory was nearly as large as England. The king named it *Pennsylvania*, a word that means "Penn's Woods." King Charles was not upset at losing the land because it was not thought to be worth much. No one at that time knew that beneath Penn's Woods there were immense amounts of coal and iron that would one day be worth more than all the king's wealth.

The truth is, however, that while Penn helped King Charles out of a tough situation, Charles was also helping him. Penn belonged to a religious society called the Society of Friends. The group is more popularly known as the Quakers. The Quakers believe that God will reveal His will to them if they are peaceful and patient enough to receive it. While the Quakers consider the Bible to be an authority for their lives, they believe the inner light they receive directly from God is more authoritative. That belief, combined with the unusual worship services they had (in which they were

Persecution of Quakers

known to sit in silence for hours until someone received the direct revelation) and their belief in pacifism (or refusal to fight in wars), led to their being persecuted in both Europe and North America. Thus, when Penn was given a free piece of land, he knew exactly what he wanted to do with it.

Penn wanted the land to be a safe haven for his fellow Quakers. Penn later bought the entire state of New Jersey for the same purpose. The Quakers suffered badly in England. They were often whipped and unjustly thrown in prison, where many died from the bad treatment they received. Penn himself had been placed in jail four times because of his religion. Although he was no longer in such danger because of his friendship with the king, he wanted to ensure that the Quakers had a place where they could live and worship in peace.

Penn Becomes Friends with the Indians. Another feature of the Quaker religion that set it apart from other religions was its attempt to befriend and understand others. For example, at a time when only men led churches, Quakers gave women equal power. More famously, however, was the way in which the Quakers treated the Indians. Penn rejected the method of simply taking Pennsylvania from the Indians, even though King Charles thought he owned it. Instead, Penn offered the Indians a fair price for the land, and he established a good relationship with them as a result.

William Penn Makes a Treaty with the Indians

The story goes that when William Penn reached America in 1682, he said, "We intend to sit down lovingly among the Indians." In the beginning, he held a great meeting with them under a wide-spreading elm that stood in what is now a part of Philadelphia. Here Penn and the Indians made a treaty in which they promised each other that they would live together as friends as long as the water should run in the rivers, or the sun shine in the sky.

The legend continues that not long after the great meeting under the elm, Penn visited some of the Indians in their wigwams, where they treated him to a meal of roasted acorns. After their feast, some of the young warriors began to run and jump in order to show the Englishman what they could do. Penn used to be quite an athlete himself, and the display inspired him to join in the fun. His ability to keep up with the younger Indians caused them to like him even more.

For sixty years after that treaty was established, the Pennsylvania settlers and the Native Americans were good friends. The Indians said, "The Quakers are honest men; they do no harm; they are welcome to come here." Thus, there were no wars with the Indians in Pennsylvania as there had been in New England.

Pennsylvania Grows but Penn Dies Tragically. Pennsylvania grew very quickly. The people were attracted by Penn's offer of cheap land and the freedom to govern themselves, especially the freedom to worship God as they pleased. Persecuted religious minorities from throughout Europe came to Pennsylvania: French Protestants, Mennonites, Amish, Catholics, Lutherans from German Catholic lands, and Jews.

First Continental Congress

Due to its central location, Philadelphia became one of the most important American cities during the colonial time period. When the War for American Independence began, representatives from all the states gathered there to decide what should be done in response to the British threat. This meeting was called the First Continental Congress, and it was held in the old State House, a building that still stands today. There in 1776, Congress declared the United States of America independent of England.

Philadelphia also grew because of Penn's generosity. He gave much of his own money to ensure that Pennsylvania not just survived, but thrived. Unfortunately, after Penn returned to England, he was wrongly put in prison by an angry former employee. Penn was innocent, and he proved that the man that accused him was nothing more than a thief. Shortly after he was freed, Penn died as a result of his stay in prison. When he died, some Indians from Pennsylvania sent his widow some beautiful furs in remembrance of their "Brother Penn," as they called him. They said that the furs were "to protect her while she passed through this thorny wilderness without her guide."

About twenty-five miles west of London, on a country road within sight of the towers of Windsor Castle, there stands a Friends' meetinghouse, or Quaker church. In the backyard of the meetinghouse, William Penn lies buried. For 100 years or more, there was no mark of any kind to show where he was buried. Now a small stone bearing his name points out the grave of the founder of the great state of Pennsylvania.

William Penn in Prison

Summary. Pennsylvania was a unique colony for many reasons. Because William Penn was a Quaker, and Quakers were persecuted badly in Europe, Pennsylvania was established to be a very tolerant colony. Thus, Pennsylvania drew a wide variety of people from all over Europe, and it became a very important state in the birth of the American nation.

Comprehension Questions

1. To whom did King Charles II owe a large sum of money?
2. How did King Charles pay his debt?
3. What did William Penn want Pennsylvania to be for the Quakers?
4. Why did the Indians not trouble the Quakers?
5. What are two reasons people came to settle in Pennsylvania?

Chapter 13
James Oglethorpe (1696–1785)

James Oglethorpe Makes a New Settlement in Georgia. We have seen that the first real colony or settlement made in America by the English was in Virginia in 1607. By the beginning of 1733, or in about 125 years, eleven more had been made—twelve in all. They stretched along the seacoast, from the farthest coast of Maine to the northern boundary of Florida, which was then owned by the Spaniards.

The two colonies farthest south were North Carolina and South Carolina. In 1733, James Oglethorpe, a brave English soldier who later became Major-General Oglethorpe, came over to North America to make a new settlement. This new one, which made a total of thirteen colonies, was called Georgia in honor of King George II, who gave a piece of land for it on the seacoast below South Carolina.

Oglethorpe had a friend in England who was cast into prison for debt. There the unfortunate man was so cruelly treated that he became sick and died, leaving his family in great trouble.

James Oglethorpe felt the death of his friend so much that he began to investigate how other poor debtors lived in the London prisons. He soon found that great numbers of them suffered terribly. The prisons were crowded and filthy. The men shut up in them were ragged and dirty; some of them were held with heavy chains; a good many actually died of starvation.

Oglethorpe could not bear to see strong men killed off in this manner. He thought that if the best of them (those who were honest and willing to work) could have the chance to earn their living, they would soon do as well as any men. During his effort to help them, he persuaded the king to give the land of Georgia.

Oglethorpe took thirty-five families to America in 1733. They settled on a bank of the Savannah River, about twenty miles from the sea. Oglethorpe laid out a town with broad, straight, elegant streets and with many small squares or parks. He called the settlement Savannah, from the Indian name of the river on which it stands.

General James Oglethorpe

In 1738, George Whitefield, the great Welsh (Calvinistic) Methodist preacher, traveled to Georgia at the request of Oglethorpe and the Wesley brothers; there he preached a series of revival messages to the colonists. When Whitefield returned to America in the fall of 1739, he preached almost every day for several months to large crowds as he traveled throughout the colonies, especially in the New England area. In 1740, he established the Bethesda Home for Boys, which still exists in Savannah, Georgia.

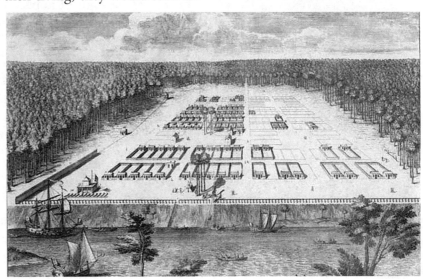

City of Savannah , 1734

The people of Charleston, South Carolina, were glad to have some English neighbors south of them to help them fight the Spaniards of Florida, who hated the English and wanted to drive them out. They gave the newcomers 100 head of cattle, a group of hogs, and twenty barrels of rice.

The emigrants began to work with a will, cutting down the forest trees, building houses, and planting gardens. There were no lazy people to be seen at Savannah. Even the children found something to do that was helpful.

Nothing disturbed the people but the alligators. They climbed up the bank from the river to see what was happening. But the boys soon taught them not to be too curious. When one monster was found impudently prowling around the town, they thumped him with sticks until they almost beat the life out of him. Soon the alligators decided not to pay any more visits to the settlers.

Georgia Grows. After a time, some German Protestants, who had been cruelly driven out of their native land on account of their religion, came to Georgia. Oglethorpe gave them a hearty welcome. He had bought land from the Indians, and so there was plenty of room for all. The Germans went up the river, and then went back several miles into the woods; there they picked out a place for a town. They called their settlement by the Bible name of Ebenezer, which means "The Lord hath helped us."

The "Blazed" Trees

There were no roads through the forests, so the new settlers "blazed" the trees; that is, they chopped a piece of bark off, so that they could find their way through the thick woods when they wanted to go to Savannah. Every tree so marked stood like a guidepost; it showed the traveler which way to go until he came in sight of the next one.

The settlers hoped to be able to get large quantities of silk to send to England because the mulberry tree grows wild in Georgia, and its leaves are the favorite food of the silkworm. At first, it seemed as if the plan would be successful, and Oglethorpe took over some Georgia silk as a present to the queen of England. She had a handsome dress made of it for her birthday; it was the first American silk dress ever worn by an English queen. But, after a while it was found that silk could not be produced in Georgia as well as it could in Italy and France, and so in time cotton became the favorite crop.

The people of Georgia did a good work in keeping out the Spaniards, who were trying to take over the country located just north of Florida. Later, like the settlers in North Carolina and South Carolina, they did their full share in helping to make America free from the rule of the king of England. When the War for American Independence began, the king had a lot of powder stored in Savannah. The people broke into the building, rolled out the kegs, and carried them off. Part of the powder they kept for themselves, and part they may have sent to Massachusetts; it is likely that the men who fought at Bunker Hill may have loaded their guns with some of the powder given to them by their friends in Savannah. Therefore, the king got it back, but in a different way than he expected.

In 1765, Oglethorpe was honored with the rank of a senior general. General Oglethorpe spent the closing years of his life in England. He lived to a very old age. Up to the last, he had eyes as bright and keen as a boy's. After the War for Independence was over, the king made a treaty, or agreement, by which he promised to let the United States of America live in peace. General Oglethorpe was able to read that treaty without glasses. He had lived to see the colony of Georgia, which he had settled, become a free and independent state. He died at Cranham Hall, Cranham, England.

In 1739, Oglethorpe was responsible for a number of successful raids on Spanish forts, as well as the siege of St. Augustine (see image above). This was during the War of Jenkins' Ear, which was fought between English Georgia and Spanish Florida. In 1743, Oglethorpe was promoted to the rank of brigadier general. In 1750, he left the colony, which opened the door to slavery being legalized.

Summary. In 1733, General James Oglethorpe brought over some emigrants from England and settled Savannah, Georgia. Georgia was the thirteenth English colony; it was the last one established in North America. General Oglethorpe lived to see it become one of the United States of America.

Comprehension Questions

1. At the beginning of 1733, how many English colonies were there in America?
2. Who was General Oglethorpe?
3. What did General Oglethorpe wish to do for the poor debtors?
4. Did the colony of Georgia raise more cotton or silk?
5. What good work did the people of Georgia do?
6. What event did General Oglethorpe see in his old age?

Chapter 14
George Whitefield (1714–1770)

When a simple farmer named Nathan Cole heard that George Whitefield was coming to preach in his home town of Middletown, Connecticut, on October 23, 1740, he "dropped [his] tool … and ran home to [his] wife, telling her to make ready quickly to go on and hear Mr. Whitefield preach." Mr. Cole and his wife then rode their horse twelve miles as fast as they could to where Whitefield was preaching. There they discovered that just about everyone in the surrounding area had come to hear this famous man preach a sermon.

But why? What had caused everyone to get so excited about a preacher coming to town? And what was it about this Whitefield that had helped create such expectation in this small town in Connecticut? The answer is actually quite simple: In the early 1700s, America was swept up in a series of religious revivals called the Great Awakening, and Whitefield was the most famous revivalist (or preacher) of them all.

Whitefield's Role in the Great Awakening. The Great Awakening was the first event that unified the American colonies. It did not matter if you were from Georgia or Maine, you heard about the Great Awakening and, chances are, you were affected by it. In both the big cities and the smallest of towns, revivals (religious meetings marked by a lot of enthusiasm and, Lord willing, a lot of conversions) occurred. The revivals had actually started before Whitefield came to America, but they were mostly local. The citizens of Massachusetts had their experience while the citizens of South Carolina had their own experience as well.

Whitefield changed all of that. He was able to fundamentally change the impact of the Great Awakening because he became America's first celebrity. Although we usually think of movie stars and sports figures as celebrities today, preachers were very important in America during the eighteenth century. But if you cannot believe that a preacher would be a celebrity, you would be even more amazed knowing a little something about Whitefield. He grew up poor in England. He basically had to beg his way through college. And he was not a good-looking man. Since getting a case of the measles when he was a child, Whitefield was permanently cross-eyed. In fact, people who did not like him often called him "Dr. Squintum." So despite the odds being stacked against Whitefield, he obviously succeeded.

Whitefield's Success. The key in Whitefield's success was the *way* he preached. Basically, no one in America (or even the world) had ever heard anyone preach the way Whitefield preached. The people were used to having their preachers read the sermons, staying behind the pulpit the entire time. But Whitefield, using skills he gained in his past as an actor, really *delivered* a sermon. For one thing, he preached his sermons *ex tempore*, or, off the top of his head. This freed him to emphasize the dramatic and emotional parts of the message. He would literally act out being born again, and he would often burst into tears. Another gift that Whitefield possessed was an incredible voice. Benjamin Franklin, who eventually became very good friends with Whitefield, estimated that about 30,000 people at a time could hear Whitefield preach. That is amazing considering he did not have a speaker system or anything else to make his voice louder.

Moreover, it was not unusual for thousands of people to go hear Whitefield preach. They did not just go because of Whitefield's revolutionary preaching style. They went because they expected him. Even though Whitefield was the most entertaining preacher they had ever heard, he was also the first preacher to recognize how powerful the press could be in helping publicize his ministry. So Whitefield promoted himself constantly. Newspapers published parts of Whitefield's diary, stories about his successes in various cities and towns, and updates of his schedule. Whitefield was front-page news. He helped sell papers and the papers helped promote Whitefield. It was a perfect "You scratch my back and I'll scratch your back" relationship.

Another factor that played into Whitefield's popularity was the fact that he practiced what he preached. Even though we see a lot of celebrities using their fame to get richer today, Whitefield was not like that at all. On his first trip to America, Whitefield established an orphanage in Georgia and did everything in his power to support it. He took an offering after every sermon he preached, collecting thousands

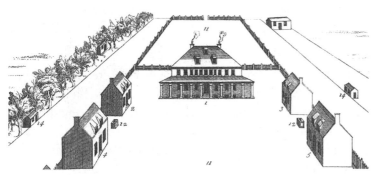

Bethesda Home for Boys, 1740

An Excerpt from Franklin's Autobiography

In 1739 arrived among us from Ireland the Reverend Mr. Whitefield, who had made himself remarkable there as an itinerant preacher. He was at first permitted to preach in some of our churches; but the clergy, taking a dislike to him, soon refus'd him their pulpits, and he was oblig'd to preach in the fields. The multitudes of all sects and denominations that attended his sermons were enormous, and it was matter of speculation to me, who was one of the number, to observe the extraordinary influence of his oratory on his hearers, and how much they admir'd and respected him.... *It was wonderful to see the change soon made in the manners of our inhabitants. From being thoughtless or indifferent about religion, it seem'd as if all the world were growing religious, so that one could not walk thro' the town in an evening without hearing psalms sung in different families of every street* [italics added]....

Mr. Whitefield, in leaving us, went preaching all the way thro' the colonies to Georgia. The settlement of that province had lately been begun, ... with families of broken shop-keepers and other insolvent debtors, ... taken out of the jails, who ... perished in numbers, leaving many helpless children unprovided for. The sight of their miserable situation inspir'd the benevolent heart of Mr. Whitefield with the idea of building an Orphan House there, in which they might be supported and educated. Returning northward, he preach'd up this charity, and made large collections, for his eloquence had a wonderful power over the hearts and purses of his hearers, of which I myself was an instance.....

Benjamin Franklin

A Cartoon Ridiculing George Whitefield's Preaching

of dollars, and then he passed every penny he could on to the orphanage. This simple act of kindness helped his listeners to believe the message he was preaching even more.

Whitefield's Critics. Not everyone was excited about Whitefield's success, however. And just as there are many reasons to explain why Whitefield became popular, there are also many reasons to explain why people did not like him. One of the most basic reasons was simple jealousy. While Whitefield achieved almost instant national success, many preachers had worked for years with little or no recognition outside their own church. That seemed unfair to them.

Other preachers were not too concerned with how famous Whitefield was, but they were concerned with the preaching style he used. They argued that Whitefield depended too much on the emotional response he created among his listeners. The problem, they believed, was that emotion only lasts a short time. Therefore, once Whitefield left town with all the excitement that came with him, people would go on living the way they had lived before he had come. Whitefield's critics argued that a calm and orderly presentation of biblical truths was the best way to give a sermon since that method actually helped people *learn more* about God. Whitefield's simple response was that true Christians were more like friends of God than students of God.

George Whitefield Preaching Outdoors

Finally, the most serious problem some other preachers had with Whitefield was how he ignored the way the church was used to doing things. That is why Whitefield preached outdoors. He wanted to preach to as many people as possible instead of being restricted by the limits a building would place on him. He also wanted to preach to more than one church's people at a time, and his ability to do that would be limited using the traditional method of preaching. He ignored it because, as far as he was concerned, doing what worked was more important than tradition (historical beliefs or customs).

But some preachers were uncomfortable with the way Whitefield redefined their job by ignoring the way it had been done for centuries. They believed they had biblical reasons for leading their churches the way they did. But because Whitefield was so popular, they had to work harder to keep people in their churches. Those preachers realized that either they would have to become more like Whitefield or lose their people to preachers who were willing to become more like Whitefield. The result was that some preachers who were more concerned with entertaining their congregations became more popular than those who tried to preach the correct biblical truths. Even today preachers struggle with that same problem.

Whitefield's Impact. The Great Awakening and Whitefield created a lot of controversy in their day, and they are still argued about today. But while everyone cannot agree as to whether they were good for America, everyone does agree that they were very important in American history. One important idea developed during the Great Awakening by Whitefield was the concept of freedom. Whitefield gave many people the idea that following traditions was not necessarily the best way of doing things. In fact, he even argued that traditions were holding the people back from experiencing true religion. A few decades later, most of the people who agreed with Whitefield on that point argued that British traditions were holding them back, and the War for American Independence started as a result. Basically, Whitefield helped prepare the American people to fight the war that would establish them as their own nation. It does not get much more influential than that.

Summary. George Whitefield unified the Great Awakening in America, preaching to multitudes of all sects and denominations in the open air. In spite of being ridiculed, he powerfully delivered his sermons that pointed men's sinful souls to the Savior. Whitefield also practiced what he preached by establishing the Bethesda Home for Boys (1740) in Georgia. He also faced criticism from some who were jealous, others who were concerned with tradition, and those who thought his emotional preaching would not bear lasting fruit. Nevertheless, Whitefield's impact on America was great, encouraging freedom and preparing the people for independence.

In conclusion, the Great Awakening was the first national event in America's history, and it introduced America's first celebrity, George Whitefield. While this revival was a controversial event, and Whitefield was a controversial figure, everyone agrees that both were very important in American history. We owe that to the gifts that God gave George Whitefield and his willingness to use them for God's glory.

Comprehension Questions

1. What is a revival?

2. What job did Whitefield have before becoming a preacher that helped his preaching?

3. Where did Whitefield send all the money he received from the offerings he took after his sermons?

4. Why did Whitefield like to preach outdoors?

5. How did Whitefield help prepare America for the War for American Independence?

From "The Seed of the Woman, and the Seed of the Serpent," a Sermon by George Whitefield

[Genesis 1] Verse 9. "And the Lord God called unto Adam, and said unto him, Adam, where art thou?"

"The Lord God called unto Adam." (for otherwise Adam would never have called unto the Lord God) and said, "Adam, where art thou? How is it that thou comest not to pay thy devotions as usual?" Christians, remember the Lord keeps an account when you fail coming to worship. Whenever therefore you are tempted to withhold your attendance, let each of you fancy you heard the Lord calling unto you, and saying, "O man, O woman, where art thou? It may be understood in another and better sense; "Adam, where art thou?" What a condition is thy poor soul in? This is the first thing the Lord asks and convinces a sinner of; when he prevents and calls him effectually by his grace; he also calls him by name; for unless God speaks to us in particular, and we know where we are, how poor, how miserable, how blind, how naked, we shall never value the redemption wrought out for us by the death and obedience of the dear Lord Jesus. "Adam, where art thou?"

Unit 3

Founding of a New Nation

Chapter 15
Benjamin Franklin (1706–1790)

Benjamin Franklin in Philadelphia. By the year 1733, when the people of Savannah were building their first log cabins, Philadelphia had grown to be the largest city in the North American Colonies—though it would take more than seventy such cities to make one as great as Philadelphia is today.

Next to William Penn, the person who did the most for Philadelphia was a young man who had come from Boston to make his home among the Quakers. He lived in a small house near the market. On a board over the door, he had painted his name and business: *Benjamin Franklin, Printer.*

Franklin was then publishing a small newspaper called the *Pennsylvania Gazette.* Today we print newspapers with computer-controlled electric power at the rate of one or two thousand a minute; but Franklin, standing in his shirtsleeves at a little press, printed slowly with his own hands. It was slow, hard work, as you could see by the drops of sweat that stood on his forehead. The young man not only wrote most of what he printed in his paper, but he often made his own ink; sometimes he even made his own type. When he ran out of paper, he would take a wheelbarrow, go out and buy a load, and wheel it home. Today there are more than one dozen newspapers printed in Philadelphia; then there were only two, and Franklin's was the better of them.

In addition to this paper, he published an almanac, which thousands of people bought. In it he printed such sayings as these: "He who would thrive must rise at five," and "If you want a thing well done, do it yourself." But Franklin was not contented with simply printing these sayings; he practiced them as well.

Sometimes his friends would ask him why he began work so early in the morning, and kept at it so many hours. He would laugh and tell them that his father used to repeat to him this saying of Solomon's: "Seest thou a man diligent in his business? He shall stand before kings; he shall not stand before mean men" (Proverbs 22:29).

The site of the house in which Benjamin Franklin was born and spent his early years is opposite the Old South Meeting House.

At that time, the young printer never expected to stand in the presence of a king; but years later, he met with five. One of them, his friend, the king of France, gave him his picture covered with diamonds.

Franklin's Boyhood. Franklin's father was a poor man with a large family. He lived in Boston and made soap and candles. Benjamin went to school two years; then, when he was ten years old, his father set him to work in his factory, and he finished the rest of his schooling at home. He was now kept busy filling the candle molds with melted tallow, cutting off the ends of the wicks, and running errands.

The boy did not like this type of work; and as he was very fond of books, his father sent him to work in the printing shop of James Franklin, one of Benjamin's brothers. James Franklin paid a small sum of money each week for Benjamin's housing; but the boy told him that if he would let him have half the money to use as he wished, he would house himself. James was glad to do this. Benjamin then stopped eating meat, and while the others went out to dinner, he would stay in the printing office and eat a boiled potato or a handful of raisins. In this way he saved up several coins every week; and when he had saved enough money, he would buy a book.

James Franklin was not only a selfish man, but also a hot-tempered one. When he became angry with his young apprentice, he would beat and knock him around. At length, the lad, who was now seventeen, made up his mind that he would run away and go to New York.

Young Franklin Moves to Philadelphia. Young Franklin sold some of his books, and with the money paid his passage to New York City on a sailing vessel, for in those days there were no airplanes or railroads in America. He could not find work in New York, however, so he decided to move on to Philadelphia. He started to walk across New Jersey to Burlington on the Delaware River, a distance of about fifty miles; there he hoped to get a sailboat going down the river to Philadelphia. Shortly after he set out, it began to rain hard, and the lad was soon soaked to the skin and splashed with red mud; but he continued until noon, and then took a rest. On the third day, he reached Burlington and found passage down the river.

Franklin landed in Philadelphia on a Sunday morning in 1723. He was tired and hungry; he had but a single dollar in the world. As he walked along, he saw a bakeshop open. He went in and bought three great, puffy rolls for a penny each. Then he started up Market Street, where he was one day to have his newspaper office. He had a roll like a small loaf of bread tucked under each arm, and he was eating the other as though it tasted good to him. As he passed a house, he noticed a nice-looking young woman. She seemed to want to laugh, and well she might, for Franklin appeared like a youthful tramp who had been robbing a baker's shop. The young woman was Miss Deborah Read. Several years later, Franklin married her. He always said that he could not have been blest with a better wife.

Franklin continued in his walk until he came to the Delaware River. He took a little drink of river water to settle his breakfast and then gave away the two rolls he had under his arm to a poor woman with a child. On his way back from the river, he followed some people to a Quaker meeting-house. At the meeting no one spoke. Franklin was tired out, and not having any preacher to keep him awake, he soon fell asleep, and slept until the meeting was over. He says, "This was the first house I was in or slept in, in Philadelphia."

The next day, the young man found some work in a printing office. Six months afterward, he decided to go back to Boston to see his friends. He started on his journey with a good suit of clothes, a silver watch, and a well-filled purse.

Franklin's First Day in Philadelphia

While in Boston, Franklin went to call on a minister who had written a little book that he had been very fond of reading. As he was coming away from the minister's house, he had to go through a low passageway under a large beam. "Stoop! Stoop!" cried out the gentleman; but Franklin did not understand him, and so hit his head a sharp knock against the beam. "Ah," said his friend, as he saw him rubbing his head, "you are young, and have the world before you; stoop as you go through it, and you will miss many hard thumps." Franklin says that this sensible advice, which was thus beat into his head, was of great use because he learned then how to stoop to conquer. Even the Bible tells us that "...he who humbles himself shall be exalted" (Luke 18:14).

Franklin Goes to London. Franklin soon went back to Philadelphia. When Franklin was only seventeen, the governor of Pennsylvania then persuaded him to go to London, telling him that he would help him to get a printing press and type to start a newspaper in Philadelphia.

When Franklin reached London, he found that the governor was one of those men who promise great things, but do nothing. Instead of buying a press, Franklin had to go to work in a printing office to earn his bread. He stayed in London more than a year. At the office where he worked, the men were great beer drinkers. One of his companions bought six pints a day. He began with a pint before breakfast. Then he took another pint at breakfast, a pint between breakfast and dinner, a pint at dinner, a pint in the afternoon, and last of all, a pint after he had finished work. Franklin drank nothing but water. The others laughed at him, and nicknamed him

Stoop! Stoop!

Ben Franklin's *Pennsylvania Gazette*, January 2, 1750

the "Water-American"; but after a while, they had to confess that he was stronger than they were who drank so much strong beer.

The fact was that Franklin could beat them, both at work and at play. When they went out for a bath in the Thames River, they found that their "Water-American" could swim like a fish. He so astonished them that a rich Londoner tried to persuade him to start a swimming school to teach his sons; but Franklin had stayed in England long enough, and he now decided to go back to Philadelphia.

Franklin Becomes Successful in Philadelphia. After his return to America, Franklin labored so diligently that he was soon able to establish a newspaper of his own. He tried to make it a good one, but some people thought that he spoke his mind too freely. They complained of this to him, and explained that if he did not make his paper to please them, they would stop taking it or advertising in it.

Franklin heard what they had to say and then invited them all to come and have supper with him. They went expecting a feast, but they found nothing on the table but two dishes of cornmeal mush and a big pitcher of cold water. Only very poor people then ate that kind of mush. Because it was yellow and coarse, it was nicknamed "sawdust pudding."

Franklin gave everybody a heaping plateful; and then, filling his own, he made a hearty supper of it. The others tried to eat, but could not. After Franklin had finished his supper, he looked up and said quietly, "My friends, anyone who can live on 'sawdust pudding' and cold water, as I can, does not need much help from others." After that, no one went to the young printer with complaints about his paper. Franklin, as we have seen, had learned to stoop; but he certainly did not wish to go stooping through life.

Benjamin Franklin worked hard to make his newspaper truly serve the needs of the American people. In an effort to provide his readers with access to important and uplifting spiritual information, Franklin reprinted a number of articles and booklets that were written by influential British evangelist George Whitefield. These articles helped Whitefield play a leading role in a wonderful period of revival in the American colonies known as the First Great Awakening. Rev. Whitefield visited the colonies several times from 1739-1770, and many newspaper editors like Franklin helped to spread the important truths that Whitefield was trying to bring to the hearts of the American people.

Not many young men can see their own faults, but Franklin could see his. More than that, he tried hard to get rid of them. He kept a little book in which he wrote down his faults. If he wasted half an hour of time or a shilling of money, or said anything that he should not have said, he wrote it down in his book. He carried that book in his pocket all his life, and he studied it as a boy at school studies a hard lesson. From it, he learned three things: first, to do the right thing; next, to do it at the right time; last of all, to do it in the right way.

As he never tired of helping himself to get upward and onward, so, too, he never tired of helping others. He started the first public library in Philadelphia, which was also the first in America. He began the first fire engine company and the first military company in that city. He led the people to pave the muddy streets with stone. He helped to build the first academy, now called the University of Pennsylvania, and he also helped to build the first hospital.

Franklin's Experiments. While doing these things and publishing his paper besides, Franklin found time to make experiments with electricity. Very little was then known about this wonderful power, but a Dutchman living in Leyden, Holland, had discovered a way of bottling it up in what is called a Leyden jar. Franklin had one of these jars, and he never tired of seeing what new and strange thing he could do with it.

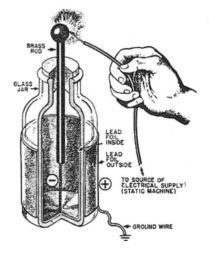

Leyden Jar Being Charged

He made a picture of the king of England with a movable gold crown on his head. Then he connected the crown by a long wire with the Leyden jar. When he wanted some fun, he would dare anyone to go up to the picture and take off the king's crown. "Why that's easy enough," a man would say; and would walk up and seize the crown. But as soon he touched it, he would get an electric shock that would make his fingers tingle as they had never tingled before. With a loud "Oh! Oh!" he would let go of the crown and stand back in amazement, not knowing what had hurt him.

But Franklin's greatest experiment was conducted seriously with a kite. He believed that the electricity in the bottle, or Leyden jar, was the same thing as the lightning we see in a thunderstorm. He knew well enough how to get an electric spark from the jar, for with such a spark he had once killed a turkey for dinner. Could he get such a spark from a cloud in the sky?

He thought about it for a long time; then he made a kite out of a silk handkerchief and fastened a sharp iron point to the upright stick of the kite. One day, when a thunderstorm was coming up, Franklin and his son went out to the fields. The kite was raised; then Franklin tied an iron key to the lower end of the string. After waiting some time, he saw the little hair-like threads of the string begin to stand up like the bristles of a brush. He felt certain that the electricity was coming down the string. He put his knuckle close to the key, and a spark flew out. Next, he took his Leyden jar and collected the electricity in it. He had made two great discoveries: he had found out that electricity and lightning are the same thing; and he had also found how to fill his bottle directly from the clouds, which no one had ever done before.

But Franklin did not stop his work. He reasoned that if he could draw down electricity from the sky with a kite string, he could draw it better still with a tall, sharp, pointed iron rod. He put up such a rod on his house in Philadelphia; it was the first lightning rod in the world. Soon other people began to put them up, so this was another gift of his to the city that he loved. Every good lightning rod that has since been built to protect buildings has been, in some degree, a copy of that first one invented by Franklin.

People now began to talk, not only in this country but also in Europe, about his electrical experiments and discoveries. The oldest college in Scotland—the University of St. Andrews—gave him a title of honor and called him Doctor—a word which means a learned man—in 1759, and one of England's most famous universities—the University of Oxford—gave him another honorary degree in 1762. After receiving these honors, Franklin the printer was no longer plain Mr. Franklin, but Dr. Franklin.

Dr. Franklin did not think that he had found out all that could be found out about electricity; he believed that he had simply made a beginning, and that other men would discover still greater things that could be done with it. Do you think he was mistaken about that?

JOIN, or DIE.

Franklin the Statesman. As Franklin became successful as a printer and author, people in the colonies began to look to him as a leader in colonial affairs. In 1753, he was appointed deputy postmaster general for the British colonies in North America and sought to improve the mail system in the colonies. The next year, he proposed a plan of union among the British colonies as they faced war between Britain and France in North America. His motto for the plan was "Join, or Die." The plan was rejected, but it was the first serious effort at unity in America.

Franklin later spent many years in England as an agent representing some of the colonies before the British government. He was first appointed by the Pennsylvania assembly to bring the colony's concerns before Parliament and the king. He was later appointed by the colonies of Georgia, New Jersey, and Massachusetts to do the same thing. Franklin became a major voice representing American interests in England. Tensions between the colonies and Britain became so bad, however, that Franklin decided to return to Pennsylvania in 1775.

When the War for American Independence broke out, Dr. Franklin did a great work for his country. He did not fight battles like George Washington, but he did something just as useful. First, he helped write the Declaration of Independence, by which the Americans declared themselves free from the rule of the king of England. Next, he went to France to get aid for America, where he stayed until 1785. The colonies were then too poor to pay their soldiers; he convinced the king of France to let them have the money to pay their soldiers. He convinced the French to make a treaty of alliance with America in 1778.

Committee for Drafting the Declaration of Independence

Franklin lived to see the War for Independence ended and America free in 1783. He even helped make the treaty with the British that ended the fighting. Franklin fulfilled a final service for his country by being a member of the Constitutional Convention that wrote the Constitution. When he died, full of years and of honors, he was buried in Philadelphia. Twenty thousand people went to his funeral.

If you wish to see what the country thinks of him, you have only to look at a large map of the United States and count how many times you find his name on it. You will find that more than 200 counties and towns are named Franklin.

Summary. Benjamin Franklin was born in Boston over 200 years ago. He went to Philadelphia when he was seventeen. He started a newspaper there, opened the first public library, and did many other things to help the city. He discovered that lightning and electricity are the same thing, and he invented the lightning rod to protect buildings. During the War for Independence, he received large sums of money from the king of France to pay the soldiers and help General Washington fight the battles that won America's freedom.

Comprehension Questions

1. Who did a great deal for Philadelphia?
2. What saying of Solomon's did Franklin's father often repeat to him?
3. Name three things that Franklin did for the city of Philadelphia.
4. What title did a college in Scotland give Franklin?
5. Did Franklin think that anything more would be discovered about electricity?
6. What two things did Franklin do in the Revolution?

Chapter 16
John Witherspoon (1723–1794)

The church was very active during the War for Independence, both in support of the patriots but also in opposition to them. One of their strongest supporters was John Witherspoon, a Presbyterian minister and college president. Even though he had only been in America for a few years, he became the only minister to sign the Declaration of Independence. In contrast with those who believed it was more important to stay loyal to the king, Witherspoon believed that the colonists had the right to fight anyone who tried to take away their liberty.

Church Support of the War for American Independence. Many Christians in America were concerned about the efforts of the British to exert greater control over their American colonies. While the political leaders became angry when the king tried to tax them more without their consent, religious leaders were afraid that Britain was going to take away the religious freedom they enjoyed in America. Thus, many religious and political leaders came to believe that independence from Britain was the only way to protect their freedoms.

Isaac Backus (1724–1806)

Many different religious leaders united in their defense of the colonists in their sermons, even though they represented many different church backgrounds. For example, the Sunday after the battles of Lexington and Concord, Isaac Backus, a Calvinistic Baptist minister from Massachusetts, preached that "it was a foundation point in the constitution of the English government that the people's property shall not be taken from them without their consent...." Therefore, Backus concluded that "our cause was just." Also, Congregational (or Puritan) pastor Moses Mather wrote a tract in 1775 entitled "America's Appeal to the Impartial World," supporting colonial claims against Parliament.

In 1744, at the age of twenty-five years old, Moses Mather became the minister of the First Congregational Church of Middlesex Parish (Darien), Connecticut.

Church support for the war extended beyond individual pastors, however. Entire church assemblies of different traditions expressed their support for American independence. The Presbyterian Synod of New York and Philadelphia wrote a letter on May 20, 1775, encouraging its ministers and church members to support the actions of the Continental Congress against British colonial policies. Later, in 1783, the Synod sent a letter to its churches thanking them for their support for the cause of American independence and asking them "to render thanks to Almighty God, for all of His mercies, spiritual and temporal, and in particular for establishing the Independence of the United States of America." After learning about the American victory at Yorktown, Virginia, those attending the meeting of the Philadelphia Baptist Association got up at sunrise on October 23, 1781, to thank God for His blessings on this country.

One of the religious traditions most supportive of the patriot cause was the Presbyterians. A Hessian captain, who served with the British army in Pennsylvania, argued that the war was "not an American rebellion, it is nothing more or less than an Irish-Scotch Presbyterian Rebellion." The Hessian may have reached that conclusion because of men like Rev. James Caldwell, the pastor of a Presbyterian church in New Jersey. During a skirmish near his church, Continental soldiers were running low on paper to use as wadding in their muskets. Caldwell ran into his church and brought out copies of Isaac Watts's hymnals for them to tear apart for wadding. According to legend, as he did so, he told the soldiers, "Now boys, give 'em Watts!"

The British or the Loyalists often targeted Christians who supported American independence. Because of Rev. Moses Mather's fervent support for American independence, he was captured on two different occasions by Loyalists and kept in prison in New York City for several months. The almost unanimous support of Presbyterians for the patriot cause often led the British to vent their anger on Presbyterians and their property. The Synod letter of 1783, mentioned above, spoke of their "burnt and wasted churches, and our plundered dwellings, in such places as fell under the power of our adversaries."

John Witherspoon's Life and Impact. One of the most fervent Presbyterian supporters of American independence was John Witherspoon, president of the College of New Jersey (now known as Princeton University). He was also an unlikely supporter for independence, however, because he was a relatively new resident of America. Witherspoon had even opposed a Scottish rebellion against King George II in 1745 when he still lived in his native country.

Rev. Witherspoon was born in Scotland in 1723 and lived there until 1768, when he moved to the American colonies to become president of the college. His mother initially taught him at home, learning to read from the Bible at age four. Being an extremely gifted student, Witherspoon sped through grammar school, college, and seminary. He received his seminary degree by the age of twenty and was well prepared to take a pastor's job at that point.

He followed his father into the ministry of the Church of Scotland and pastored two different Presbyterian churches for a total of seventeen years. He married his first wife during his first pastorate. Witherspoon was a faithful pastor who stressed the need for biblically-based sermons, taught that salvation is by grace alone, spoke of the need for the elect to give an evidence of their faith through good works and morality, and emphasized local control of the church. This combination of beliefs made him an attractive candidate to be a leader in the American Presbyterian church. On the one hand, the Presbyterians who appreciated George Whitefield's revivals (and considered his success in the Great Awakening to be an inspiration) really liked Witherspoon's evangelical zeal and his emphasis on

Rev. James Caldwell
at the Battle of Springfield

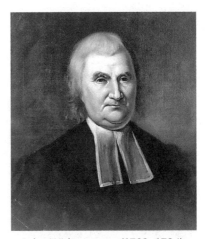

John Witherspoon (1723–1794)

morality and Christian living. On the other hand, the more traditional Presbyterians respected Witherspoon's concern to be biblically accurate. Thus, he was acceptable to all major factions within the American Presbyterian churches.

Witherspoon had a significant influence on America through his work at the College of New Jersey. He served as president from 1768 to 1794, teaching several classes and filling the position of professor of divinity at the college. He lived on campus and preached regularly at the Presbyterian church next to his house. Of the 478 men to graduate during his tenure as president of the college, many went on to play important roles in the life of the United States. Many became ministers, and several served their states and country in important political and legal positions. His most famous graduate was James Madison, who went on to become Secretary of State and later the fourth President of the United States.

College of New Jersey

Rev. Witherspoon's impact, however, was not limited to his work at the college or his labors in the pulpit. History remembers him best as an active supporter of American independence. He delivered one of the more famous sermons in American history on May 17, 1776, less than two months before becoming the only minister to sign the Declaration of Independence. The sermon, titled "The Dominion of Providence over the Passions of Men," argued that Britain was unjustly requiring total submission by the colonies. Witherspoon believed that man had the obligation to fight in the defense of his God-given right to both political and religious freedom. He also reminded his congregation that no matter how bad things looked God was always in control. Witherspoon's strong leadership skills led him to be elected as a delegate from New Jersey to the Continental Congress, where he served from 1776 to 1782.

After leaving Congress, he spent the next several years at the college but was again elected to public office in 1789, serving in the New Jersey legislature and heading a committee on abolishing the slave trade in New Jersey. His first wife died in October 1789, but he remarried two years later, at the age of sixty-eight. He died on November 15, 1794, after being blind for three years.

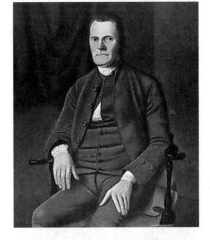

Roger Sherman (1721–1793)

Other Supporters of American Independence. As stated, Presbyterians were not the only Christians who played an important role in securing American independence. Baptists, such as John Hart (a deacon and signer of the Declaration of Independence), and Congregationalists, such as Roger Sherman, were also heavily involved in the effort. Sherman was described by John Adams as "an old Puritan, as honest as an angel and as firm in the cause of American independence as Mount Atlas." His influence is most clearly seen in that he was the only person to sign the Articles of Association (1774), the Declaration of Independence (1776), the Articles of Confederation (1777), and the United States Constitution (1787).

Ironically, many members of the Church of England (known as Anglicans in Britain and Episcopalians in America) were very important to the success of the War for American Independence. While their church membership committed them to be loyal to the British royalty, Episcopalians still made up two thirds of the signers of the Declaration of Independence. Some of the more notable signatures on that document include George Washington (commander of the American armies during the War for American Independence and the first U.S. President), Alexander Hamilton (army officer in the war, delegate to the Constitutional Convention, and the first Secretary of the Treasury under President Washington), and Patrick Henry (governor of Virginia best known for his stirring call, "Give me liberty or give me death!").

Christian Support for Britain. While many Christians supported the war, not all did. These men were known as Loyalists. While most of the signers of the Declaration of Independence were Episcopalian, many Americans who came from that same church tradition also provided the British Army a lot of support. Many believed that the Word of God required submission to their ruler and to the laws of the land. Therefore, they believed that rebellion against England was wrong. In addition, ministers of the Church of England had to swear that they would not support any effort to harm or depose the English monarch, and they regularly included prayers for the king in the worship services. Those that signed the Declaration of Independence clearly believed freedom was more important than those vows or prayers.

Even though the Methodist church was extremely small in America before the War for Independence, a large majority of the members were Loyal-

Francis Asbury (1745–1816)

Thomas Fitzsimmons (1741–1811)

ists. The founders of the Methodist movement, Charles and John Wesley, strongly opposed the War for Independence. In fact, all but one of the Methodist missionaries left America and returned to England. Only Francis Asbury remained in America because he strongly disagreed with the Wesleys' support for the Loyalist cause. Another exception was Richard Bassett from Delaware. Mr. Bassett was a devout Methodist and friend of Francis Asbury who served in the Delaware militia and government during the War for American Independence. He later was a delegate from Delaware at the Constitutional Convention in 1787 and served in the United States Senate.

Many Roman Catholics were also sympathetic to the British. Protestants distrusted the Catholics because of the Catholic belief that everyone was supposed to obey the pope. The Protestants thought that the Catholics would take away their religious liberty if they were given the chance to do so. Because of this mistrust, Catholics and Protestants did not always get along. Not all Catholics reacted this way, however. Individual Catholics such as Daniel Carroll of Maryland and Thomas Fitzsimmons of Pennsylvania were both active in efforts to support the American war effort and later were delegates to the Constitutional Convention.

Many Loyalists left the thirteen colonies, either permanently or temporarily. Many settled in Canada, establishing a large English settlement there. They left because they did not wish to live in a country that they believed had unlawfully revolted against its rightful ruler. Others left because of persecution by supporters of American independence.

Christian Pacifism. While most Christians in America could be considered either Patriots or Loyalists, some attempted to remain neutral throughout the war because they opposed the use of military force. Such people are generally known as pacifists.

The best-known and oldest group of pacifists in America was part of the Quakers. They had established themselves in Pennsylvania, following the lead of history's most famous Quaker and the state's namesake, William Penn. All but a few Quakers opposed military service or even the hiring of substitutes to fight for them. They also objected to paying any war taxes or fines for not having served in the military or provided substitutes. The Quaker church disciplined several hundred individual Quakers for paying these war taxes and fines. They also questioned the appropriateness of giving oaths of loyalty to state governments that had come into being through rebellion against their rulers.

Other pacifists that had come to America during the eighteenth century included the Mennonites, Moravians, and Dunkers (the name comes from their mode of baptism). The Mennonites held beliefs that were similar to those of the Quakers, but the others tended to be more flexible. Unlike the Quakers, they were willing to pay war taxes and fines, and hire substitutes; some even participated in the war in noncombatant roles such as working in hospitals or driving wagons. Moravians were even willing to fight in their own self-defense in some instances.

Most pacifists eventually supported the patriot position in spite of their rejection of military service and the persecution some received from patriots for their positions. The Moravians tended to be more sympathetic to the loyalist cause because they appreciated the greater freedom given them under British rule as opposed to the persecution they had suffered in continental Europe (mostly Germany). Also, they had taken oaths of loyalty to Britain when they came to America, and they did not take those oaths lightly.

Summary. American Christians were divided in their response to the War for American Independence. Many actively supported the independence of the colonies from England while some remained loyal to Britain. A small minority tried to remain neutral because they were opposed to all military action. If it had not been for the prayers and work of men like Rev. John Witherspoon, the cause of American independence could have been lost.

Comprehension Questions

1. What did the Loyalists do to Rev. Mather?
2. What church assembly got up at sunrise to thank God for the American victory at Yorktown, Virginia?
3. Why did Rev. Witherspoon support the American Revolution?
4. How many ministers signed the Declaration of Independence?
5. Which church brought all but one of its missionaries home to England during the Revolutionary War?
6. Name one of the pacifist groups in America during the Revolutionary War.

Count Nicholas Ludwig von Zinzendorf (1700–1760)

Count Zinzendorf is known for preaching a religion marked by emotional expression and personal piety. This was in reaction to the intellectual and liturgical practices of the German state church (Lutheran).

In 1752, Count Zinzendorf arranged the purchase of nearly 100,000 acres of land from the Earl of Granville, who owned the northern portion of North Carolina. This arrangement allowed Moravians to settle in the hilly Piedmont region of North Carolina. In this area, the count helped establish six Moravian communities, with the hope of escaping their religious enemies in Europe, separating themselves from the sinful temptations of the world, and earning profits.

After meeting a slave who had been converted, Count Zinzendorf became burdened to share the gospel around the world. In obedience to the Great Commission, he sent missionaries to the Native Americans and even traveled to America to meet with Indian chiefs.

Chapter 17
George Washington (1732–1799)

George Washington (1732–1799)

George Washington is one of the most important persons in American history. He led America to victory over the British during the War for American Independence and later led the United States in peace as its first President. He was highly thought of by his countrymen for his ability, integrity, and commitment to duty. After Washington's death, Charles Lee, an army comrade and congressman, gave the following tribute to Washington: "First in war, first in peace, and first in the hearts of his countrymen…." He was truly the "Father of His Country."

A Virginia Boy. In 1732, when Franklin was at work on his newspaper, a boy was born on a plantation in Virginia who was one day to become even greater than the Philadelphia printer.

That boy when he grew up was to be chosen leader of the armies of the War for Independence; he was to be elected the first President of the United States; and before he died he was to be known and honored throughout the world. The name of that boy was George Washington.

Washington's father died when George was only eleven years old, leaving him, with his brothers and sisters, to the care of a most excellent and sensible mother. It was that mother's influence, more than anything else, except the influence of the Holy Spirit, which made George the man he became.

George went to a little country school, where he learned to read, write, and work math. By the time he was twelve, he could write a clear, bold letter. In one of his first books, he copied many good rules or sayings. Here is one: Labor to keep alive in your breast that little spark of heavenly fire called conscience.

But young Washington was not always copying good sayings, for he was a tall, strong boy, fond of all outdoor sports and games. He was a well-meaning boy, but he had a hot temper; and at times, his blue eyes flashed fire.

In all trials of strength and all deeds of daring, George took the lead; he could run faster, jump farther, and throw a stone higher than anyone else in the school. When the boys played "soldier," they liked to have "Captain George" as commander. When he drew his wooden sword, and shouted "Come on!" they would all rush into battle with a wild hurrah. Years afterward, when the real war came, and George Washington drew his sword in real battle, some of his school companions may have fought under their old leader.

Once, however, Washington had a battle of a different kind. It was with a high-spirited young horse that belonged to his mother. Nobody had ever been able to do anything with that colt, and most people were afraid of him. Early one morning, George and some of his brothers were out in the pasture. George looked at the colt prancing about and kicking up his heels. Then he said, "Boys, if you'll help me put a bridle on him, I'll ride him." The boys managed to get the colt into a corner and to slip on the bridle. With a leap, George seated himself firmly on his back. Then the fun began. The colt, wild with rage, ran, jumped, plunged, and reared straight up on his hind legs, hoping to throw his rider off. It was all useless; he might as well have tried to throw off his own skin, for the boy stuck to his back as though he had grown there. Then, making a last desperate bound into the air, the animal burst a blood vessel and fell dead. The battle was over, George was victor, but it had cost the life of Mrs. Washington's favorite colt.

When the boys went in for breakfast, their mother, knowing that they had just come from the pasture, asked how the colt was getting on.

"He is dead, madam," said George. "I killed him."

"Dead!" exclaimed his mother.

"Yes, madam, dead," replied her son. Then he told her just how it happened.

When Mrs. Washington heard the story, her face flushed with anger. Then, waiting a moment, she looked steadily at George, and said quietly, "While I regret the loss of my favorite horse, I rejoice in my son, who always speaks the truth."

Washington Makes the Acquaintance of Lord Fairfax. George's eldest brother, Lawrence Washington, had married the daughter of a gentleman named Colonel William Fairfax of Belvoir, who lived on the banks of the Potomac. Lawrence had a fine home a few miles away on the same river; he called his place Mount Vernon. When he was fourteen, George went to Mount Vernon to stay with his brother.

Lawrence Washington took George down the river to call on the Fairfaxes. There the lad made the acquaintance of Lord Fairfax, an English nobleman who had come from London. He owned an immense piece of land in Virginia. Lord Fairfax and George soon became great friends. He was a gray-haired man nearly sixty, but he enjoyed having this boy of fourteen as a companion. They spent weeks together on horseback in the fields and woods, hunting deer and foxes.

Lawrence Washington (1718–1752)

Lord Fairfax's land extended westward more than 100 miles. It had never been carefully surveyed; and he was told that settlers were moving in beyond the Blue Ridge Mountains, and were building log cabins on his property without asking permission. By the time Washington was sixteen, he had learned surveying; and so Lord Fairfax hired him to measure his land for him. Washington was glad to undertake the work, for he needed the money.

Early in the spring, Washington, in company with another young man, started off, on foot, to do this business. They crossed the Blue Ridge Mountains and entered the Valley of Virginia, one of the most beautiful valleys in America.

The two young men would work all day in the woods, with a long chain, measuring the land. When evening came, Washington would make a map of what they had measured. Then they would wrap themselves up in their blankets, stretch themselves on the ground at the foot of a tree, and go to sleep under the stars.

Every day they shot some animals: squirrels or wild turkeys, or even a deer. They kindled a fire with flint and steel, and roasted the meat on sticks held over the coals. For plates, they had flat pieces of wood; and since a few blows with an axe could always make wood plates, they never washed any dishes but just threw them away and had a new set for each meal.

While in the valley, they met a band of Indians, who stopped and danced a war dance for them. The music seemed strange to their ears because most of it was made by drumming on a deerskin stretched across the top of an old iron pot. Moreover, their dancing was lively; the Indians leaped into the air, swung their hatchets, gashed the trees, and yelled until the woods rang.

When Washington returned from his surveying trip, Lord Fairfax was greatly pleased with his work; and the governor of Virginia made him one of the public surveyors. By this new job, he could get work that paid very well.

Fighting the French. By the time Washington was twenty-one, he had grown to be over six feet in height. He was as straight as an arrow and as tough as a cannon. He had keen blue eyes that seemed to look into the very heart of things, and his fist was like a blacksmith's sledgehammer. He knew all about the woods, all about Indians, and he could take care of himself anywhere. Best of all, however, he had a humble and caring spirit that helped him avoid the sin of pride.

At this time, the English settlers held the country along the seashore as far back as the Allegheny Mountains. West of those mountains, the French from Canada were trying to get possession of the land. They had made friends with many Indians, and with their help, the French hoped to drive out the English and get the whole country for themselves.

In order to hold this land in the West, the French had built several forts south of Lake Erie, and they were getting ready to build forts on the Ohio River. The governor of Virginia was determined to put an end to this. He had given young Washington the military title of major; he now sent Major Washington to see the French commander at one of the forts near Lake Erie. Washington was to tell the Frenchman that he had built his forts on land belonging to the English, and that he and his men must either leave or fight.

Map of Operations of the French and Indian War (1754–1763)

Major Washington dressed himself like an Indian and, attended by several friendly Indians and by a white man named Gist, who knew the country well, he set out on his journey through what was called the Great Woods.

The entire distance to the farthest fort and back was about 1,000 miles. Washington could travel by horseback part of the way, but there were no regular roads, and he had to climb mountains and swim rivers. After several weeks' travel, he reached the fort, but the French commander refused to surrender the land. He said that he and his men had come to stay, and that if the English did not like it they must fight.

On the way back, Washington had to leave his horses and come on foot with Gist and an Indian guide sent from the fort. This Indian guide was in the pay of the French, and he intended to murder Washington in the woods. One day he shot at him from behind a tree, but by God's grace, did not hit him. Then Washington and Gist managed to get away from him and set out to go back to Virginia themselves. There were no paths through the thick forest; but Washington had his compass with him, and with that he could find his way just as the captain of a ship finds his way at sea.

George married Martha Custis on January 6, 1759, at her home, which was called "The White House." Both were twenty-seven years old.

In 1754, George Washington was commissioned lieutenant colonel, which ranks above a major and below a colonel.

When they reached the Allegheny River, they found it full of floating ice. They worked all day and made a raft of logs. As they were pushing their way across with poles, Washington's pole was struck by a big piece of ice that jerked him out into water ten feet deep. A short time later, the two men managed to get to a little island, but as there was no wood on it, they could not make a fire. The weather was bitterly cold and Washington, who was soaked to the skin, had to take his choice between walking around all night or trying to sleep on the frozen ground in his wet clothes.

When Major Washington returned to Virginia, the governor made him a lieutenant colonel. With 150 men, Colonel Washington was ordered to set out for the West. He was to "make prisoners, kill or destroy," all Frenchmen who tried to take possession of land on the Ohio River. He built a small log fort, which he named Fort Necessity. Here the French attacked him, with five times as many soldiers as Washington had. Colonel Washington fought like a man who liked to hear the bullets whistle past his ears (as he said he did), but in the end he had to surrender the fort.

Then General Braddock, a noted English soldier, was sent to Virginia by the king to drive the French out of the country. He started with a fine army, and Washington went with him. Washington warned General Braddock that the French and the Indians would hide in the woods and fire at his men from behind trees. But Braddock paid no attention to the warning. On his way through the forest, the enemy suddenly struck down the brave English general; and half of his soldiers were killed or wounded, and the rest put to flight. Washington had two horses shot from under him, and four bullets went through his coat. It was a narrow escape for the young man. One of those who fought in the battle said, "I expected every moment to see him fall." But God preserved George Washington for greater work.

Braddock's Defeat

Trouble with England. The war with the French lasted several years. It ended with the English gaining possession of the whole of America from the Atlantic Ocean to the Mississippi River. George III, king of England, ruled all this part of America. The king now determined to send over more soldiers, and to keep them in America to prevent the French in Canada from trying to win back the country they had lost. He wanted the people in the thirteen colonies to pay the cost of keeping these soldiers. The colonists were not willing to do this because they felt that they could protect themselves without help of any kind. Then the king said, "If the Americans will not give the money, I will take it from them by force, for pay it they must and shall." This was more than the king would have dared say about England; for there, if he wanted money to spend on his army, he had to ask the people for it, and they could give it or not, as they thought best. The Americans said, "We have the same rights as our brothers in England, and the king cannot force us to give a single copper against our will. If he tries to take it from us, we will fight." Some of the greatest men in England agreed with them and said that they would fight, too, if they were in their place.

But, George III thought that the Americans did not mean what they said. He tried to make them pay the money through unjust taxes, but they would not. From Maine to Georgia, all the people were of one mind. Then the king tried a different way. Quantities of tea were sent to New York, Boston, Philadelphia, Charleston, and Annapolis. If the tea should be landed and sold, then everyone who bought a pound of it would have to pay six cents more than the regular price. That six cents was a tax, and it went into the king's pocket. The people said, "We won't pay that six cents." When the tea reached New York, the citizens sent it back to Eng-

An Artist's Rendering of the Boston Tea Party (December 16, 1773)

land. They did the same thing at Philadelphia. At Charleston, the tea was landed, but it was stored in damp cellars. People would not buy any of it any more than they would buy so much poison, so it all rotted and spoiled. At Annapolis, the citizens forced the owner of the tea ship *Peggy Stewart* to burn his vessel, tea and all. At Boston, they had a grand "tea party." Several men dressed themselves up like Indians, went on board the tea ships at night, broke open the chests, and emptied the tea into the harbor.

This act of the Bostonians made the king terribly angry, and orders were given to close the port of Boston so that no ships, except the king's warships, could come in or go out. Nearly all trade stopped in the city. Many of the inhabitants began to suffer for lack of food. Throughout the colonies, the people tried their best to help them. The New England towns sent herds of sheep and cattle, New York sent wheat, South Carolina gave 200 barrels of rice; the other colonies gave liberally in money and provisions. Even in England much sympathy was felt for the distressed people of Boston, and in London a large sum of money was raised to help those whom the king was determined to starve into submission.

George III, King of England

General Thomas Gage (1719–1787)

Paul Revere warned the colonists that the British were coming.

Washington's Home, Mount Vernon

The colonies now sent some of their best men to Philadelphia to consider what should be done. As this meeting was made up of those who had come from all parts of the country, it took the name of the General or Continental Congress.

About this time, too, a great change happened. People throughout the country began to call themselves Americans, and to speak of the English troops that the king sent over as British soldiers.

In Boston, General Gage had command of these soldiers. He knew that the Americans were getting ready to fight, and that they had stored up powder and ball at Concord, about twenty miles from Boston. One night he secretly sent out a group of soldiers to march to Concord and destroy what they found there.

But Paul Revere, a Boston man, was on the watch; and as soon as he found out which way the British were going, he set off at a gallop for Lexington, on the road to Concord. All the way out, he roused people from their sleep with the cry, "The British are coming!" This daring ride helped to warn the American colonists that British soldiers were coming.

When the king's soldiers reached Lexington, they found the Americans, under Captain John Parker, ready for them. Captain Parker said to his men, "Don't fire unless you are fired on; but if they want a war, let it begin here." The fighting did begin there, April 19, 1775; and when the British left the town on their way to Concord, seven Americans lay dead on the grass in front of the village church. At Concord that same day, there was still harder fighting; and on the way back to Boston, many of the British were killed.

Washington Is Put in Command of the American Army. Not quite two months later, June 17, 1775, a battle was fought near Bunker Hill in Charlestown, just outside Boston (see map on page 89). General Gage thought the Americans wouldn't fight; but they did fight, in a way that General Gage never forgot. Though the Americans eventually had to retreat because their powder gave out, the British lost more than 1,000 men. The contest at Bunker Hill was the first great battle of the War for American Independence, also called the American Revolution, the war that overturned the British power in America and made the Americans a free people. Many Englishmen thought the king was wrong. They would not fight against the Americans, and he was forced to hire many German soldiers and send them to America. These Germans had to fight the Americans, whether they wanted to or not, for their king ordered them to come.

At the time the Battle of Bunker Hill was fought, Colonel George Washington was living quietly at Mount Vernon. His brother Lawrence had died, and Mount Vernon was now his home. Washington was very well off; he had a fine estate and plenty of servants to do the work on it; but when he received the call of duty to command the American army, he freely gave up his comforts for the cause of freedom.

Congress now made Colonel Washington general-in-chief of all the forces and sent him to Cambridge, a town just outside Boston, to take command of the American army. It was called the Continental Army because it was raised, not only to fight for the people of Massachusetts, but for all the Americans on the continent, north and south. Washington took command of the army under a great elm on what was then the Commons. Six months later, he raised the first American flag over the camp at Cambridge.

Men now came from all parts of the country to join the Continental Army. Many of them were sharpshooters. In one case, an officer set up a board with the figure of a man's nose chalked on it, for a mark. A hundred men fired at it at long distance, and sixty hit the nose. The newspapers gave them great praise for their skill and said, "Now, General Gage, look out for your nose."

Washington wanted to drive General Gage and the British soldiers out of Boston; but for months he could not get either cannon or powder. Benjamin Franklin said that the Americans would have to fight as the Indians had, with bows and arrows.

The Battle of Bunker Hill took place on June 17, 1775, on Breed's Hill, as part of the Siege of Boston.

While Washington was waiting, a small American force marched against the British in Canada; but when cold weather came on, they nearly starved to death. During this time, the men would sometimes take off their moccasins and gnaw on them while they danced in the snow to keep their bare feet from freezing.

Eventually, Washington received both cannon and powder. He dragged the cannon up to the top of the hills overlooking Boston Harbor (see dashed lines on the map). He then sent word to General William Howe (who had replaced General Gage) that if he did not leave Boston, his ships would

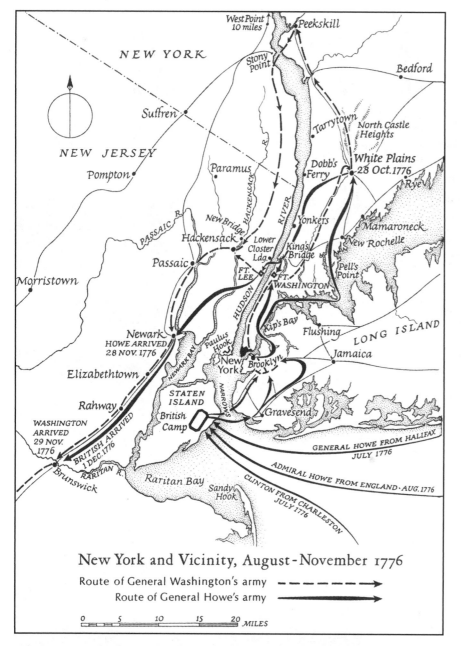

New York and Vicinity, August - November 1776
Route of General Washington's army - - - →
Route of General Howe's army ——→

0   5   10   15   20 MILES

Washington Crossing the Delaware (December 25, 1776)

be blown to pieces. The British saw that they could not help themselves, so they quickly marched on board their vessels and sailed away. They never came back to Boston again, but went to New York City.

The Declaration of Independence. Washington got to New York first. While he was there, Congress, on the fourth of July, 1776, declared the United States independent; that is, entirely free from the rule of the king of England. In New York, there was a gilded lead statue of King George III on horseback. When the news of what Congress had done reached that city, the cry rose: "Down with the king!" That night some men pulled down the statue, melted it in a furnace, and cast it into bullets. The next month, there was a battle on Long Island, just across from New York City; the British gained the victory. Washington had to leave New York, and Lord Charles Cornwallis, one of the British generals, chased him and his little army clear across the state of New Jersey. It looked at one time as though the men would all be taken prisoners; but Washington managed to seize a number of small boats on the Delaware River and get across into Pennsylvania. As the British had no boats, they could not follow.

Lord Cornwallis left 1,500 German soldiers at Trenton on the Delaware. He intended, as soon as the river froze over, to cross on the ice and attack Washington's army. But Washington did not wait for him. On Christmas night (1776), he took many boats, filled them with soldiers, and secretly crossed over to New Jersey. The weather was intensely cold, the river was full of floating ice, and a furious snowstorm set in. Many of the men were ragged

90

and had only old, broken shoes. They suffered terribly, and two of them were frozen to death. However, General Washington never heard one complaint from these brave men.

The Germans at Trenton had been having a jolly Christmas and had gone to bed, suspecting no danger. Suddenly Washington, with his men, rushed into the little town and captured 1,000 German soldiers. It was all done so quickly that the men found themselves prisoners almost before they knew what had happened. The rest of the Germans escaped to tell Lord Cornwallis how the Americans had beaten them. When Washington had been driven out of New York, many Americans had feared he would be captured. Now they were filled with joy. The Battle of Trenton was the first battle won by the Continental Army.

Washington took his 1,000 prisoners over into Pennsylvania. A few days later, he again crossed the Delaware River into New Jersey. While Cornwallis was fast asleep in his tent, Washington slipped around him, got to Princeton, and there beat a part of the British Army. Cornwallis woke up and heard Washington's cannon. "That's thunder," he said. He was right; it was the thunder of another American victory.

On December 19, 1777, Washington settled into Valley Forge, Pennsylvania, with his poorly fed, ill-equipped army, which proved to be a strategic move.

But before the next winter set in, the British had taken Philadelphia, which was then the capital of the United States. Washington's army was freezing and starving on the hillsides of Valley Forge, about twenty miles northwest of Philadelphia.

Good news was coming, however. The Americans won a great victory at Saratoga, New York, over the British general, Burgoyne. Benjamin Franklin was then in Paris. When he heard that Burgoyne was beaten, he hurried to the palace of the French king to tell him about it. The king of France hated the British, and he agreed to send money, ships, and soldiers to help the Americans. When the men at Valley Forge heard the news, they leaped for joy. Not long after that the British left Philadelphia, and the Americans entered it in triumph.

The War in the South. While these things were happening in the North, the British sent a fleet of vessels to take Charleston, South Carolina. They hammered away with their big guns at a little log fort under the command of Colonel William Moultrie. In the battle, a cannon ball struck the flagpole on the fort and cut it in two. The South Carolina flag fell to the ground outside the fort.

General Nathanael Greene
(1742–1786)

Sergeant William Jasper leaped down and, while the British shots were striking all around him, seized the flag, climbed back, fastened it to a short staff, and raised it to its place to show that the Americans would never surrender the fort. The British, after fighting all day, saw that they could do nothing against palmetto logs when defended by such men as Moultrie and Jasper. They sailed away the following day with their ships that had not been destroyed.

Several years later, Charleston was taken. Lord Cornwallis then took command of the British army in South Carolina. General Nathanael Greene of Rhode Island had command of the Americans. He sent Brigadier General Daniel Morgan with his sharpshooters to meet part of the British army at Cowpens; they did meet them, and sent them flying. Then Cornwallis determined to whip General Greene or drive him out of the state. Instead, General Greene forced Cornwallis to retreat into Virginia. He had found North and South Carolina like two hornets' nests, and the farther he ran away from those hornets, the better he was pleased.

When Lord Cornwallis came into Virginia, he found General Benedict Arnold waiting for him. Arnold had been a general in the American Army; Washington gave him the command of the fort at West Point, on the Hudson River, and trusted him as though he were his brother. Arnold deceived him and secretly offered to surrender the fort to the British. We call a man who is false to his friends and to his country a traitor; it is the most shameful name we can fasten on him. Arnold was a traitor. If the Americans could have caught him, they would have hanged him, but he was clever enough to run away and escape to the British. Now he was burning houses and towns in Virginia and doing all that he could to destroy those who had once been his best friends. He wanted to stay in Virginia and help Cornwallis, but that general was a brave and honorable man. He despised Arnold and did not want to have anything to do with him.

A young nobleman named Lafayette had come earlier from France to help the Americans fight against the British. Cornwallis laughed at him and called him a "boy," but he found that General Lafayette was a "boy" who knew how to fight. The British commander moved toward the seacoast so that British forces in New York could reinforce him. Lafayette followed him, and, at length, Cornwallis shut himself up with his army in Yorktown.

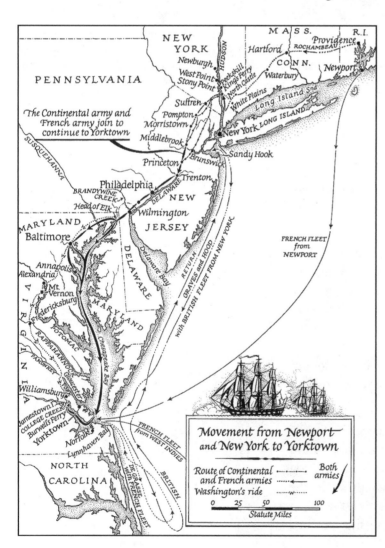

Movement from Newport and New York to Yorktown

Route of Continental and French armies — · — · —
Washington's ride · · · · · · ·
Both armies

0 25 50 100
Statute Miles

92

Washington Marches Against Yorktown. Washington, with his army, was then near New York City, watching the British there. The French king had done as he agreed and had sent over warships and soldiers to help the Americans; but until this time they had never been able to do much. Now was the chance. Before the British knew what Washington was doing, he quickly marched south with most of his own army and a large number of French soldiers to attack Yorktown by land. At the same time, French Admiral François Joseph Paul de Grasse brought his fleet and more French soldiers north from the West Indies to Virginia. After landing the soldiers, he defeated a British fleet that had come to help Cornwallis. With the defeat of the British ships, Cornwallis could no longer receive more soldiers or supplies, nor could he escape Yorktown by sea.

When Washington arrived at Yorktown with his army, he placed his cannon around the town and began battering it to pieces. For more than a week, he kept firing night and day. One house had over 1,000 cannon balls go through it. Eventually, Cornwallis could not hold out any longer, and on October 17, 1781, his army came out and gave themselves up as prisoners.

Two days later, the Americans formed a line more than a mile long on one side of the road, and the French stood facing them on the other side. The French had on bright clothes and looked very handsome; the clothes of Washington's men were patched and faded, but their eyes shone with a wonderful light—the light of victory. The British marched out slowly, between the two lines. Somehow they found it more pleasant to look at the bright uniforms of the French than to look at the eyes of the Americans.

People at a distance noticed that the cannon had suddenly stopped firing. They looked at one another and wondered what it meant. Suddenly a man appeared on horseback, riding with all his might toward Philadelphia. As he dashed past, he rose in his stirrups, swung his cap, and shouted with all his might, "Cornwallis is taken! Cornwallis is taken!" Then it was the

Gilbert du Motier,
Marquis de Lafayette (1757–1834)

François Joseph Paul,
Marquis de Grasse Tilly (1722–1788)

Cornwallis signed official surrender papers on October 19, 1781.

93

people's turn to shout, and they made the hills ring with "Hurrah! Hurrah! Hurrah!"

Poor Lord Fairfax, Washington's old friend, had always stood by the king. He was now over ninety. When he heard the cry, "Cornwallis is taken!" it was too much for the old man. He said to his servant, "Come, Joe; carry me to bed, for I'm sure it's high time for me to die."

The war did not end when Cornwallis surrendered at Yorktown, but that was the last big battle. The War for American Independence had lasted seven years, until peace was signed in 1783. These were terrible years—years of sorrow, suffering, and death. But now the end had come, and America was free. When the British left New York City in December 1783, they nailed the British flag to a high pole on the wharf. An American sailor soon climbed the pole, tore down the flag of England, and hoisted the Stars and Stripes in its place. That was more than 200 years ago. Now the English and the Americans have become good friends, and the English people see clearly that the War for Independence ended in the way that was best for both sides.

The Signing of the United States Constitution on September 17, 1787

Further Service. When it was certain there would be no more fighting, Washington resigned from the army and went back to Mount Vernon. He had hoped to spend the rest of his life there, but the country still needed him. The government of the United States seemed ineffective, without a president or judges and having only a weak congress. Many people were concerned that the country was falling apart. Congress decided to call a convention together to suggest changes. Therefore, from May to September 1787, some of the most important men in America met in Philadelphia to discuss making a new government for the United States. George Washington was a delegate to the meeting from Virginia and was elected president of the convention. It was this convention that developed the system of government the United States enjoys today.

After the states agreed to this new form of government, it was time to select the nation's first President. George Washington was the logical choice; he had led the country in war and had presided over the Constitutional Convention. The nation, therefore, chose Washington as the first President of the United States. He was elected unanimously; the only person ever elected without opposition. Washington assumed the presidency in 1789 in New York City, which was then the capital of the United States. A French gentleman, who was there, tells us how Washington, standing in the presence of thousands of people, placed his hand on the Bible and solemnly swore that with the help of God he would protect and defend the United States of America.

Washington sought to establish the government on a sound footing. He had several well-known and talented men in his government, including John Adams as the Vice President, Alexander Hamilton as Secretary of the Treasury, and Thomas Jefferson as Secretary of State. Washington ran an efficient government that sought to improve the national economy, uphold the nation's laws, and keep peace with other countries.

Washington did more, however, than simply run a good government. He established a pattern for other Presidents to follow. He refused to accept majestic terms of address, preferring to be called "Mr. President." He was elected President twice, but refused a third term, establishing a practice that was voluntarily followed by all Presidents until Franklin Roosevelt and is now part of the Constitution. He showed that the federal government was prepared to take vigorous action to uphold national laws when he led military forces to bloodlessly put down the Whiskey Rebellion.

Washington retired from the presidency in March 1797 and went home to Mount Vernon. However, he did not have much longer to live. He died just over two years later. When he died in 1799, many of the people in England and France joined America in mourning for him, for all men honored his memory.

Lafayette, the brave young Frenchman who fought for America in the War for Independence, came to visit the United States many years afterward. He went to Mount Vernon, where Washington was buried. There he went down into the vault and, kneeling by the side of the coffin, covered his face with his hands, and shed tears of gratitude to think that he had known such a man as Washington, and that Washington had been his friend.

Summary. George Washington, the son of a Virginia planter, became the leader of the armies of the United States in the War for Independence. At the close of the war, after he had helped to make America free, he was elected the first President. His name stands today among those of the greatest men in the history of the world. He truly was, as Charles Lee put it: "First in war, first in peace, and first in the hearts of his countrymen…."

On April 30, 1789, the Electoral College unanimously elected George Washington as the President of the United States at Federal Hall in New York City. John Adams was elected as Vice President. In 1792, Washington was chosen for a second term.

George Washington received the honor of becoming the first President under the Constitution for the United States of America. Moreover, he remains the only President to receive 100% of the votes of the Electoral College.

Comprehension Questions

1. Where was George Washington born?
2. What job did Lord Fairfax give to Washington when he was only seventeen years old?
3. Describe the event known as the "Boston Tea Party."
4. What was the name of Washington's plantation home?
5. Where was the final decisive battle of the Revolutionary War fought?
6. Name three well-known men in George Washington's government.

Chapter 18
George Rogers Clark (1752–1818)

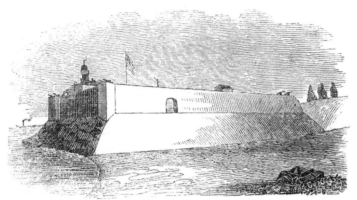

Fort Niagara

Fort Detroit

General John Sullivan (1740–1795)

War on the Frontier. While Washington was fighting the battles of the War for Independence in the East, the British in the West were not sitting still. They had many forts in the Wilderness, as the country west of the Allegheny Mountains was then called. Their two most important forts were at Niagara in New York and Detroit in what is now Michigan. Other British forts were at Vincennes, in what is now Indiana, and at Kaskaskia, in what is now Illinois. From Niagara and Detroit, the British planned attacks against American frontier settlements. Pro-British Indians and Loyalists, often led by British officers, made raids along much of the frontier, from New York to Kentucky.

Sir Guy Johnston in Niagara supported the Iroquois tribes that were opposed to the American settlers. Although not all of the Iroquois tribes fought for the British, most did. They, along with Loyalist troops, attacked settlements along much of the frontier of New York and northeastern Pennsylvania. After a series of massacres in 1778, Congress ordered George Washington to send troops from the regular army to put a stop to these raids; militia forces were proving unable to stop the attacks.

In 1779, Washington ordered General John Sullivan to take several thousand soldiers into the Iroquois territory to destroy their towns and defeat their warriors. There was only one battle, in which the Americans defeated a combination of British, Loyalist, and Indian forces, but General Sullivan destroyed many of the Iroquois towns and their crops. While the Sullivan Expedition—as it came to be called—did not end Indian attacks in Pennsylvania and New York, it significantly weakened the pro-British Iroquois tribes.

Further west, Colonel Henry Hamilton, the British commander at Detroit, was determined to drive the American settlers out of the West. During the beginning of the War for Independence, both sides tried to get the support of the various Indian tribes or at least to get them to stay out of the war. It was not too hard, however, for the British to gain the support of several of the Indian tribes due to earlier fights the Indians had had with the settlers. In 1777, Hamilton was told to encourage Indian raids against frontier settlements. Many did not like this new policy because they knew it would result in civilian casualties. In spite of these concerns, Hamilton effectively carried out his orders to encourage raids in western Pennsylvania, western Virginia, and what is now Kentucky and Illinois.

The Indians would often creep up secretly, by night, and attack the farmers' homes. They killed and scalped the settlers in the West, burned their log cabins, and carried off the women and children as prisoners. On occasion, they would also attack fortified settlements, such as Boonesborough in Kentucky. Hamilton sometimes sent Canadian militia and British officers with the Indians on their raids. He became known as Henry "The Hair Buyer" Hamilton because he paid bounties for prisoners and scalps brought in by the Indians.

George Rogers Clark Gets Help from Virginia. Daniel Boone, the famous explorer of Kentucky, had a friend in Virginia named George Rogers Clark, who believed that he could take the British forts in the West and drive out the British from that part of the country. Virginia then owned most of the Wilderness territory. For this reason, Clark went to Patrick Henry, governor of Virginia, and asked for help. The governor liked the plan and let Clark have money to hire men to go with him to try to take Fort Kaskaskia.

George Rogers Clark (1752–1818)

Clark started in the spring of 1778 with about 150 men. They built boats on the banks of the Allegheny River just above Pittsburgh and floated down the Ohio River, a distance of over 900 miles. They went ashore in what is now the state of Illinois and marched toward Fort Kaskaskia.

It was 100 miles to the fort, and half of the way the men had to find their way through thick woods, full of underbrush, briers, and vines. The British, thinking that the fort was perfectly safe from attack, had left it in the care of a French officer. Clark and his soldiers reached Kaskaskia at night. They found no one to stop them. The soldiers in the fort were having a dance, and the Americans could hear the merry music of a violin and the laughing voices of girls.

Clark left his men just outside the fort and, finding a door open, he walked in. He reached the room where the fun was happening and, stopping there, he stood leaning against the doorpost, looking on. The room was lighted with torches; the light of one of the torches happened to fall full on Clark's face. An Indian sitting on the floor caught sight of him; he sprang to his feet and gave a terrible war whoop. The dancers stopped as though they had been shot; the women screamed; the men ran to the door to get their guns. Clark did not move, but said quietly, "Go on; only remember you are dancing under Virginia, and not under Great Britain." The next moment, the Americans rushed in, and Clark and his "Long Knives," as the Indians called his men, had full control of the fort.

The Settlement at Kaskaskia

Clark's Moves on Fort Vincennes

Clark wanted next to march against Fort Vincennes, but he did not have enough men. There was a French Catholic priest at Kaskaskia, and Clark's kindness to him had made him his friend. He said, "I will go to Vincennes for you, and I will tell the French, who hold the fort for the British, that the Americans are their real friends, and that, in this war, they are in the right." He went to Vincennes. The French listened to him and then pulled down the British flag and ran up the American flag in its place.

The British Return. The next year, the British, led by Colonel Henry Hamilton of Detroit, took Fort Vincennes back. When Clark heard of this, he said, "Either I must take Hamilton, or Hamilton will take me."

Just then Francis Vigo, a trader from St. Louis, came to see Clark at Kaskaskia. Hamilton had held Vigo as a prisoner, so he knew all about Fort Vincennes. Vigo said to Clark, "Hamilton has only about eighty soldiers; you can take the fort, and I will lend you all the money you need to pay your men what you owe them."

Clark, with about 200 men, started for Vincennes. The distance was nearly 150 miles. The first week, everything went pretty well. It was in the month of February; the weather was cold, and it rained a great deal, but the men did not mind that. They would get wet during the day, but at night they built roaring log fires, gathered round them, roasted their buffalo meat or venison, smoked their pipes, told jolly stories, and sang lively songs.

The next week, they came to a branch of the Wabash River. Then they found that the constant rains had raised the streams so that they had overflowed their banks; the whole country was under water three or four feet deep. This flooded country was called the "Drowned Lands." By the time Clark and his men had crossed these lands, they were nearly drowned themselves.

For about a week, the Americans had to wade in ice-cold water, sometimes waist deep and sometimes nearly up to their chins. While wading, the men were obliged to hold their guns and powder horns above their heads to keep them dry. Now and then, a man would stub his toe against a root or a stone and would go sprawling headfirst into the water. When he came up, puffing and blowing from such a dive, he was lucky if he still had his gun. For two days no one could get anything to eat; but hungry, wet, and cold, they kept moving slowly on.

The last part of the march was the worst of all. They were now near the fort, but they still had to wade through a sheet of water four miles across. Clark took the lead and plunged in. The rest, shivering, followed. A few looked as though their strength and courage had given out. Clark saw this and, calling to Captain Joseph Bowman, one of the bravest of his officers, he ordered him to kill the first man who refused to go forward.

Finally, with frozen hands and cold feet, all made it across. Some of the men were so weak and blue with cold that they could not take another step. They fell flat on their faces in the mud. These men were so nearly dead that no fire seemed to warm them. Clark ordered two strong men to lift each of these poor fellows up and run them up and down until they began to get warm. By doing this, he saved everyone.

Clark Captured Fort Vincennes, 1779

"Conqueror of the Northwest." After a desperate fight, Clark took Fort Vincennes on February 23, 1779, and raised the Stars and Stripes over it in triumph. Henry Hamilton was captured at Vincennes and sent to Virginia as a prisoner. The British never took Vincennes back, but they still had Fort Detroit and continued sending raiding parties against the settlers. Clark was never able to capture Detroit, but he continued the fight against the British and their Indian allies in what is now Kentucky and Ohio.

With Clark's victories, he became known as the "Conqueror of the Northwest." When the war ended, the Americans controlled the whole western wilderness up to Detroit. The British did not want to give the United States any part of America beyond the thirteen states on the Atlantic coast. But the Americans said, "The whole West, clear to the Mississippi, is ours. We fought for it, we took it, we hoisted our flag over its forts, and we mean to keep it."

There is a grass-grown grave in a burial ground in Louisville, Kentucky, which has a small headstone marked with the letters G. R. C., and nothing more. That is the grave of General George Rogers Clark, the man who did more than anyone else to expand the United States westward. Clark died feeling lonely and in great poverty. In 1895, a fine monument was erected in Indianapolis, Indiana, to his memory.

Summary. During the War for Independence, George Rogers Clark, of Virginia, with a small number of men, captured Fort Kaskaskia in Illinois and Fort Vincennes in Indiana. Clark drove out the British from that part of the country. When peace was made, the United States kept the West (the country beyond the Allegheny Mountains as far as the Mississippi River). Had it not been for Clark and Governor Patrick Henry, the United States might not have gained this territory.

All of Clark's military victories came before his thirtieth birthday.

Comprehension Questions

1. Name three British forts in the western wilderness and their locations.
2. Who was the governor of Virginia in 1778?
3. Who led the American expedition against the Iroquois in 1779?
4. In what year was a monument erected for Clark in Indianapolis?
5. Why was Henry Hamilton called "The Hair Buyer"?
6. Was Daniel Boone a friend of George Rogers Clark?
7. Tell how George Rogers Clark captured Fort Kaskaskia.

Chapter 19
Daniel Boone (1734–1820)

Daniel Boone (1734–1820)

Daniel Boone's Life in North Carolina. Before Washington began to fight the battles of the War for Independence in the East, Daniel Boone and other famous hunters were fighting bears and Indians in what was then called the West. By that war in the woods, these brave and hardy men helped us to settle that part of the country.

Daniel Boone was born in Pennsylvania. His father moved to North Carolina, and Daniel helped cut down the trees around their log cabin in the forest. He plowed the land, which was thick with stumps, hoed the corn that grew up among those stumps, and then, as there was no mill nearby, pounded it into meal for Johnnycake. He learned how to handle a gun at the same time he did a hoe. The unfortunate deer or raccoon that saw young Boone coming toward him, if he had only been bright enough, might have known that he had seen his best days and that he would soon have the whole Boone family sitting round him at the dinner table.

When Daniel had grown to manhood, he wandered off with his gun on his shoulder and, crossing the mountains, entered what is now the state of Tennessee. That whole country was then a wilderness, full of large animals and Indians, and Boone had many a hard fight with each.

More than 245 years ago, he cut these words on a beech tree still standing in eastern Tennessee: "D. Boon killed a bar on this tree in the year 1760." You will see if you examine the tree, on which the words can still be read, that Boone could not spell very well; but he could do what the bear cared about a good deal better—he could shoot straight.

Boone Goes to Kentucky. Nine years after he cut his name on that tree, Boone, with a few companions, went to a new part of the country. The Indians called it Kentucky. There he saw buffalo, deer, bears, and wolves enough to satisfy the best hunter in America.

This region was a kind of "No Man's Land" because, though many tribes of Indians roamed over it, none of them claimed to own it. These bands of Indians were always fighting and trying to drive each other out, so Kentucky was often called the "Dark and Bloody Ground." But, as much as the Indians

Boone's Bear Tree

hated each other, they hated the white men, or the "palefaces," as they called them, still more.

The hunters were on the lookout for these Indians, but the Indians practiced all kinds of tricks to get the hunters near enough to shoot them. Sometimes Boone would hear the gobble of a wild turkey. He would listen a moment, then he would say, "That is not a wild turkey, but an Indian, imitating that bird; but he won't fool me and get me to come near enough to put a bullet through my head."

One evening an old hunter, on his way to his cabin, heard what seemed to be two young owls calling to each other. But his keen ear noticed that there was something not quite natural in their calls and, what was stranger still, that the owls seemed to be on the ground instead of being perched on trees, as all well-behaved owls should be. He crept cautiously along through the

Fort Boonesborough

bushes until he saw something ahead that looked like a stump. He did not like the looks of the stump. He aimed his rifle at it and fired. The stump, or what had seemed to be one, fell over backward with a groan. He had killed an Indian, who had been waiting to kill him.

In 1775, Boone, with a party of thirty men, chopped a path through the forest from the mountains of eastern Tennessee to the Kentucky River, a distance of about 200 miles. This was the first path in that part of the country leading to the great West. It was called the "Wilderness Road." Over that road, which thousands of emigrants traveled afterward, Boone took his family, with other settlers, to the Kentucky River. There they built a fort called Boonesborough. That fort was a great protection to the early settlers in Kentucky. In fact, it is hard to see how the state could have grown up without it. So, in one way, we can say with truth that Daniel Boone, the hunter, fighter, and road-maker, was a state-builder as well.

Captured by the Indians. One day Boone's daughter was out, with two other girls, in a canoe on the river. Suddenly, some Indians pounced on them and carried them off. One of the girls, as she went along, broke off

---

Wilderness Road

In 1775, Daniel Boone hired a group of men to widen a path through the Cumberland Gap to help pioneers settle the frontier, which included present-day Kentucky and Tennessee. The trail was widened in the 1790s to accommodate wagon traffic.

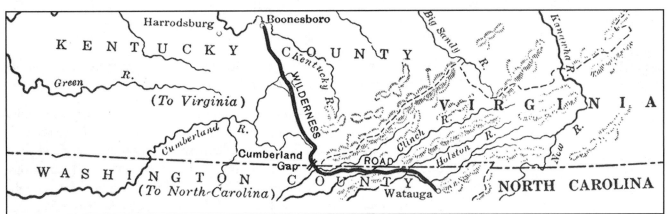

On Sunday, July 14, 1776, three teenage girls from Boonesborough—Jemima Boone and Elizabeth and Frances Callaway—were captured as they were floating in a canoe on the Kentucky River.

Boone Trailing Indians

twigs from the bushes, so that her friends might be able to follow her track through the woods. An Indian caught her doing it, and told her that he would kill her if she did not stop. Then she slyly tore off small bits of her dress and dropped a piece from time to time.

Boone and his men followed the Indians like bloodhounds. They picked up the bits of dress and easily found which way the men had gone. They came up to the Indians just as they were sitting down around a fire to eat their supper. Creeping toward them behind the trees as softly as a cat creeps up behind a mouse, Boone and his men aimed their rifles and fired. Two of the Indians fell dead, the rest ran for their lives, and the girls were carried back in safety to the fort.

Later, Boone himself was caught and carried off by the Indians. They respected his courage so much that they would not kill him, but decided to adopt him; that is, take him into the tribe as one of their own people, or make an Indian of him.

They pulled out all his hair except one long lock, called the "scalp-lock," which they left to grow in Indian fashion. The women and girls braided bright feathers in this lock. Then the Indians took him down to a river. There they stripped him and scrubbed him with all their might, to get his white blood out, as they said. Next they painted his face in stripes with red and yellow clay, so that he looked, to their minds, more handsome than he had ever looked before. When all had been done, and they were satisfied with the appearance of their new Indian, they sat down to a great feast and had fun.

After a time, Boone managed to escape, but the Indians were so fond of him that they could not rest until they found him again. One day he was at work in a type of shed, drying some tobacco leaves. He heard a slight noise and, turning round, saw four Indians with their guns pointed at him.

"Now, Boone," said they, "we got you. You no get away this time."

"How are you?" said Boone pleasantly. "Glad to see you; just wait a minute till I get you some of my tobacco."

He gathered two large handfuls of the leaves; they were as dry as powder and crumbled to dust in his hands. Coming forward, as if to give the welcome present to the Indians, he suddenly sprang on them and filled their eyes, mouths, and noses with the stinging tobacco dust. The Indians were half choked and nearly blinded. While they were dancing about, coughing, sneezing, and rubbing their eyes, Boone slipped out of the shed and ran to a place of safety. The Indians were as mad as they could be, yet they could hardly help laughing at Boone's trick; for cunning as the Indians were, he was more cunning still.

The End of Boone's Life. Boone lived to be a very old man. After the war ended, Boone had owned a good deal of land in the West, but he had lost possession of it due to conflicting land claims and the need to pay off debts. When Kentucky began to fill with people and the animals were killed off, Boone moved across the Mississippi into the Spanish territory of Missouri in 1799, where the Spanish gave him land. He said that he went because he wanted "more elbow room" and a chance to hunt buffalo again.

After Missouri became part of the United States in 1804 as part of the Louisiana Purchase, Boone lost most of his land in Missouri to pay off old Kentucky debts. In his remaining years, Boone hunted and trapped as much as his health would allow. He died in Missouri in 1820.

There are a number of stories about Boone's final days. Some have him returning to Kentucky for a final visit and possibly to ask the state of Kentucky to give him a small piece of land, where he could "lay his bones." Another has him going with a group of men on a long hunt to the Yellowstone River, which flows through parts of Wyoming and Montana.

In 1845, people from Kentucky came to Missouri to dig up Daniel Boone's body. They wanted to rebury him in a cemetery in Frankfort, Kentucky, within sight of the river on which he built his fort at Boonesborough. Boone's family, however, claimed that the wrong body was dug up and, therefore, Daniel Boone is still buried in Missouri. No one truly knows where he is currently buried.

Summary. Daniel Boone, a famous hunter from North Carolina, opened up a road through the forest, from the mountains of eastern Tennessee to the Kentucky River. It was called the "Wilderness Road," and over it thousands of emigrants went into Kentucky to settle. Boone, with others, built the fort at Boonesborough, Kentucky, and went there to live. That fort protected the settlers against the Indians, and so helped that part of the country to grow until it became the state of Kentucky.

Comprehension Questions

1. What did Boone cut on a beech tree?
2. Why was the Wilderness Road important?
3. What purpose did the fort at Boonesborough serve?
4. Tell the story of the tobacco dust.
5. Why did Boone move to Missouri?

In 1799, Boone moved across the Mississippi River into Spanish Louisiana, settling in what is known today as Missouri. In 1800, Emperor Napoleon Bonaparte of France acquired Louisiana from Spain in hopes of expanding his empire in the New World; however, the Spanish were allowed to continue ruling until November of 1803. At the request of the Spanish Governor, Boone served as a judge and military leader until the United States officially acquired the Louisiana Territory from France on March 10, 1804. Boone spent his final years in Missouri hunting and trapping. He died on September 26, 1820, at his youngest son's (Nathan Boone) home near St. Charles, Missouri.

Chapter 20
James Madison (1751–1836)

James Madison (1751–1836)

James Madison's Early Years. Many of the greatest men of the early days of American history came from Virginia. One of the most important was James Madison. He was born at Port Conway, Virginia, and was raised at Montpelier, Virginia, his father's plantation.

He was initially educated at home by his grandmother, mother, and local tutors. At age eleven, he went off to a boarding school for five years. After returning home, he spent three more years studying with the pastor of his local church. In 1769, James Madison went to Princeton to study at the College of New Jersey (now known as Princeton University). After completing his college education in 1772, he returned home for further study in preparation for the ministry.

While Madison went into law and politics instead of the ministry, he never lost his concern for religious matters, especially as they concerned the law. Even though he was an Episcopalian, he defended local Baptists against minor acts of persecution from the legal and religious establishment of Virginia. He also supported religious liberty issues in the Virginia Convention of 1776 and the Virginia legislature in 1786.

Madison's political career began in 1775 with his election to the Orange County Committee of Safety. Between that election and the Constitutional Convention of 1787, he served in many responsible positions: the Virginia Constitutional Convention in 1776, the Virginia legislature, Virginia state government, the Continental Congress, the Mount Vernon Conference in 1785, and the Annapolis Convention of 1786.

"Father of the Constitution." Soon after the establishment of American independence, it became evident to many that the government under the Articles of Confederation was not strong enough to hold the states together in peace. It was very plain that, unless some remedy could be found, the Union would go to pieces, and that, instead of one republic, there would be thirteen.

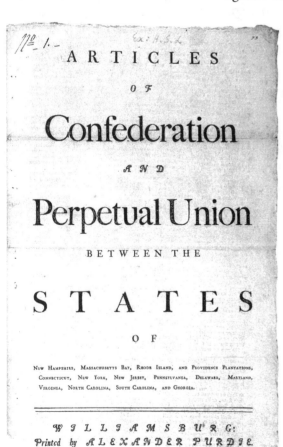

One of those who saw this need was James Madison. His participation in the Continental Congress showed him that there was a great need for a change in the government. He became a strong supporter of improving the government and did what he could to encourage efforts at reform.

All felt the need of union, but the states were so jealous of their own rights that it was doubtful whether they could be induced to give any additional powers to the national government. At that time, the enforcement of any law passed by Congress was left entirely to the states. Therefore, the authority of the central government was very limited.

An effort was made in 1786 to get the states to send delegates to a convention in Annapolis, Maryland, to revise the Articles of Confederation. However, only five states responded to the call. One of the few to attend this convention was James Madison. A second effort was more successful. All the states except Rhode Island sent delegates to the convention, which met in Philadelphia on May 14, 1787. George Washington, of Virginia, was chosen president of the convention.

The assembling of the convention to revise the Articles of Confederation was due to the earnest efforts of three men—James Madison and George Washington, of Virginia, and Alexander Hamilton, of New York. The formation and adoption of the Constitution was due to James Madison more than to any other one man. His experience in state and national government made him invaluable in the work of the convention. He was the author of many of the Constitution's chief features and has been called the "Father of the Constitution."

Details About the Constitution. Some of the delegates to the convention wished to establish a strong national government. But the majority would not even allow the word "national" to appear in the new Constitution. They were willing to greatly enlarge the powers of the federal government, but they were determined to adhere to the idea of a confederation.

The Constitutional Convention was held in Carpenters' Hall, Philadelphia.

After four months of careful labor, the new plan of union, called the Constitution of the United States, was ready to be offered to the people of the several states. Under this plan, the states gave to the federal government much larger powers than it had possessed before; but each state reserved to itself the right to manage its domestic affairs and to pass any law that did not interfere with the rights of other states or of the federal government.

Under the first union, Congress exercised all the powers given to the government. Under the new plan, the government was to consist of three branches—the legislative, which is to make the laws; the judicial, which is to explain the laws; and the executive, which is to see that the laws are carried out.

The Congress makes
the laws

The President carries out
the laws

The Supreme Court judges
the laws

The law-making power is vested in Congress, which consists of two houses, the Senate and the House of Representatives. The number of representatives allowed to each state depends upon the population of the state. These representatives are elected by the people and hold office for two-year terms. Two senators are allowed to each state, are elected by the people from each state, and hold office for six-year terms. Congress is allowed to control all matters that pertain to the general interest of all the states. Its main job is to make laws for the nation.

Congress can also affect the executive and judicial branches through its confirmation and impeachment powers. Congress can remove the President, Vice President, and all civil officers (including federal judges) from office through the impeachment process. The Senate has the responsibility to confirm the appointments by the President to all important offices in the Executive branch and the appointment of all federal judges.

The judicial branch consists of one Supreme Court and of such inferior courts as may be established by Congress. The Supreme Court is made up of the Chief Justice and eight associate justices. If the justices on the Supreme Court declare that any law of Congress or of any of the states does not agree with the Constitution, then such law becomes at once null and void.

The executive branch consists of the President, the Vice President, and the federal bureaucracy. As chief executive, the President is responsible to execute the laws passed by Congress and administers the vast bureaucracy, the most important of which is the Executive Office of the President and the Cabinet departments. The President is also the commander-in-chief of the armed forces of the United States and diplomatic leader of the nation. The President can attempt to stop Congress from passing a new law by vetoing it. A veto, however, can be overridden by a two-thirds vote in each house of Congress.

The Cabinet consists of a group of important advisors to the President, who also head important executive departments. Congress establishes the Cabinet departments, and the Senate must confirm the appointment of those whom the President has appointed to head these various departments. The Cabinet currently consists of the Secretaries of State, Defense, Agriculture, Veterans Affairs, the Treasury, Education, Energy, Health and Human Services, Housing and Urban Development, Commerce, Interior, Labor, and Transportation; the Attorney-General, who heads the Department of Justice, is also a Cabinet member.

The Vice President has a limited formal role in the American government. The most important role of the Vice President is to take the place of the President upon his death or disability. The Vice President also serves as the President of the Senate, but has no vote in the Senate unless there is a tie vote. The President may assign other duties to him.

The Constitution can be amended by the consent of three fourths of the states. However, no amendment can be made that would deprive any state without its own consent of its equal vote in the Senate.

Ratification of the Constitution. Under the Articles of Confederation, no change could be made without the consent of all the states. The Preamble to the Constitution, as at first adopted by the convention, mentioned each state by name. However, it became evident that there would be great difficulty in getting all the states to accept the new Constitution. Therefore, it was determined by the convention that the consent of nine states should suffice for its establishment between the states that ratified it. As it was uncertain which of the states would ratify the Constitution and thus constitute the new Union, the Preamble was altered so as to read: "We the people of the United States...."

The seventh and last article of the Constitution as submitted by the convention reads: "The ratification of the conventions of nine states shall be sufficient for the establishment of this Constitution between the states so ratifying the same." Thus no state would be, without its own consent, bound by the new Constitution. Only those states that actually ratified the Constitution would be part of the new government.

Patrick Henry and others were concerned that the new Constitution, with a Preamble that included the phrase "We the people," meant a consolidated government instead of a confederation. For this reason, Patrick Henry earnestly opposed its ratification by Virginia. But in answer to his objection, Mr. Madison said: "Who are parties to it [the Constitution]? The people [are], but not the people as composing one great body, but the people as composing thirteen sovereignties. Were it a consolidated government, the

Patrick Henry (1736–1799)

Although the required nine states (New Hampshire being the last of the nine) had now ratified the Constitution, the approval of Virginia and New York was necessary for a viable Union—the former because of its importance and the latter because of its geographical position.

Debate continued in the Virginia Convention. Madison, Edmund Randolph, and John Marshall worked hard to subdue Antifederalist opposition. Washington worked for ratification indirectly, but his influence was important. Five days after New Hampshire, Virginia ratified the Constitution on June 26, 1788. The Federalists won by only ten votes in the Virginia Convention.

Members of the New York Convention debated for another month. Alexander Hamilton, John Jay, Robert Livingston, and other Federalist leaders fought for ratification with political skill. The New York Convention ratified by a narrow margin of three votes on July 26, 1788.

North Carolina and Rhode Island remained outside the federal Union.

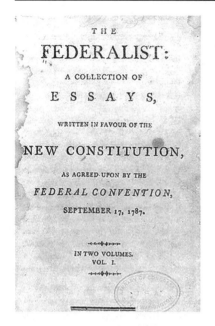

Alexander Hamilton (1755–1804)

John Jay (1745–1829)

assent of a majority of the people would be sufficient for its establishment, and as a majority have adopted it already, the remaining states would be bound by the act of the majority, even if they reprobated it; but, sir, no state is bound by it, as it is, without its own consent."

In response to the opposition to ratification of the Constitution in the state of New York, James Madison, Alexander Hamilton, and John Jay wrote a famous series of articles, known as *The Federalist*, in favor of the Constitution. Madison also took an active role in the debate over the Constitution in the Virginia ratification convention.

After much opposition, eleven states ratified the Constitution. The method was the same in each state. Delegates were chosen to meet in convention and decide the question according to the wish of the people who had elected them. The 70,000 people of the little state of Delaware had precisely the same weight—one vote—in the ratification of the Constitution as the more than 700,000 of Virginia or the 400,000 of Pennsylvania.

By July 26, 1788, the conventions of eleven states had ratified the Constitution. The following list gives the names of the eleven states so ratifying it, and the dates of their ratification:

Delaware, December 7, 1787

Pennsylvania, December 12, 1787

New Jersey, December 18, 1787

Georgia, January 2, 1788

Connecticut, January 9, 1788

Massachusetts, February 6, 1788

Maryland, April 28, 1788

South Carolina, May 23, 1788

New Hampshire, June 21, 1788

Virginia, June 26, 1788

New York, July 26, 1788

Virginia accompanied her ratification with the assertion of the right of the people to resume the powers granted under the Constitution, whenever the same should be used for their injury or oppression. As each state ratified the Constitution separately, the word "people" here meant the people of that particular state, who were then ratifying the Constitution in behalf of that state. The natural inference would be that, if the people of Virginia had that right, the people of each of the other ratifying states had the same right. New York's convention made a declaration similar to that of Virginia.

North Carolina and Rhode Island had not ratified. Steps were immediately taken for the establishment of the new government by the eleven ratifying states. In all of these eleven states, except New York, the necessary elections were held. George Washington of Virginia received every electoral vote cast for the office of President, and John Adams of Massachusetts was elected Vice President by a majority of the electoral votes. On April 30, 1789, in the city of New York, the inauguration took place amid imposing ceremonies. Under the guidance of the beloved Washington, whom all Americans of every section have delighted to honor as the "Father of His Country," the United States entered upon a brilliant career.

The new Union formed the most perfect model of a confederated republic, as both Washington and Hamilton styled it, that the wisdom of man ever devised. There were, as we have seen, only eleven states in the new republic. North Carolina and Rhode Island had thus far refused to adopt the Constitution. But there was no claim on the part of the eleven states that had formed the more perfect union to control the action of the other two. Their accession to the Union was desired, but their right to do as they pleased in this matter was never questioned. There was no inclination to violate the very principle for which they had contended in the War for Independence by attempting to coerce any state that did not see fit to unite with them.

In September 1789, while Rhode Island was still holding aloof from the new Union, President Washington received and sent in to the Senate of the United States a letter from the General Assembly of Rhode Island, addressed to "the President, the Senate, and the House of Representatives of the eleven United States of America in Congress assembled." This letter is interesting because it shows the relationship then existing between Rhode Island and the United States. It was a request that trade and commerce might be free and open between that state and the United States.

On November 21, 1789, North Carolina, after becoming satisfied that the most important of the amendments and "Declaration of Rights" that North Carolina and other states had proposed would be adopted, agreed to "adopt and ratify" the Constitution. On May 29, 1790, Rhode Island gave its long-withheld assent to the Constitution, after becoming fully convinced that certain proposed amendments would be adopted.

When Washington announced to Congress that North Carolina had ratified the Constitution of 1787, he expressed his gratification at the accession of that state. On June 1, 1790, he announced by special message the like accession of the state of Rhode Island and congratulated Congress on the

On April 30, 1789, George Washington was inaugurated as the first President of the United States of America and became known as the "Father of His Country."

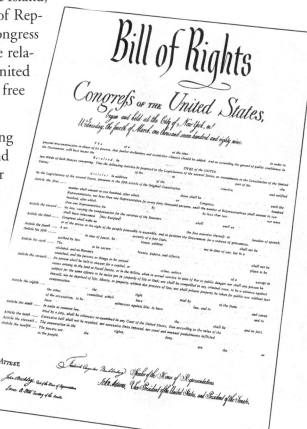

happy event that "united under the General Government all the states which were originally confederated."

The Bill of Rights. During the fight over ratification of the Constitution, it became clear that many people believed that the Constitution needed to include a list of rights. Many states ratified the Constitution with the understanding that a bill of rights would be added later. Some states even sent proposed lists of rights to Congress for its consideration.

In response, James Madison took the lead in drawing up a list of proposed amendments to the Constitution. Twelve amendments were submitted to the states in September 1789. Ten of these amendments were ratified in December 1791 and became known as the Bill of Rights.

Many important rights are listed in the Bill of Rights. Examples of some of these well-known rights are: freedom of religion, freedom of the press, freedom of speech, the right to bear arms, and the right to a speedy trial by jury. One of the least understood of the amendments is the Tenth Amendment, which specifically limits the powers of the United States government and is a safeguard to state authority. The Tenth Amendment states: "The powers not delegated to the United States by the Constitution, nor prohibited by it to the states, are reserved to the states respectively, or to the people."

Samuel Adams, of Massachusetts, said of the Tenth Amendment: "It is consonant with the second article in the present Confederation, that each state retains its sovereignty, freedom, and independence, and every power, jurisdiction, and right, which is not by this Confederation expressly delegated to the United States in Congress assembled." Thus, we see the founding fathers, while anxious to form a more perfect union, guarded carefully the sovereignty of the states. President Washington referred to the country as a "nation of nations."

James Madison's Public Service to His Country. Following the ratification of the Constitution, Madison served as a representative from Virginia in the House of Representatives from 1789 through 1797. While in Congress, he was largely responsible for the writing and passage of the Bill of Rights. During his time in Congress, he married Dolley Payne Todd. After four years of private life, Madison became Secretary of State under President Thomas Jefferson. As Secretary of State, he helped to arrange for the purchase of the Louisiana Territory.

In 1809, Madison became the fourth President of the United States and served two terms, retiring in 1817. President Madison led the United States in its second war with Britain during the War of 1812. As President, he

Dolley Payne (née Todd) Madison
(1768–1849)

authorized the seizure of West Florida from Spain, supported the chartering of the second Bank of the United States, and encouraged Congress to pass a new protective tariff law.

Madison continued his public service after leaving office. He became a member of the board of the University of Virginia and served as its rector from 1826 to 1834. He served as a delegate to the Virginia Constitutional Convention in 1829 and was called upon to give advice during various political controversies. He also edited his *Notes of Debates in the Federal Convention of 1787*, which was published after his death. Madison died on June 28, 1836, having provided his country with long and faithful service.

Even long after his death, Madison continues to affect the United States government. One of the two amendments Madison suggested that the states ratify, but which were not made part of the Bill of Rights, has become the Twenty-seventh Amendment of the Constitution. This amendment, which was originally proposed to the states by Congress in 1789, finally was made part of the Constitution in 1992, after Michigan became the thirty-eighth state to ratify the amendment. This new amendment prohibits Congress from introducing and voting through salary increases for itself within a single congressional term.

Summary. A good deal of the credit for the formation and adoption of the United States' beloved Constitution and Bill of Rights belongs to James Madison. On several occasions, Madison was the only leader who continued to press for the passage of the key constitutional amendments known as the Bill of Rights. His faithfulness to the people gained him the respect and honor of all Americans past and present. He truly deserves the title of "Father of the Constitution." Madison also became the fourth President of the United States and led the nation to victory during the War of 1812.

James Madison was the principal author of the Constitution and became known as the "Father of the Constitution." On March 4, 1809, he was inaugurated the fourth President of the United States. Madison led the nation to victory during the War of 1812 against Great Britain.

Comprehension Questions

1. Where did James Madison receive his early education?

2. When did Madison begin his political career?

3. How many branches of government make up our federal government?

4. Who wrote the articles entitled *The Federalist*?

5. What state was the last to ratify the Constitution?

6. How did the Tenth Amendment promote the role of the states in the United States system of government?

Chapter 21
James McGready (1758–1817)

Methodist Information

James McGready

Naturally, the Americans were very excited that they had won the War for Independence, especially because they had beaten the powerful British Army. And while many gave credit for the victory to God, people seemed to lose their religious enthusiasm pretty quickly after the war. There were at least two reasons for this rapid shift. First, a few famous people (including Thomas Jefferson and Benjamin Franklin) raised questions about traditional beliefs in God. For example, Jefferson went so far as to argue that the miracles in the Bible did not happen. Secondly, the church had a hard time keeping up with how quickly the people were moving to the western territories. In order to reach those people more effectively, the church turned to the old, but proven, method of revivals. These revivals (which came to be known as the Second Great Awakening) did succeed in creating a lot of spiritual excitement in the West, but they also stirred up a lot of controversy.

Camp Meetings. It was clear that the West was in need of some good churches. The men who settled the West had to practically make it on their own since they were so far from established towns. The rough lives they had often meant rough lifestyles, however. In other words, since they were so far from civilization, they did not have a church or pastor to make sure they were living in a godly way.

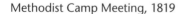

Methodist Camp Meeting, 1819

Fortunately, there were a number of pastors who were not content to leave things that way. Since the people were spread all over the West (which at this time only went as far as Indiana), it was impossible to bring church to where they were. Instead, they invited the people to one central location where they held camp meeting revivals. These revivals were called camp meetings because the people who came often stayed for days (even months) to hear the pastors preach, and they were forced to bring tents to stay in.

The response of the people to the camp meetings was electrifying. Thousands of people from all over the South and West, and from every different religious denomination, streamed to them. While many likely went to see what the big deal was about these camp meetings, many also came to hear the Word of God being preached, and they were converted as a result. What made the camp meetings so electrifying, however, was how the people responded to the preaching. People were known to dance, laugh, run around, and fall when they were caught up in the emotion of the moment. Many believed that these emotional responses seen in the camp meetings proved that the Holy Spirit was there. Others believed that these emotional responses proved that things had gotten out of control.

James McGready's Role. Many preachers from various Christian denominations were instrumental in rekindling the fire of social and theological reformation in the early nineteenth century. However, few preachers had as much influence during this period as James McGready, who was a fiery and tough Presbyterian preacher. McGready had the reputation for preaching the eternal truths of God in a bold and uncompromising way. He stressed the need for the people to repent and be converted. His style, although at times crude, was well received by the simple country people who often attended his revival meetings.

In 1796, James McGready became the pastor of three Presbyterian churches in notoriously immoral Logan County, Kentucky. Here, under his preaching, the great western revival began.

McGready was joined by several Presbyterian and Methodist preachers; and by 1800, the success of the outdoor revival meetings he led was amazing. During that year, a massive revival meeting at Red River, Kentucky, drew thousands of people from hundreds of miles in every direction to hear the gospel of Jesus Christ. Great numbers of people were converted to the Christian faith at that time.

Francis Asbury (1745–1816)

Despite creating some controversy in the Presbyterian church, McGready continued to use camp meeting revivals to spread the gospel. He pushed as far west as Indiana, where he eventually died in 1817.

During this same period, similar revivals were taking place in the eastern part of the United States. Many of these revivals were led or influenced by Francis Asbury, a powerful Methodist bishop who encouraged men to travel from town to town on horseback to preach to the people. The men who took Asbury's advice became known as "circuit-riding" preachers, and they were so effective that the Methodist denomination was the fastest growing church in America during the Second Great Awakening. The Methodists had about 300 people in 1771 and grew to over 200,000 by 1816.

Criticism of the Second Great Awakening. As stated earlier, however, not everyone was excited about the Second Great Awakening. The critics of the camp meetings saw problems in both how the Word was being preached and also in the people's response to the Word being preached. First, the critics argued that the preachers were working too hard to get an emotional reaction out of the people. They believed that the Word created enough emotion on its own without any extra help from the preachers. In addition, because of the camp meeting preachers'

A Circuit Rider Preacher

emphasis on the emotional response, the critics feared that they would deemphasize the true teachings about God. Evidence for that criticism was found in the fact that camp meetings would use pastors from many different denominations. To the critics, that meant that all the pastors were willing to dismiss rather large differences in order to have a successful revival.

Those big differences that existed also explain the second problem the critics had with the camp meetings; that is, the emotional reaction of the people. While the critics were not opposed to emotion being expressed during church, they were careful to make sure that it was proper emotion. In other words, they believed genuine religious emotion can only come from true biblical teaching. The critics were fearful that many people simply were caught up in the moment at the camp meetings, and they were not aware of the teaching that lay behind the emotions they were feeling.

The Calm Revivalist. During the Second Great Awakening, the revivalists who provoked strong emotional reactions, such as James McGready and Charles Finney, received the most attention. However, there were revivalists who rejected "enthusiastic" methods of preaching and still achieved impressive success.

Asahel Nettleton (1783–1844)

Asahel Nettleton was one of these "calm revivalists." He believed that the emotion created by revivals was temporary, and he feared that those 'converted' at those revivals would go back to their former way of life once the emotion wore off. He also feared that the revival minister gave the people too much power in their argument that they had the ability to choose for or against God (known as "free will"). Thus, Nettleton preached in a very controlled and calm way, always emphasizing the traditional belief that God alone has the power to save. Instead of being annoyed at Nettleton's reluctance to use the more "popular" revival techniques, the people flocked to wherever he preached. Some estimate that 30,000 people converted as a result of his ministry.

Nettleton represented a firm response to the excesses of the Second Great Awakening. Along with his extensive preaching efforts, Nettleton helped

found the Theological Institute of Connecticut to help train young ministers. Thus, while the enthusiastic revivalists and the doctrine of free will carried the day during the Second Great Awakening, Nettleton helped ensure that skeptics of its success would have a voice.

The Impact of the Second Great Awakening. Whether one liked the camp meetings or not, there is no debate about their impact on America. As revival spread, church membership increased and public morality generally improved. The disinterest in spiritual things that had been observed after the War for American Independence had been destroyed. America had become a very religious nation, and it even remains one to this day.

A spiritually thirsty America responded to the dynamic preaching of leaders like James McGready and Francis Asbury. People who visited America during the early nineteenth century also noticed the effects of this great spiritual awakening. The famous French author and historian Alexis de Tocqueville visited America in the early 1830s and wrote his famous book *Democracy in America* based on what he observed during his visit. The book explained why Tocqueville believed America not only survived but also thrived at such an early point in its history. In his book, this keen social observer and gifted author wrote:

> There is no country in the world where the Christian religion retains a greater influence over the souls of men than in America; and there can be no greater proof of its utility and of its conformity to human nature than that its influence is powerfully felt over the most enlightened and free nation of the earth. The secret to America's greatness is its moral goodness. If America ever ceases to be good, it will cease to be great.

Summary. The Second Great Awakening was key in establishing America as one of the most religious nations on earth. The success of the revivals allowed the church to establish itself in the Wild West. Men such as James McGready and Francis Asbury were tireless in their efforts to bring the gospel to whoever would hear, wherever they were. Critics questioned the revivals, however, wondering whether the preachers were more concerned about getting an emotional reaction from the people than they were about preaching the truth.

Comprehension Questions

1. Why were the revivals that took place during the Second Great Awakening called camp meetings?

2. In what state did Rev. McGready begin his revival meetings?

3. Who was Francis Asbury?

4. According to critics of the Second Great Awakening, what were the preachers working too hard to get?

5. Who was known as a "calm revivalist"

6. Who was Alexis de Tocqueville?

7. What did Tocqueville believe was the key to America's greatness during this period?

Unit 4
Growth of the Nation

Chapter 22
America Adds New States (1791–1803)

New States. After America won its independence from Great Britain, people began moving into the territories to establish new homes and communities. Between 1791 and 1803, four new states joined the Union. The first new state was Vermont, which is between New York and New Hampshire. During the colonial period, the Vermont territory was claimed by both New York and New Hampshire. In 1776, the people of Vermont decided they wanted to be independent of both New York and New Hampshire, and, for a time, Vermont governed itself. However, once the United States Constitution was ratified and the new government organized, Vermont petitioned Congress to become a new state. In 1791, Vermont became the fourteenth state in the new federal Union—the first new state of the nation.

One of Vermont's most famous early citizens was Ethan Allen. His family was one of the early settlers of Vermont, moving from Connecticut shortly after Allen was born in 1738. He served in the colonial militia during the French and Indian War. In 1775, Vermont militia forces—called the Green Mountain Boys—commanded by Ethan Allen helped capture Fort Ticonderoga, which is on Lake Champlain in New York, from the British without firing a shot.

The Consitution of Vermont was the founding document of the Vermont Republic, which existed from 1777 to 1791. Vermont's army was essentially made up of the militia, called the Green Mountain Boys, led by Ethan Allen.

In 1775, Ethan Allen and Benedict Arnold led a raid to capture Fort Ticonderoga.

Ethan Allen (1738–1789)

The next territory to become a state was Kentucky, which had been part of Virginia and joined the Union in 1792 as the fifteenth state. We have already learned how Daniel Boone helped bring settlers over the mountains into Kentucky. After the War for Independence, the settlers of Kentucky asked to be separated from Virginia. Once Virginia agreed to the separation, Kentucky was accepted as a new state.

William Tryon (1729–1788)
"Great Wolf of North Carolina"

Trouble in North Carolina. When Daniel Boone first went to Kentucky (1769), he had a friend named James Robertson in North Carolina, who was, like himself, a mighty hunter. The British governor of North Carolina at that time was William Tryon. He lived in a palace built with money that he had forced the people to give him. The people disliked him because of his greed and cruelty, so they nicknamed him the "Great Wolf of North Carolina."

Eventually, many of the settlers vowed that they would not give the governor another penny. When he sent tax collectors to get money, they drove them away. They flogged one of the governor's friends with a rawhide until he had to run for his life.

The governor then collected some soldiers and marched against the people in the West. A battle was fought near the Alamance River in 1771. The governor had the most men, and cannon besides, so he gained the day. He took seven of the people prisoners and hanged them. They all died bravely, as men do who die for liberty.

After the Battle of Alamance, James Robertson and his family decided they would not live any longer where Governor Tryon ruled. They resolved to go across the mountains into the Western wilderness. Sixteen other families joined the Robertsons and went with them. It was a long, hard journey. They had to climb rocks and find their way through deep, tangled woods. The men went ahead with their axes and their guns; then the older children followed, driving the cows; last of all came the women with the little children, with beds, pots, and kettles packed on the backs of horses.

John Sevier (1745–1815)

Settlers in Tennessee. When the little party had crossed the mountains into what is now the state of Tennessee, they found a delightful valley. Through this valley there ran a stream of clear, sparkling water called the Watauga River; the air of the valley was sweet with the smell of wild crab apples.

On the banks of that river, the emigrants built their new homes. Their houses were simple, rough log huts, but they were clean and comfortable. When the settlers put up these cabins, they chopped down every tree near them that was big enough for an Indian to hide behind. They knew that they might have to fight the red men; but they would rather do that than be robbed by tax collectors. In the wilderness, Governor Tryon could not reach them. They were free—free as the deer and the squirrels were. That one thought made them happy.

The year after this little settlement was made, John Sevier went from Virginia to Watauga, as it was called. He and Robertson became best friends, for one brave man can always see something to respect and like in another brave man. Robertson and Sevier hunted together and worked together. After a while, they called a meeting of the settlers and agreed on some excellent laws known as the Watauga Association, so that everything in the log village might be done decently and in order; for, although these people lived in the woods, they did not want to live like savages or wild beasts.

Sevier gained an impressive reputation as an Indian fighter and militia officer. He built Fort Watauga in 1775 as protection for the settlement against Indian attacks and commanded the forces that successfully defended the fort against an attack by Cherokee Indians the next year. A few years later, in 1780, Colonel Sevier commanded part of the force of American militia troops that went over the mountains into South Carolina to defeat the British at the Battle of Kings Mountain.

Hand-to-hand combat on King's Mountain as Lt. Col. Ferguson tries to break through American lines

In the meantime, Robertson moved further west. He led a large group of emigrants to the Cumberland River, where he built Fort Nashborough on its banks. The settlement founded near the fort became the city of Nashville, the current capital city of the state of Tennessee.

Out of this settlement on the Watauga River grew the state of Tennessee. In 1796, Tennessee became the sixteenth state of the Union. Both Robertson and Sevier were honored for their service to their country and their state. President Washington gave James Robertson the rank of general for what he had done for his country.

Sevier was elected as the first governor of the state of Tennessee and served several terms in office, as well as other positions in the state and federal governments. Many years ago, a small monument was erected to Sevier in the cemetery at Nashville. Also, a noble monument to Sevier's memory has been erected in Knoxville, the first capital of Tennessee.

Moving to Ohio. While Vermont, Tennessee, and Kentucky were being settled, others began to consider the great Northwest Territory, which George Rogers Clark had won for the United States during the War for American Independence. In the spring of 1788, a group of emigrants from New England, veterans from the War for Independence and their families, built a boat at a place on a branch of the Ohio River just above Pittsburgh, Pennsylvania. They named this boat the *Mayflower* because they were Pilgrims going west to make their home there.

At that time, there was not a European settler in what is now the state of Ohio. Most of that country was covered with thick woods. There were no roads through those woods; and there was not an airport, an automobile, or a railroad in America or, for that matter, in the whole world. If you look on the map and follow down the Ohio River from Pittsburgh, you will come to the place where the Muskingum River flows into it. There the *Mayflower* stopped, and the emigrants landed and began to build their settlement.

These new settlers were led by Rufus Putnam, who was originally from Massachusetts and had fought in the War for American Independence. When the British had possession of Boston at the beginning of the war,

Rufus Putnam (1738–1824)

George Washington asked Rufus Putnam, who became a great builder of forts, to help him drive them out. Putnam began to work one dark, stormy night and built a fort on some high land overlooking Boston Harbor.

When the British commander woke up the next morning, he saw the American cannon pointed at his ships. He was so astonished that he could hardly believe his eyes. "Why," said he, "the rebels have done more in one night than my whole army could have done in a week." Another officer, who had command of the British vessels, said, "If the Americans hold that fort, I cannot keep a ship in the harbor." The Americans did hold that fort, and the British had to leave Boston. Next to General Washington, Rufus Putnam was the man who made them go because not many officers in the American Army could build such a fort as he could.

Putnam went on to build other important forts and also served during the Battle of Saratoga. In 1783, shortly before the war was over, he was promoted to brigadier general in reward for his valuable service. He went back to Massachusetts after the war, but later decided to help settle Ohio.

During the War for American Independence, the beautiful Queen Marie (Antoinette) of France was a firm friend, and she was very kind and helpful to Dr. Franklin when he went to France for America. Since many of the emigrants to Ohio had fought in the War for Independence, the company of settlers decided to name the town Marietta, in honor of the queen.

When the Marietta settlers celebrated the Fourth of July, Major Ebenezer Denny, who commanded a fort just across the river, came to visit them. He said, "These people appear to be the happiest folks in the world." President Washington said that he knew many of them and that he believed they were just the kind of men to succeed. He was right; for these people, with those who came later to build the city of Cincinnati, were the ones who laid the foundation of the great and rich state of Ohio.

War with the Indians. The people of Marietta had hardly begun to feel at home in their little settlement before a terrible Indian war broke out. The village of Marietta had a high fence built around it, and if a man walked outside that fence, he went at the risk of his life. The Indians were always hiding in the woods ready to kill any settler they saw. When the settlers worked in the cornfield, they had to carry their guns as well as their hoes; and one man always stood on top of a high stump in the middle of the field, to keep a sharp lookout.

Marie Antoinette (1755–1793)

On the Ohio River, below Marietta, there is a lofty rock that is still called Indian Rock. It was given this name because the Indians used to climb to the top and watch for emigrants coming down the river in boats. When they saw a boat, they would fire a shower of bullets at it, hoping to leave it full of dead and wounded men to drift down the stream. In the western part of Ohio, on the Miami River, the Indians killed so many people that the settlers called that part of the country by the terrible name of the "Miami Slaughter House."

This situation could not be allowed to continue. A loose alliance of Indian tribes had been formed to oppose the settlement of territory north of the Ohio River and had even been able to defeat American military forces in 1790 and 1791. President Washington decided, therefore, to send a man to Ohio who would make the Indians beg for peace. This man was General Wayne; he had fought in the War for Independence, and fought so furiously that he was called "Mad Anthony Wayne." Wayne created a new army called the Legion of the United States and trained his men carefully. When his men were ready, Wayne and his troops entered Ohio to deal with the Indian alliance.

The Indians said that Wayne never slept. They named him "Black Snake," because that is the quickest and boldest snake there is in the woods, and, in a fight with any other creature of his kind, he is pretty sure to win the day. General Wayne won the Battle of Fallen Timbers in 1794, and the Indians agreed the next year to move off and give up a very large part of Ohio to the settlers.

After Wayne's victory and the treaty with the Indians, there was not much trouble, and new emigrants moved in by the thousands. So many settlers came in fact, that Ohio was able to become the seventeenth state in 1803. Ohio was the first part of the Northwest Territory to become part of the Union.

On the Lookout

Summary. Soon after the establishment of the Constitution, the United States began to grow as people moved into the frontier to establish new lives for themselves and their families. It was not an easy life for the newcomers, but they built new homes and towns. Within twenty years after America won its independence, four new states—Vermont, Kentucky, Tennessee, and Ohio—had joined the Union. Many more were to follow.

Comprehension Questions

1. Name the states that joined the Union between 1791 and 1803.
2. What territory was claimed by both New York and New Hampshire?
3. Which territory did Daniel Boone help to settle?
4. Where did James Robertson and his party first settle? How did they get there?
5. What state grew out of the Watauga settlement?
6. To which territory did Rufus Putnam lead emigrants? How did they get there?
7. Why did George Washington send General Wayne to Ohio?

Chapter 23
Eli Whitney (1765–1825)

Eli Whitney (1765–1825)

Eli Whitney's Early Years. Near Westboro, Massachusetts, there was an old farmhouse that was built before the War for American Independence. Close to the house was a small wooden building; on the door you could read a boy's name, just as he cut it with his pocketknife more than 100 years ago. Here is the door with the name. If the boy had added the date of his birth, he would have cut the figures 1765; but, just as he was about to try, his father appeared and said sharply:

"Eli, don't be cutting that door."

"No, sir," said Eli, with respect; and shutting his knife up with a snap, he hurried off to do his chores.

Eli Whitney's father used that little wooden building as a workshop, where he mended chairs and did many other small jobs. Eli liked to go to that workshop and make little things for himself, such as toy guns and windmills; for it was as natural for him to use tools as it was to whistle.

Once, when Eli's father was gone from home for several days, the boy was very busy all the while in the little shop. When Mr. Whitney came back, he asked his housekeeper, "What has Eli been doing?"

"Oh," she replied, "He has been making a fiddle."

His father shook his head and said that he was afraid Eli would never succeed in the world. However, Eli's fiddle, though it was rough looking, was well made. It had music in it, and the neighbors liked to hear it. Somehow it seemed to say, through all the tunes played on it, "Whatever is worth doing, is worth doing well."

When Eli was fifteen, he began making nails. We have machines today that will make more than 100 nails a minute; but Eli made his, one by one, by pounding them out of a long, slender bar of red-hot iron. Whitney's handmade nails were not handsome, but they were strong and tough; and as the War for American Independence was then happening, he could sell all he could make.

After the war was over, the demand for nails declined. Then Whitney threw down his hammer and said, "I am going to college." He had no money; he worked his way through Yale College, partly by teaching and partly by doing little jobs with his tools. A carpenter who saw him at work one day noticed how neatly and skillfully he used his tools and said, "There was one good mechanic spoiled when you went to college."

Whitney Goes to Georgia. When the young man had finished his course of study, he went to Georgia to find a job teaching. On the way to Savannah, he became acquainted with Mrs. Greene, the widow of the famous General Nathanael Greene of Rhode Island. General Greene had done such excellent fighting in the South during the War for Independence that, after the war was over, the state of Georgia gave him a large piece of land near Savannah.

Mrs. Catharine Littlefield Greene invited young Whitney to stay and work at her house. As he had been disappointed in not finding a place to teach, he was very glad to accept her kind invitation. While he was there, he made her an embroidery frame. It was much better than the old one that she had been using, and she thought the maker of it was wonderfully skillful.

Not long after this, a number of cotton planters were at Mrs. Greene's house. In speaking about raising cotton, they said that the man who could invent a machine for stripping off the cottonseeds from the plant would make his fortune.

Raw cotton or "cotton wool," as it grows in the field, has numerous little green seeds clinging to it. Before the cotton wool can be spun into thread and woven into cloth, those seeds must be pulled off.

At that time, the Southern planters had their black slaves do most of this work. When they had finished their day's labor of gathering the cotton in the cotton field, the men, women, and children would sit down and pick off the seeds, which stuck so tight that getting them off was no easy task.

After the planters had talked awhile about this work, Mrs. Greene said, "If you want a machine to do it, you should apply to my young friend, Mr. Whitney; he can make anything."

"But," said Mr. Whitney, "I have never seen a cotton plant or a cottonseed in my life," for it was not then the time of year to see it growing in the fields.

Gen. Nathanael Greene (1742–1786)

Whitney Invents the Cotton Gin. After the planters had gone, Eli Whitney went to Savannah and hunted about until he found, in some store or warehouse, a little cotton wool with the seeds left on it. He took this back with him and began to work to make a machine that would strip off the seeds.

He said to himself, "If I fasten some upright pieces of wire in a board, and set the wires very close together, like the teeth of a comb, and then pull the cotton wool through the wires with my fingers, the seeds, being too large to come through, will be torn off and left behind." He tried it and found that the

The cotton gin (*gin* is short for "engine") is a machine that quickly and easily separates cotton fibers from their seeds and seedpods. This machine uses a wire screen and small wire hooks to pull the cotton through the screen, while brushes continuously remove the loose cotton lint to prevent jams.

As a Yale graduate, Whitney was well-connected. In 1817, Whitney married Henrietta Edwards, the granddaughter of the famous evangelist Jonathan Edwards. Henrietta was also the daughter of Pierpont Edwards, head of the Democratic party in Connecticut and first cousin of Yale's president, Timothy Dwight.

After Whitney died, his armory was turned over to his capable nephews, Eli Whitney Blake and Philos Blake. The Blake brothers went on to invent the mortise lock and stone-crushing machine.

cotton wool came through without any seeds on it. "Now," said he, "if I should make a wheel, and cover it with short steel teeth, shaped like hooks, these teeth would pull the cotton wool through the wires better than my fingers do, and much faster as well."

He made such a wheel, which was turned by a crank, and it did the work perfectly. Therefore, in the year 1793, he had invented the machine the planters wanted.

Before that time, it used to take a plantation worker all day to clean a single pound of cotton of its seeds, by picking them off one by one; now Eli Whitney's cotton gin, as he called his machine, would clean 1,000 pounds in a day. This new invention and many others like it helped American workers produce things cheaper and better than ever before.

"**King Cotton.**" Today nothing is much cheaper than common cotton cloth. You can buy it for very little money per yard; but before Whitney invented his cotton gin, it sold for a great deal of money per yard. Two hundred years ago, the planters in the South raised very little cotton, for few people could afford to wear it; but after this wonderful machine was made, the planters kept making their fields bigger and bigger. Eventually, they raised so much more of this plant than of any other crop that they said, "Cotton is king." It was Eli Whitney who built the throne for that king. Although he did not make a fortune from his machine, he received a lot of money for its use in some southern states.

Later, Mr. Whitney built a gun factory near New Haven, Connecticut, at a place now called Whitneyville. At that factory, he made thousands of the muskets that were used in the second war with England in 1812—the famous war that gave us the stirring song called *The Star Spangled Banner* and secured American independence on the sea, as the War for American Independence did on the land.

Summary. About 200 years ago (1793), Eli Whitney of Westboro, Massachusetts, invented the cotton gin, a machine for pulling off the green seeds from cotton wool, so that it may be easily woven into cloth. That machine made thousands of cotton planters and cotton manufacturers rich, and it made cotton cloth so inexpensive that everybody could afford to use it.

Comprehension Questions

1. What was the name of the lady that Eli Whitney met when he went to Savannah?

2. What name did Eli Whitney give to his invention that pulled the seeds out of cotton?

3. What was the name of the college that Whitney attended?

4. What did Mr. Whitney build at Whitneyville, Connecticut?

The National Anthem of the United States:

The Star-Spangled Banner

by Francis Scott Key

Oh, say, can you see, by the dawn's early light,

What so proudly we hailed at the twilight's last gleaming?

Whose broad stripes and bright stars, through the perilous fight,

O'er the ramparts we watched were so gallantly streaming!

And the rocket's red glare, the bombs bursting in air,

Gave proof through the night that our flag was still there.

O say does that star-spangled banner yet wave

O'er the land of the free and the home of the brave!

On the shore, dimly seen through the mists of the deep,

Where the foe's haughty host in dread silence reposes,

What is that which the breeze, o'er the towering steep,

As it fitfully blows, half conceals, half discloses?

Now it catches the gleam of the morning's first beam,

In full glory reflected now shines on the stream.

'Tis the star-spangled banner; Oh, long may it wave

O'er the land of the free and the home of the brave!

Oh, thus be it ever, when freemen shall stand

Between their loved homes and the war's desolation!

Blest with victory and peace, may the heaven-rescued land

Praise the Power that hath made and preserved us a nation.

Then conquer we must, when our cause it is just,

And this be our motto: "In God is our trust,"

And the star-spangled banner in triumph shall wave

O'er the land of the free and the home of the brave!

Francis Scott Key (1779–1843)

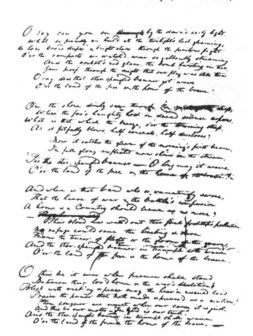

Francis Scott Key's handwritten notes of his poem "The Star-Spangled Banner."

Chapter 24
Thomas Jefferson (1743–1826)

Thomas Jefferson (1743–1826)

Before Eli Whitney invented his machine, the United States sent hardly a bale of cotton abroad. Now America sends so much in one year that the bales can be counted by millions. If they were laid end to end, in a straight line, they would reach over 17,000 miles—that is, traveling from New York City to Los Angeles seven times! Eli Whitney did more than any other man to build up this great trade. But at the time when he invented his cotton gin, the United States did not own New Orleans or, for that matter, any part of Louisiana or of the country west of the Mississippi River. The man who bought New Orleans and Louisiana for the United States was President Thomas Jefferson.

Thomas Jefferson's Early Years. Thomas Jefferson was the son of a rich planter who lived near Charlottesville in Virginia. When his father died, he came into possession of a plantation of nearly 2,000 acres of land, with forty or fifty slaves on it.

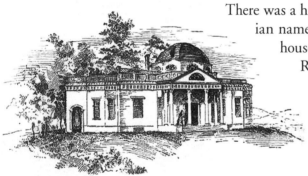

Monticello, Estate of Thomas Jefferson

There was a high hill on the plantation, to which Jefferson gave the Italian name of Monticello, or the little mountain. Here he built a fine house. From it, he could see the peaks and valleys of the Blue Ridge Mountains for an immense distance. No man in America had a more beautiful home, or enjoyed it more, than Thomas Jefferson.

Jefferson's slaves thought that no one could be better than their leader. He was always kind to them, and they were ready to do anything for him. Yet, Jefferson hoped and prayed that the time would come when every slave in the country might be set free.

Patrick Henry (1736–1799)

Jefferson was educated to be a lawyer. He was not a good public speaker himself, but he liked to hear men who were good speakers. Just before the beginning of the War for American Independence (1775), the people of Virginia sent men to Richmond to hold a meeting in old St. John's Church. They met to see what should be done about defending those rights which the king of England had refused to grant the Americans.

One of the speakers at that meeting was a famous Virginian named Patrick Henry. When he stood up to speak, he looked very pale, but his eyes shone like coals of fire. He made a great speech. He said, "We must fight! I repeat it, sir, we must fight!" The other Virginians agreed with Patrick Henry; and George Washington and Thomas Jefferson, along with other noted men who were present at the meeting, began at once to prepare to fight.

The Declaration of Independence. Shortly after this, the great war began. About a year after the first battle was fought, the Continental Congress asked Thomas Jefferson, Benjamin Franklin, and some others to write the Declaration of Independence. Mr. Jefferson was called the "Pen of the Revolution," for he could write as well as Patrick Henry could speak.

The Declaration was printed and was then carried by men mounted on fast horses all over the United States. When men heard it, they rang the church bells and sent up cheer after cheer. General Washington had the Declaration read to all the soldiers in his army; and if powder had not been so scarce, they would have fired off every gun for joy.

Jefferson as President of the United States. Several years after the war was over, Jefferson was elected President of the United States; while he was President (1801-1809) he did something for the country that will never be forgotten.

Louisiana Territory, the city of New Orleans, and the lower part of the Mississippi River all belonged to the French. At that time, the United States reached west only as far as the Mississippi River. Because New Orleans stands near the mouth of that river, the French could say, if they chose, which vessels could go out to sea, and which could come in. So far as that part of America was concerned, the United States was like a man who owns a house while another man owns one of the main doors to it. The man who has the door could say to the owner of the house, "I shall stand here on the steps, and you must pay me so many dollars every time you go out and every time you want to go into your house."

Jefferson saw that as long as the French held the door of New Orleans, Americans would not be free to send cotton down the river and across the ocean to Europe. He said they must have that door, no matter how much it cost.

Robert R. Livingston, one of the signers of the Declaration of Independence, was in France at that time, and Jefferson sent him instructions to try to buy New Orleans for the United States. Napoleon Bonaparte then ruled France. He said, "I want money with which to buy warships so that I can fight England; I will sell not only New Orleans, but all Louisiana besides, for fifteen million dollars." That was cheap enough, and so in 1803 President Jefferson bought it.

If you look on the map, you will see that Louisiana then was not simply a good-sized state, as it is now, but a huge territory reaching all the way to the Rocky Mountains. It was larger than the whole United States east of the Mississippi River. So, through President

The Purchase and Its Aftermath, 1803-1819

129

Thomas Jefferson (1743–1826) was the third President of the United States (1801–1809), the principal author of the Declaration of Independence (1776), the architect of the Louisiana Purchase (1803), and the promoter of the Lewis and Clark Expedition (1804–1806).

Jefferson's purchase, the United States added so much land that it now had more than twice as much as it had before. It also had the whole Mississippi River, New Orleans, and what is now the great city of St. Louis as well.

Death of Jefferson. Jefferson lived to be an old man. He died at Monticello on the Fourth of July, 1826, just fifty years, to a day, after he had signed the Declaration of Independence. John Adams, who had been President just before Jefferson, died a few hours later. So America lost two of her great men on the same day.

Jefferson was buried at Monticello. He asked to have these words, with some others, cut on his gravestone: Here Was Buried Thomas Jefferson, Author of the Declaration of American Independence.

Summary. Thomas Jefferson of Virginia wrote most of the Declaration of Independence. After he became President of the United States, he bought Louisiana. The purchase of Louisiana, with New Orleans, gave the United States the right to send ships to sea via the Mississippi River, which now also belonged to the United States. Louisiana added so much land that it more than doubled the size of the United States.

Comprehension Questions

1. Did the United States own New Orleans or Louisiana when Whitney invented his cotton gin?

2. Who bought them for the United States?

3. What elected office did Thomas Jefferson hold from 1801-1809?

4. For what profession was Jefferson educated?

5. How did Patrick Henry help the people become free?

6. What important paper did Thomas Jefferson help to write?

7. How much did the United States pay to France for the Louisiana Territory?

Chapter 25
Robert Fulton (1765–1815)

The Louisiana Territory. Even before the United States bought the great Louisiana Territory, the country had more land than the people then could use. After the United States had bought it, it seemed to some people as though they would be unable to use what they had bought for more than 100 years. Such people thought that the United States was like a man with a small family who lives in a house much too large for him; but who, not contented with that, buys his neighbor's house, which is bigger still, and adds that to his own.

If a traveler in those days went across the Allegheny Mountains to the West, he found some small settlements in Ohio, Kentucky, and Tennessee, but hardly anything else. The region that is now covered by the great states of Indiana, Illinois, Michigan, and Wisconsin was then a wilderness; and this was true also of what are now the states of Alabama and Mississippi.

If the same traveller, pushing westward on foot or on horseback (for there were no cars, buses, or trains) crossed the Mississippi River, he could hardly find a settler outside what was then the little town of St. Louis. The country stretched west for more than 1,000 miles, with nothing in it but wild beasts and Indians. In much of it there were no trees, no houses, no human beings. If you shouted as hard as you could in that solitary land, the only reply you would hear would be the echo of your own voice.

But during the nineteenth century (1801–1900), that great empty land in the West filled with people. Thousands upon thousands of emigrants entered the Louisiana Territory. They built towns and cities and railroads and telephone lines. What made such a wonderful change? Well, one man helped to do a great deal toward it. His name was Robert Fulton. He saw how difficult it was for people to travel west, for if emigrants wanted to travel with their families in wagons, they had to chop roads through the forests. That was slow, hard work. Fulton found a way that was quick, easy, and cheap. Let us see who he was and how he found that way.

Robert Fulton's Boyhood. Robert Fulton was the son of a poor Irish farmer in Pennsylvania. He did not care much for books, but liked to draw pictures with pencils, which he hammered out of pieces of lead.

Like most boys, he was fond of fishing. He used to go out in an old scow, or flat-bottomed boat, on a river near his home. He and another boy would push the scow along with poles. But Robert said, "There is an easier way to make this boat move. I can put a pair of paddle wheels

Robert Fulton's Paddle Wheel Scow

131

on her, and then we can sit comfortably on the seat and turn the wheels by a crank." He tried it and found that he was right. The boys now had a boat that suited them exactly.

When Robert was seventeen, he went to Philadelphia. After his father's death, Robert earned his living and helped his mother and sisters by painting pictures. He stayed in Philadelphia until he was twenty-one. By that time, he had saved up enough money to buy a small farm for his mother, so that she might have a home of her own.

Fulton Goes to England and France. Soon after buying the farm for his mother, young Fulton went to England and then to France. He stayed in those countries twenty years. In England, Fulton built some famous iron bridges, but he was more interested in boats than in anything else.

While he was in France, he made what he called a diving boat. It would go underwater almost as well as it would on top, so that, wherever a big fish could go, Fulton could follow him. His object in building such a boat was to make war in a new way. When a swordfish attacks a whale, he dives under him and stabs the monster with his sword. Fulton said, "If an enemy's warship should come into the harbor to cause trouble, I can get into my diving boat, slip under the ship, fasten a torpedo to it, and blow the ship sky high."

Fulton's Diving Boat

Napoleon Bonaparte liked nothing more than war, so he let Fulton have an old vessel to see if he could blow it up. He tried it, and everything happened as he expected; nothing was left of the vessel but the pieces.

Then Fulton went back to England and tried to do the same thing there. He went out in his diving boat and fastened a torpedo under a vessel; when the torpedo exploded, the vessel, as he said, went up like a "bag of feathers," flying in all directions.

The English people paid Fulton $75,000 for showing them what he could do in this way. Then they offered to give him a great deal more, enough to make him a very rich man, if he would promise never to let any other country know just how he blew vessels up. But Fulton said, "I am an American; and if America should ever want to use my diving boat in war, she shall have it first."

Fulton and the Steamboat. While Fulton was doing these things with his diving boat, he was always thinking of the paddle-wheel scow he used to fish in when a boy. "I turned those paddle wheels by a crank," he said, "but what is to keep me from putting a steam engine into such a boat, so it can turn the crank for me?" That would be a steamboat. Such boats had already been tried, but for one reason or another, they had mostly failed. Robert R. Livingston was still in France, and he helped Fulton build his first steamboat. It was put on a river there; it barely moved.

But Robert Fulton and Mr. Livingston both believed that a steamboat could be built that would go, and that would keep going. So they went to New York City and built one there.

In the summer of 1807, a great crowd gathered to see the boat start on her voyage up the Hudson River. They joked and laughed as crowds will at anything new. They called Fulton and Livingston fools. But when Fulton, standing on the deck of his steamboat, waved his hand, and the wheels began to turn, and the vessel began to move up the river, the crowd became silent with astonishment. Now it was Fulton's turn to laugh, and in such a case the man who laughs last has a right to laugh loudest.

Fulton's Steamer on the way to Albany

Up the river Fulton kept going. He passed the Palisades, the Highlands, and still he continued. Eventually, he reached Albany, 150 miles from New York City.

Nobody had ever seen such a sight as that boat moving up the river without the help of oars or sails, but from that time people saw it every day. When Fulton came back to the city of New York in his steamboat, everybody wanted to shake hands with him. The crowd, instead of shouting jeers, now whispered among themselves that Fulton was truly a very great man.

The "Big Fire Canoe." Four years later, Fulton built a steamboat for the West. In the autumn of 1811, it started from Pittsburgh to go down the Ohio River, and then down the Mississippi to New Orleans. The people of the West had never seen a steamboat before, and when the Indians saw the smoke puffing out, they called it the "Big Fire Canoe."

Steamboat on the Mississippi

On the way down the river, there was a terrible earthquake. In some places it changed the course of the Ohio, so that where there had been dry land there was now deep water, and where there had been deep water there was now dry land. One evening, the captain of the "Big Fire Canoe" fastened his vessel to a large tree on the end of an island. In the morning, the people on the steamboat looked out, but could not tell where they were. The island was gone; the earthquake had carried it away. The Indians called the Great Earthquake of 1811, the "Big Shake"; it was a good name, for it kept on shaking that part of the country and doing all sorts of damage for weeks.

When the steamboat reached the Mississippi, the settlers on that river said that the boat would never be able to go back because the current was so strong. At one place, a crowd had gathered to see her as she turned against the current, in order to come up to the landing place. An old man stood watching the boat. It looked as if, in spite of all the captain could do, she would be carried down stream, but at last steam conquered, and the boat came up to the shore. Then the old man could hold in no longer: he threw up his ragged straw hat and shouted, "Hooray! hooray! the old Mississippi's just met her master this time!"

Soon steamboats began to run regularly on the Mississippi; and after a few years they began to move up and down the Great Lakes and the Missouri River. Emigrants could now go to the West and the Far West quickly and easily; they had Robert Fulton to thank for that.

Robert Fulton lies buried in New York City, in the shadow of the tower of Trinity Church. There is no monument or mark over his grave; but every time we think of the great growth of the United States we will remember this great inventor.

Summary. In 1807, Robert Fulton of Pennsylvania built the first steamboat that ran on the Hudson River, and four years later he built the first one that navigated the rivers of the West. His boats helped to fill the whole western country with settlers.

Comprehension Questions

1. List the names of three states that were once a part of the great Western wilderness.
2. What man helped Robert Fulton build the first successful steamboat?
3. In what countries did Robert Fulton build his diving boat?
4. What did the Indians call Fulton's steamboat?
5. Where was Mr. Fulton buried?
6. How did the steamboat help people during this time?

Chapter 26
William Henry Harrison (1773–1841)

War with the Indians. During the year 1811, in which the first steamboat went west, a great battle was fought with the Indians. The battleground was on the Tippecanoe River, in what is now the state of Indiana.

The Shawnee Indians fought because they were tired of being pushed farther west. They wanted to keep the West for themselves. One day, a military officer came to the wigwam of an old Indian chief to tell him that he and his tribe must go still farther west. The chief said, "General, let's sit down on this log and talk it over." So they both sat down. After they had talked a short time, the chief said, "Please move a little farther that way; I haven't room enough." The officer moved along. In a few minutes, the chief asked him to move again, and he did so. Presently, the chief gave him a push and said, "Do move farther on, won't you?"

"I can't," said the general.

"Why not?" asked the chief.

"Because I've come to the end of the log," replied the officer.

"Well," said the Indian, "now you see how it is with us. You settlers have kept pushing us until you have pushed us clear to the end of our country, and yet you come now and say move on, move on."

What Tecumseh and His Brother, the "Prophet," Tried to Do. A famous Shawnee Indian warrior named Tecumseh determined to bring the different Indian tribes together and drive out the American settlers from the West.

Tecumseh had a brother Tenskwatawa, called the "Prophet," who pretended he could tell what would happen in the future. He said, "The white traders come here, give the Indians whiskey, get them drunk, and then cheat them out of their lands. Once we owned this whole country; now, if an Indian strips a little bark from a tree to shelter him when it rains, a settler steps up with a gun in his hand and says, 'That's my tree, let it alone.'"

Then the "Prophet" said to the Indian warriors, "Stop drinking fire-water, and you will have strength to kill off the 'pale-faces' and get your land back. When you have killed them off, I will bless the earth. I will make pumpkins grow to be as big as wigwams, and the corn shall be so large that one ear will be enough for a dinner for a dozen hungry Indians." The Indians liked to hear these things; they wanted to taste those pumpkins and that corn, and so they prepared to fight.

William H. Harrison (1773–1841)

"Move On"

135

Tecumseh (1768–1813)

Governor William Henry Harrison. At this time, William Henry Harrison was governor of the Indiana Territory. He had fought under General Anthony Wayne in his war with the Shawnee Indians in Ohio. Everybody knew Governor Harrison's courage, and the Indians all respected him; but he tried in vain to prevent the Indians from going to war. The "Prophet" urged them on in the North, and Tecumseh had gone south to persuade the Indians there to join the northern tribes.

Governor Harrison saw that a battle must soon be fought, so he started with his soldiers to meet the Indians. He marched to the Tippecanoe River, and there he stopped.

While Harrison's men were asleep in the woods, the "Prophet" told the Indians not to wait, but to attack the soldiers immediately. In his hand, he held up a string of beans. "These beans," said he to the Indians, "are sacred. Come and touch them, and you are safe; no white man's bullet can hit you." The Indians hurried up in crowds to touch the wonderful beans.

"Now," said the "Prophet," "let each one take his hatchet in one hand and his gun in the other, and creep through the tall grass until he gets to the edge of the woods. The soldiers lie there fast asleep; when you get close to them, spring up and go for them, like a wildcat for a rabbit."

The Battle of Tippecanoe

The Indians started to do this, but a soldier on guard saw the tall grass moving as though a great snake was gliding through it. He fired his gun at the moving grass; up sprang the whole band of Indians, and, with a terrible yell, they rushed forward. In a moment the battle began.

Harrison won the victory. He not only killed many of the Indians, but he marched against their village, set fire to it, and burned it to ashes.

After that, the Indians in that part of the country would not listen to the "Prophet." They called him a liar; his beans had not saved them.

The Battle of Tippecanoe did much good because it prevented the Indian tribes from uniting and beginning a great war all through the West. Governor Harrison received high praise for what he had done and was made a general in the United States Army.

When Tecumseh came back from the South, he was terribly angry with his brother Tenskwatawa for fighting before he was ready to have him begin. He seized the "Prophet" by his long hair and shook him as a big dog shakes a rat. Tecumseh then left the United States and went to Canada to help the British, who were preparing to fight the United States.

The War of 1812. The next year began the second war with England. It is called the War of 1812. One of the major reasons the United States fought was that the British would not leave the American merchant ships alone. They stopped them at sea and took thousands of American sailors from them. The British then forced the men to serve in their warships in their battles against the French.

During the War of 1812, the British burned the Capitol at Washington, but a grander building rose from its ashes. General Harrison fought a battle in Canada in which he defeated the British and killed Tecumseh, who was fighting on the side of the English.

A Battle at Sea in the War of 1812

Many years after this battle, the people of the West said that they must have the "Hero of Tippecanoe" for President of the United States. They went to vote for him, with songs and shouts, and he was elected. A month after he went to Washington, President Harrison died (1841), and the whole country was filled with sorrow.

Summary. In 1811, General Harrison gained a great victory over the Shawnee Indians at Tippecanoe, in Indiana. By that victory, he saved the West from a terrible Indian war. In the War of 1812, with England, General Harrison beat the British in a battle in Canada and killed Tecumseh, the Indian chief who had caused so much trouble. Many years later, General Harrison was elected President of the United States.

Comprehension Questions

1. In which state was the Battle of Tippecanoe fought?

2. Who was the famous Indian warrior who had a brother called "The Prophet"?

3. What countries fought during the War of 1812?

4. Did the British burn the capitol building in Washington during the war?

5. What year did President Harrison die?

Chapter 27
Andrew Jackson (1767–1845)

Andrew Jackson (1767–1845)

Andrew Jackson Early Years. He was the son of a poor emigrant who came from the north of Ireland and settled in the Waxhaws region on the border of North and South Carolina. When Thomas Jefferson wrote the Declaration of Independence in 1776, Andrew was nine years old, and his father had long been dead. He was a tall, slender, freckled-faced, barefooted boy, with eyes full of fun; the neighbors called him "Little Andy."

He went to school in a log hut in the pine woods; but he learned more things from what he saw in the woods than from the books he studied in school.

He was not a very strong boy, and in wrestling, some of his companions could pin him three times out of four; but though they could get him down without much trouble, it was quite another thing to keep him down. No sooner was he laid flat on his back, than he bounded up like a steel spring and stood ready to try again.

He had a violent temper and when, as the boys said, "Andy was mad all over," not many cared to face him. Once some of his playmates secretly loaded an old gun almost to the muzzle and then dared him to fire it. They wanted to see what he would say when it kicked him over. Andrew fired the gun. It knocked him sprawling; he jumped up with eyes blazing with anger and, shaking his fist, cried out, "If one of you boys laughs, I'll punch him." He looked as though he meant exactly what he said, and the boys thought that maybe it would be just as well to wait and laugh some other day. Little Andrew Jackson did not as yet have the love of Christ ruling his heart. However, when Mr. Jackson was older, he came to know the Lord and was saved from his sins.

Tarleton's Attack on the Americans. When Andrew was thirteen, he learned the horrors of war. The country was then fighting the battles of the Revolution. A British officer named Sir Banastre Tarleton came suddenly upon some American soldiers near the place where young Jackson lived. Tarleton had so many men that the Americans saw that it was useless to try to fight, and they made no attempt to do so. The British should have taken them all prisoners, but instead of that, they attacked them furiously and killed them with their swords. More than 100 men were left dead, and a still larger number were so horribly wounded that they could not be moved any distance. Such an attack was not war, for war means a fair, stand-up fight; it was murder. When the people in England heard what Tarleton had done, many cried, "Shame!"

Sir Banastre Tarleton (1754–1833)

There was a little log meetinghouse near Andrew's home, and it was turned into a hospital for the wounded men. Mrs. Jackson, with other kind-hearted women, did all she could for the poor fellows who lay there groaning and helpless. Andrew carried food and water to them. He had forgotten many of the lessons he had learned at school, but here was something he would never forget.

From that time, when young Jackson went to the blacksmith's shop to get a garden tool fixed, he was sure to come back with a rude spear, or with some other weapon. Andrew Jackson longed for the day when he could fight against the cruel "red coats."

Tarleton said that no people in America hated the British as much as those who lived in that part of the country where Andrew Jackson had his home. The reason was that no other British officer was so cruel as "Butcher Tarleton," as he was called. Once, however, his men met their match. They were robbing a farm of its pigs and chickens and corn and hay. When they finished carrying things off, they were going to burn down the farmhouse; but one of the "red coats," in his haste, ran against a big hive of bees and upset it. The bees swarmed out in a fury and stung the soldiers so terribly that finally the robbers were glad to drop everything and run. If Andrew could have seen that battle, he would have laughed until he cried.

Dangerous State of the Country. Andrew knew that he and his mother lived in constant danger. Some of the people in the Carolinas were for the king, and some were for liberty. Bands of armed men, belonging sometimes to one side, and sometimes to the other, went roving about the country. When they met a farmer, they would stop him and ask, "Which side are you for?" If he did not answer to their liking, the leader of the party would cry out, "Hang him up!" In an instant, one of the group would cut down a long piece of wild grapevine, twist it into a noose, and throw it over the man's head; the next moment, he would be dangling from the limb of a tree. Sometimes the gangs would let him down again while he was still alive; sometimes they would ride on and leave him hanging there.

Even the children saw and heard so much of the war that was going on that they played at war, and fought battles with red and white corn—red for the British and white for the Americans.

At the Battle of Cowpens, Colonel William Washington fought on the American side, and Tarleton was badly beaten and had to run. Not long afterward, he happened to see some boys squatting on the ground, with a pile of corn instead of marbles. They were playing the Battle of Cowpens. A red kernel stood for Tarleton, and a white one for Colonel Washing-

ton. The boys shoved the corn this way and that; sometimes the red would win, sometimes the white. At last the white kernel gained the victory, and the boys shouted, "Hurrah for Washington—Tarleton runs!"

Tarleton had been quietly looking on without their knowing it. When he saw how the game ended, he turned angrily away. He had seen enough of "the little rebels," as he called them.

Colonel William Washington
at the Battle of Cowpens

Andrew Taken Prisoner. Not long after the American victory at Cowpens, Andrew Jackson was taken prisoner by the British. The officer in command of the soldiers had just taken off his boots, splashed with mud. Pointing to them, he said to Andrew, "Here, boy, clean those boots."

Andrew replied, "Sir, I am a prisoner of war, and it is not my job to clean boots."

The officer, in great anger, whipped out his sword and hit the boy. It cut a gash on his head and another on his hand. Andrew Jackson lived to be an old man, but the marks of that blow never disappeared; he carried the scars to his grave.

Andrew was sent, with other prisoners, to Camden, South Carolina, and locked up in the jail. In this jail, many became sick and died of smallpox.

One day some of the prisoners heard that General Greene, the greatest American general in the War for Independence next to Washington, was coming to fight the British at Camden. Andrew's heart leaped for joy, for he knew that if General Greene would win he would let all the prisoners go free.

General Greene, with his little army, was on a hill in sight of the jail; but there was a high board fence around the jail yard, and the prisoners could not see them. With the help of an old razor, Andrew managed to dig out a knot from one of the boards. Through that knothole, he watched the Battle of Hobkirk's Hill.

Jackson and the Officer's Boots

The Americans were beaten in the fight, and Andrew saw their horses with empty saddles running wildly about. Then the boy turned away, sick at heart. Soon after that, he was seized with the smallpox and would have died if his mother had not been able to get him set free.

In the summer, Mrs. Jackson made a journey on horseback to Charleston 160 miles away. She went to carry some little comforts to the poor American prisoners, who were starving and dying of disease in the crowded and filthy British prison ships in the harbor. While visiting these sick men, she caught the fever that many of them had. Two weeks later, she was in her grave, and Andrew, then a lad of fourteen, stood alone in the world.

Years afterward, when he had risen to be a noted man, people would sometimes praise him because he was never afraid to say and do what he believed to be right. Jackson would answer, "That I learned from my good old mother. She taught me to trust in God and do what the Bible says is right."

Andrew began to study law. After he became a lawyer, he went across the mountains to Nashville, Tennessee. There he was made a judge. There were plenty of rough men in that part of the country who meant to have their own way in all things, but they soon found that they must respect and obey Judge Jackson. They could frighten other judges, but it was no use to try to frighten him. Seeing what sort of stuff Jackson was made of, they thought that they would like to have such a man to lead them in battle. And so Judge Jackson became General Jackson. When trouble came during the War of 1812, Jackson proved to be the very man they needed.

The Creek War. We have already seen how the Indian chief Tecumseh went south to stir up the tribes to make war on the settlers in the West. In Alabama he told the "Red Stick" group of the Creek Indians that if they fought, they would gain a great victory. "I see," said Tecumseh, "that you don't believe what I say, and that you don't mean to fight. Well, I am now going north to Detroit. When I get there, I shall stamp my foot on the ground and shake down every wigwam you have."

Chief Tecumseh (1768–1813)

It happened that, shortly after Tecumseh had gone north, the sharp shock of an earthquake was felt in Alabama, and the wigwams were shaken down by it. When the terrified Indians felt their houses falling to pieces, they ran out of them shouting, "Tecumseh has come to Detroit!"

These Red Stick Indians now believed all that Tecumseh had said. Not all of the Creek Indians, however, thought the Red Sticks were correct. Creeks actually began fighting each other. In 1813, the fighting spread to include Red Stick attacks on the settlers. During that summer, the Red Sticks attacked several frontier forts, destroying Fort Mims. Several hundred people were killed in what became known as the Fort Mims Massacre.

One of the Red Stick leaders was William "Red Eagle" Weatherford, whose father was Scottish and mother was a Creek princess. He participated in the Fort Mims attack, although he unsuccessfully tried to prevent the massacre of the women and children after the fort was captured. Weatherford played a prominent role in several other fights with the Americans.

The United States was busy fighting the British and their Indian allies in the North. Few troops could be sent to the South. Therefore, the states of Georgia and Tennessee, along with the Mississippi Territory (made up of the current states of Mississippi and Alabama), mobilized their militia troops to fight along with the few regular Army troops in the area and with friendly Indians against the Red Stick Creeks.

One of the early American victories was won by forces commanded by General Ferdinand L. Claiborne. The Red Stick Indians had established a village at a place their prophets called the "Holy Ground." They believed that if a white man dared to set his foot on that ground he would be struck dead, as if by a flash of lightning. The Creeks also thought that the village was protected by difficult terrain, with the Alabama River on one side and the other sides protected by swamps hard for attackers to cross.

General Claiborne and his men, however, marched to the "Holy Ground" in December 1813. The Creeks soon found that neither the difficult terrain nor the work of their prophets could keep the Americans out of their village. The head prophet had left the village when he learned that the American force was coming, leaving Weatherford in charge of its defense. Most of the Creeks fled once they realized that there was nothing holy about their ground. Soon, Weatherford found himself to be the last defender in the village, since the remaining defenders were killed. To escape, Weatherford rode his horse over a bluff about ten feet high into the cold river.

It took General Jackson, however, to end the Creek War. He had marched from Tennessee with the largest army against the Red Stick Indians. Jackson's forces beat the Red Sticks at the Battle of Horseshoe Bend on March 27, 1814. Jackson had a force of around 3,000 men against 1,000 Red Sticks. William Weatherford was again one of the Red Stick leaders. The Red Sticks were severely defeated, losing almost 800 warriors in the fight. A young Sam Houston—later a governor of Tennessee and Texas—was also wounded in the battle. Only about 200 Red Sticks, including Weatherford, escaped. Most of the Red Sticks fled to Spanish controlled Florida.

But Weatherford remained in Alabama. Not long after the Red Sticks' crushing defeat, he rode boldly up to Jackson's tent. "Kill him! Kill him!" cried Jackson's men, but the general asked Weatherford into his tent.

"You can kill me if you want to," said he to Jackson, "but I came to tell you that the

William "Red Eagle" Weatherford surrendered to Andrew Jackson after the Battle of Horseshoe Bend.

Indian women and children are starving in the woods, and to ask you to help them, for they never did you any harm." General Jackson sent Weatherford away in safety and ordered that corn should be given to feed the starving women and children. That act showed that he was as merciful as he was brave. Jackson had learned how to fulfill the teaching of Jesus Christ to "love your enemies."

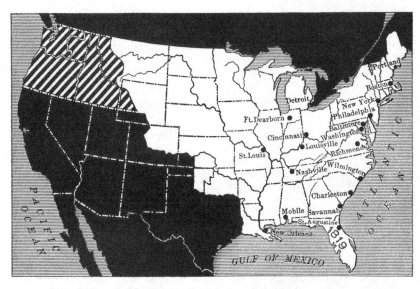

The light part of the map shows the extent of the United States in 1819, after the purchase of Florida. The striped area shows that the ownership of the Oregon Territory was still in dispute between Great Britain and the United States.

The Battle of New Orleans and the Great Victory. These things happened during the second war with England, called the War of 1812. About a year after Jackson's victory over the Indians, the British sent an army in ships to take New Orleans. General Jackson now went to New Orleans to prevent the enemy from capturing the city.

About four miles below the city, which stands on the Mississippi River, there was a broad, deep ditch, running from the river into a swamp. Jackson saw that the British would have to cross that ditch when they marched against the city. For that reason, he built a high wall on the upper side of the ditch and placed cannon along the top of the bank.

Early on Sunday morning, January 8, 1815, the British sent a rocket whizzing up into the sky; a few minutes afterward, they sent up a second one. It was the signal that they were about to march to attack Jackson's men.

Battle of New Orleans

Just before the fight began, General Jackson walked along among his men, who were getting ready to defend the ditch. He said to them, "Stand to your guns; see that every shot hits; give it to them, boys!" The "boys" did give it to them. The British soldiers were brave men. They had been in many terrible battles, and they were not afraid to die. They fought hard. They tried again and again to cross that ditch and climb the bank, but they could not do it. The fire of the guns cut them down just as a mower cuts down the tall grass. In less than half an hour, the great battle was over. Jackson had won the victory and saved New Orleans. The Americans lost only eight killed; the enemy lost over 2,000. America has never had another battle since that time with England. Hopefully, there will never be another, for two great nations like England and America, that speak the same language, should be firm and true friends.

Statue of General Jackson in front of the Jackson County Courthouse in Kansas City, Missouri

Jackson as President of the United States. After the Battle of New Orleans, General Jackson conquered the Seminole and Creek Indians in Florida, and in 1819, the United States bought that territory from Spain. This new land made the United States much larger on the south. This was the second great land purchase.

Ten years after the United States bought the Florida Territory, General Jackson became President of the United States. He had fought his way up. Here are the four steps: first the boy, Andy Jackson; then Judge Jackson; then General Jackson; last of all, President Jackson.

Shortly after he became President of the nation, the first steam railroad in the United States was built (1830). From that time, railroad tracks kept creeping farther and farther west. The Indians had frightened the settlers with their terrible war whoop. Now it was their turn to be frightened, for the locomotive whistle could beat their wildest yell. They saw that settlers were determined to get possession of the whole land. The greater part of the Eastern Indians were forced to move across the Mississippi; but the settlers kept following them and the buffalo farther and farther across the country, toward the Pacific Ocean. The railroad followed the path of the settlers as they moved westward.

Summary. Andrew Jackson of the Carolinas, but later a citizen of Tennessee, gained a great victory over the Creek Indians in Alabama and also in Florida. In 1815, in the second war with England, General Jackson beat the British at New Orleans, and so prevented their getting possession of that city. A few years later, the United States bought Florida from Spain.

After General Jackson became President, the first steam railroad was built in the United States. Railroads helped to settle the West and build up states beyond the Mississippi River.

Comprehension Questions

1. Who hit Andrew Jackson with a sword when he was a prisoner?
2. Who was William Weatherford?
3. Who won the Battle of New Orleans?
4. In what year did America buy the territory of Florida?
5. In what year did the first steam-powered railroad appear?
6. How did the railroads help the western part of the United States develop?

Chapter 28
Industrial Development (1830–1850)

Cyrus H. McCormick (1809–1884)

A Machine for Cutting Grain. The nineteenth century was a time of great inventions that greatly affected the lives of people around the world. Americans made several of the most important inventions. We have already read about a few inventors, but there are many others.

Two hundred years ago, wheat and other grains were cut by hand. A Virginia farmer said to himself, "Why can't I make a machine which my horses can pull and that can cut my wheat in less time than it takes a dozen men to do with sickles or cradles?" He built a machine, but it did not satisfy him, and he left it to rust to pieces where it stood.

Cyrus H. McCormick (1809–1884)

His son, Cyrus H. McCormick, made up his mind that he would find out why his father's reaper would not work. Cyrus had learned to do one thing at a time, and to do the hardest thing first. Now the hardest thing in this case was to discover why the reaper, when it cut the wheat, would not throw it down straight, so that it could be easily bundled for the threshing machine, which separated the grain from the straw. By patient effort, young McCormick succeeded in making a reaper that would do what was wanted. This was in 1831. He had to wait years before anyone bought one of his new machines, and even then he found that he needed to improve it. He began to make some improvements, but not many farmers there could afford to buy it.

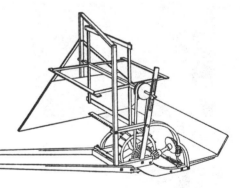

Finally, a friend said to him, "Cyrus, why don't you go to the West with your reaper, where the land is level and where it is difficult for the farmers to hire men enough to cut all the grain that grows?"

"Yes," answered Cyrus, "I will go west." He started at once, and for the first time in his life saw a prairie. It stretched out as far as the eye could see and seemed as smooth as a barn floor. Then the thought came to him, "What must this country look like when it is covered with golden fields of wheat?" "Now," said he, "I see what I really made my machine for. I must come out here and build it, for every farmer will be sure to buy it."

He traveled on until he came to Lake Michigan. On the southern shore of the lake, he stopped at a town called Chicago. "Here," said Mr. McCormick, "I shall start my business, for this town will grow, and my business will grow with it." He made no mistake that time. He built reapers and found no difficulty in selling them. He kept making improvements in his work. He improved his reapers so that they would cut the grain rapidly and smoothly and then tie it up in bundles.

Obed Hussey (1792–1860)

Who Really Invented the Reaper?

Many believe that Obed Hussey should receive the honor of being the one who invented the reaper. In 1833, Mr. Hussey moved to Cincinnati, where he began work on his new invention. During the summer, he successfully tested his reaper and patented it by the end of the year. This placed him in fierce competition with Cyrus McCormick. Both men made several patented innovations to the reaper, until Obed was ultimately driven out of business. Had Obed lived, he would have been able to establish his claim to inventing the first reaper. This humble Quaker presented his case before Congress and the United States Patent Office; however, he died tragically while traveling by train from Boston to Portland, Maine, on August 4, 1860. This came just at the time when his victory seemed certain and the future of his reaper looked bright with promise.

Having done all this, he took the last step. He made a new reaper, or Harvester, which would do all that the old one did, and would even thresh out the grain as well. This did everything that the Western farmer could want, for it filled row after row of bags with the precious wheat that gives us "our daily bread."

Elias Howe (1819–1867)

Elias Howe (1819–1867)

The Sewing Machine. While Cyrus H. McCormick was busy in the West, a young man named Elias Howe was just as busy in his house in Cambridge, Massachusetts. When someone asked him what he was trying to make, he answered, "I am trying to make a machine that will sew cloth." His answer was met by a loud laugh. Mr. Howe paid no attention to the laugh, but kept quietly at work. By the end of the winter, he was able to put together a clumsy machine that he called his "Iron Needle-woman." This was in 1845.

He hoped that in time his machine would be able to sew faster than any girl, but in the end, people found that the "Iron Needle-woman" could sew faster than ten girls. The young man expected to sell his invention to the tailors; however, they were afraid that if they bought the machines, the men they hired to do sewing by hand would refuse to use them for fear of losing their jobs. Subsequently, they refused to have anything to do with him.

Mr. Howe then traveled to London, England, thinking that maybe he could sell his invention in that city. There he was worse off than he was at home, for the tailors would try his machine, but would not pay for it. He decided that he must leave England and go back to America. He found that the only way he could get money enough to pay his passage across the ocean was to borrow it and leave his "Iron Needle-woman" as security. When he landed in New York City, he had less than a dollar in his pocket. He was discouraged. Then came an even harder experience. He learned that someone, who had no lawful right to do so, had been making and selling his invention while he had been abroad.

In fact, a man in western New York was traveling about, at that very time, showing this sewing machine to anyone who would pay twelve cents to see

Howe's Sewing Machine

it. Many ladies went to see it and bought fancy work done by this sewing machine. They carried the work home to show their friends what the wonderful "Iron Needle-woman" could do. Still, very few believed that the machine would ever prove to be of any real use in a family.

Mr. Howe was too poor to go to court to protect his rights, but he at length found means to prevent others from taking his machine away from him. Then he became prosperous, and this man, who once did not have a dollar in his pocket, began to complain that he hadn't enough pockets to hold all the dollars that poured in on him.

At the same time, several other inventors made various improvements to the sewing machine. Finally, one of them built a machine that would sew leather with a waxed thread. This opened a new field of work. Today most of our clothing is made by sewing machines, and our boots and shoes are generally stitched together by them. The result is that now both clothing and footwear are far cheaper than when they were all made by hand.

Samuel F. B. Morse (1791–1872)

Samuel F. B. Morse (1791–1872)

Samuel Morse's Early Years. The Erie Canal, in the state of New York, connects the Hudson River at Albany with Lake Erie at Buffalo. It is the greatest work of the kind in America and was completed many years ago. When the water was let into the canal from the lake, the news was flashed from Buffalo to New York City by a row of cannon, about five miles apart, which were fired as rapidly as possible, one after the other. The first cannon was fired at Buffalo at ten o'clock in the morning; the last was fired at New York at half-past eleven. In an hour and a half, the sound had travelled over 500 miles. Everybody said that was very quick work; but an inventor who lived in the mid-1800s discovered a way to send messages like this in less than a minute. The man who found out how to do this was Samuel Finley Breese Morse.

We have seen how Benjamin Franklin discovered with his kite that lightning and electricity are the same. Samuel Morse was born in Charlestown, Massachusetts, about a mile from Franklin's birthplace, the year after that great man died. He began his work where Franklin left off. He said to himself, "Dr. Franklin found out what lightning is; I will find out how to harness it and make it carry news and deliver messages."

How they flashed the news of the completion of the Erie Canal in 1825

When Samuel Morse was a little boy, he liked to draw pictures, particularly faces. After he became a man, he learned to paint. At one time, he lived in France with several other American artists. One day they were talking about how long it took to get letters from America, and they were wishing the time could be shortened. Somebody spoke of how cannon had been used when the Erie Canal was opened. Morse was familiar with all that. He had been educated at Yale College, and he knew that the sound of a gun will travel a mile while you are counting five. But, quick as that is, he wanted to find something better and quicker still. He said, "Why not try lightning or electricity?" The speed of light will go more than 1,000 miles while you are counting one.

Professor Morse and the Electric Telegraph. Some time after that, Mr. Morse set sail for America. On the way across the Atlantic Ocean, he was constantly talking about electricity and how a telegraph—that is, a machine that would write at a distance—might be invented. He thought about this so much that he could not sleep nights. At last, he believed that he knew how he could make such a machine.

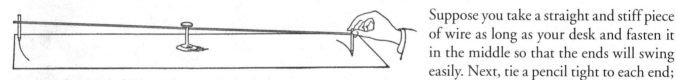

One Kind of Telegraph

Suppose you take a straight and stiff piece of wire as long as your desk and fasten it in the middle so that the ends will swing easily. Next, tie a pencil tight to each end; then put a sheet of paper under the point of each pencil. Now, if you make a mark with the pencil nearest you, you will find that the pencil at the other end of the wire will make the same kind of mark. Such a wire would be a type of telegraph because it would make marks or signs at a distance. Mr. Morse said, "I will have a wire a mile long, with a pencil, or something sharp-pointed like a pencil, fastened to the farther end; the wire itself shall not move at all, but the pencil will, for I will make electricity run along the wire and move it." Mr. Morse was then a professor or teacher in the University of New York. He put up such a wire in one of the rooms of the building, sent the electricity through it, and found that it made the pencil mark just as he wanted. Mr. Morse knew that he had invented the electric telegraph; for if he could do this over a mile of wire, then what was to stop him from doing it over 100 or even 1,000 miles?

But all this was not done in a day, for this invention cost years of patient labor. At first, Mr. Morse lived in a little room alone. There he worked, ate when he could get something to eat, and slept if he wasn't too tired to sleep. Later he had a room in the university. While he was there, he painted pictures to get money enough to buy food; there, too, he took the first photograph ever made in America (1839). Yet, with all his hard work, there were times when he had to go hungry. Once he told a young man that if he did not get some money he would be dead in a week—dead of starvation.

Alfred Lewis Vail (1807–1859)

A young man named Alfred Lewis Vail happened to see Professor Morse's telegraph. He believed it would be successful. He persuaded his father, Judge Vail, to lend $2,000, and he became Professor Morse's partner in the work. Mr. Vail was an excellent mechanic, and he made many improvements in the telegraph. He then made a model of it at his own expense and took it to Washington, D.C., and got a patent for it in Professor Morse's name. The invention was now safe in one way, for no one else had the right to make a telegraph like his. Yet, though he had this help, Professor Morse did not get rich very fast, for a few years later he said, "I have not a cent in the world; I am as poor as a church mouse."

Congress and the First Telegraph Line. Professor Morse now asked Congress to let him have $30,000 to build a telegraph line from Washington to Baltimore. He felt sure that businessmen would be glad to send messages by telegraph and to pay him for his work. But many members of Congress laughed at it and said they might as well give Professor Morse the money to build "a railroad to the moon."

Week after week went by, and the last day that Congress would sit was reached, but still no money had been granted. Then came the last night of the last day (March 3, 1843). Professor Morse stayed in the Senate Chamber of Congress until after ten o'clock; then, tired and disappointed, he went back to his hotel, thinking that he must give up trying to build his telegraph line.

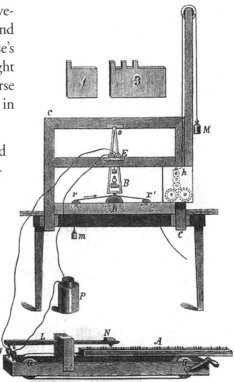

Morse's Telegraph Recorder

The next morning, Annie G. Ellsworth met him as he was coming down to breakfast. She was the daughter of his friend who had charge of the Patent Office in Washington. She came forward with a smile, grasped his hand, and said that she had good news for him, that Congress had decided to let him have the money. "Surely you must be mistaken," said the professor, "for I waited last night until nearly midnight, and came away because nothing had been done."

"But," said the young lady, my father stayed until it was past midnight, and a few minutes before the clock struck twelve, Congress voted the money; it was the very last thing that was done."

Professor Morse was then a gray-haired man over fifty. He had worked hard for years and had received little for his labor. This was his first great success. He never said whether he laughed or cried at this time; perhaps he felt a little like doing both. Hopefully, he remembered to send up a prayer of thanks to Almighty God.

When Professor Morse did speak, he said to Miss Ellsworth, "Now, Annie, when my line is built from Washington to Baltimore, you shall send the first message over it." In the spring of 1844, the line was completed, and Miss Ellsworth, by Professor Morse, sent these words over it (they are words taken from the Bible): "What hath God wrought!"

Photograph of Samuel F. B. Morse Taken in 1866

For nearly a year after that, the telegraph was free to all who wished to use it; then a small charge was made, a very short message costing only one cent. On the first of April, 1845, a man came into the office and bought a cent's worth of telegraphing. That was all the money that was taken in that day for the use of forty miles of wire. A few years later, there were nearly a million miles of telegraph wire in the United States. This is almost enough to reach thirty-six times around the earth. Americans could telegraph not only across America, but across the Atlantic Ocean, and even to China, by a line laid under the sea. Professor Morse's invention made it possible to write by electricity; but now, with the telephone, a man in New York City or Boston can talk with someone in Chicago, St. Louis, or in any other city; and the man listening at the other end of the wire can hear every word he says, and can talk with him freely. Professor Morse did not live to see this wonderful invention, which, in many ways, is an improvement over his telegraph.

Summary. Cyrus H. McCormick and Obed Hussey worked hard on inventing a reaper to harvest wheat. About the same time, Elias Howe developed the sewing machine. Professor Morse invented the electric telegraph. He received much help from Alfred Vail. In 1844, Professor Morse and Mr. Vail built the first line of telegraph in the world. It extended from Washington to Baltimore. These inventors gave the world the reaper, sewing machine, and the telegraph.

Comprehension Questions

1. What famous farm machine did Cyrus McCormick invent?
2. Name Howe's invention that could sew faster than ten girls.
3. Tell how they sent the news of the completion of the Erie Canal.
4. What is a telegraph?
5. What did Mr. Morse ask Congress to do?
6. What was the first message sent by telegraph in 1844?
7. Why is the telephone an improvement over the old telegraph?

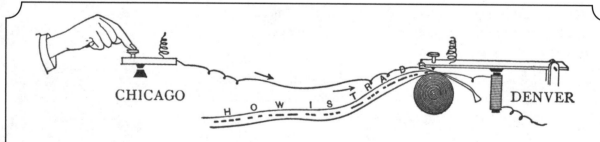

How a Message is sent by Telegraph

When the button at Chicago is pressed down, the electricity passing through the wire to Denver causes the point to be pressed down onto the roll of paper at that end, and so makes a dot or dash which stands for a letter. In this way, words and messages are spelled out. The message on the strip of paper above is the question, "How is trade?"

Chapter 29
Expanding to the Pacific (1750–1850)

Captain Gray (1755–1806)

Captain Gray Goes to the Pacific Coast. Not long after the War for American Independence had ended, some merchants from Boston sent out two vessels to Vancouver Island, on the northwest coast of North America. The names of the vessels were the *Columbia* and the *Lady Washington*, and they sailed down the long coast of North and South America and then round Cape Horn into the Pacific Ocean. Captain Robert Gray went out as commander of one of these vessels. He was born in Rhode Island and had fought in an American warship in the Revolutionary War.

Captain Robert Gray (1755–1806)

Captain Gray was sent out by the Boston merchants to buy furs from the Indians on the Pacific coast. He had no difficulty in getting all he wanted, for the Indians were glad to sell them for very little. In one case, a chief traded 200 sea otter skins(used for making ladies' coats), worth thousands of dollars, for an old iron chisel. After getting a valuable cargo of furs, Captain Gray sailed in the *Columbia* for China, where he bought a quantity of tea. He then went down the coast of Asia and Africa, and round the Cape of Good Hope into the Atlantic Ocean. He kept sailing west until he reached Boston in the summer of 1790. He had been gone about three years; and he was the first man who carried the American flag clear around the globe.

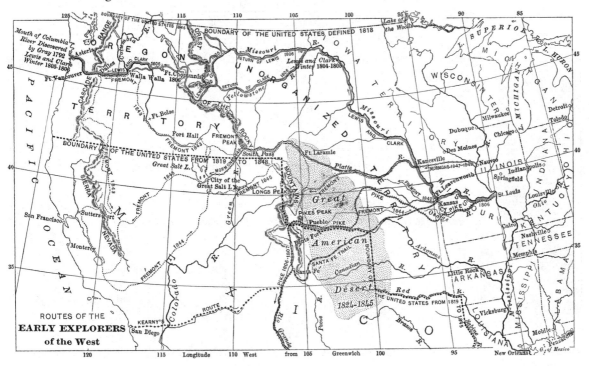

ROUTES OF THE
EARLY EXPLORERS
of the West

151

Marcus Whitman
(1802–1847)

Martyr of the West

Not long after Meriwether Lewis and William Clark finished their famous expedition to the west coast in 1806, the American church expressed interest in evangelizing the new tribes of Indians that had been discovered. Even though the task was overwhelming and the church experienced only limited success in the beginning, an important foundation to build upon was laid for future missionaries.

One of the first missionaries sent to the west coast was Marcus Whitman. Whitman was a doctor who had traveled with the missionary Samuel Parker during an evangelization trip to the Nez Perce tribe of Indians. Inspired, Whitman became a missionary himself and settled among the Cayuse tribe in the Oregon Territory. He labored among them for over ten years before he, his wife, and twelve other settlers were killed by the Cayuse in 1847. Ironically, his training as a doctor likely led to his death since the Indians seemingly blamed him for being unable to prevent a measles epidemic that decimated the tribe.

As a result, Marcus Whitman became more famous through his death than he had been during his life. His death prompted churches to send more missionaries to help settle and subdue the Wild West.

Captain Gray's Second Voyage to the Pacific Coast. Captain Gray did not stay long at Boston, for he sailed again that autumn in the *Columbia* for the Pacific coast to buy more furs. He stayed on that coast a long time. In the spring of 1792, he entered a great river and sailed on it a distance of nearly thirty miles. He seems to have been the first white man who had ever entered it. He named the vast stream the Columbia River, from the name of his vessel. It is the largest American river that empties into the Pacific Ocean south of Alaska.

The United States Claims the Oregon Country. Captain Gray returned to Boston and told the people about his voyage of exploration; this led Congress to claim the country through which the Columbia flows as part of the United States.

After Captain Gray had been dead forty years, the United States came into possession, in 1846, of the large territory then called the Oregon Country. It was through what he had done that the United States held the first claim to that country, which now forms the states of Oregon, Washington, and Idaho, and parts of Wyoming and Montana.

General Sam Houston (1793–1863)

Sam Houston and the Indians. When General Jackson beat the Creek Indians in Alabama, a young man named Sam Houston fought under Jackson and was badly wounded. It was thought that the brave fellow would surely die, but God's grace carried him through, and he lived to do many great things for the southwest part of the United States.

Although Houston fought the Indians as an adult, he was very fond of them as a boy and spent much of his time with them in the woods of Tennessee.

Long after he became a man, his love for wilderness living came back to him. While Houston was governor of Tennessee (1829), he suddenly made up his mind to leave his home and his friends, go across the Mississippi River, and start a new life with an Indian tribe in that part of the country.

General Sam Houston (1793–1863)

The chief, who had known him as a boy, gave him a hearty welcome. "Rest with us," he said. "My wigwam is yours." Houston stayed with the tribe three years.

The Texas War for Independence. At the end of that time, he said to a friend, "I am going to Texas, and in that new country I will make a man of myself." Texas then belonged to Mexico; and President Andrew Jackson had tried in vain to buy it as Jefferson bought Louisiana. Houston said, "I will make it part of the United States." About 20,000 Americans had already moved into Texas, and they felt that the Mexican rulers treated them harshly because they came from the United States.

War broke out between Texas and Mexico, and General Sam Houston led the Texan soldiers in their fight for independence. He had many noted American pioneers and hunters in his little army: one of them was the brave Colonel William Barret Travis of Alabama; another was Colonel James "Jim" Bowie of Louisiana, the inventor of the "bowie knife"; still another was Colonel David Crockett of Tennessee, whose motto is a good one for every young American: "Be sure you're right, then—go ahead." Travis, Bowie, and Crockett, with a small force, held Fort Alamo, an old Spanish church in San Antonio. The Mexicans fought against the fort with a large army of men and killed every man in it.

Colonel David Stern Crockett
(1786–1836)

Not long after that, General Houston fought a great battle near the place where the city called by his name now stands. The Mexicans had more than two men to every one of Houston's; but the Americans and Texans went into battle shouting the terrible cry, "Remember the Alamo!"; and the Mexicans fled before them. Texas then became an independent state and elected General Houston president. The people of the Republic of Texas raised a flag having on it a single star. For this reason, the state is sometimes called the "Lone Star State."

Texas was not contented to stand alone; she begged the United States to add her to its great and growing family of states. This was done in 1845. As we shall presently see, a war soon broke out (1846) between the United States and Mexico, and when that war ended the United States added a great deal more land in the West.

The War Between the States. We have noted the actions that General Sam Houston took in getting new country to add to the United States. He lived in Texas for many years after that. When the great war broke out between the North and the South in 1861, General Houston was governor of the state. He withdrew from office and went home to his log cabin in

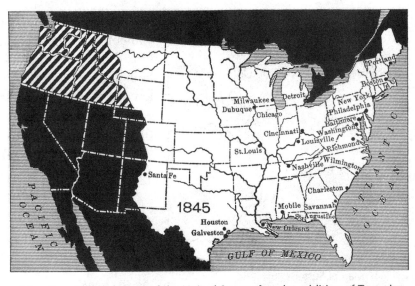

Map showing the extent of the United States after the addition of Texas in 1845. The striped portion shows that the ownership of the Oregon Territory was still in dispute between the United States and Great Britain.

Huntsville, Texas. He refused to take any part in the war, for he loved the Union—that is, the whole country, North and South together—and he said to his wife, "My heart is broken." Before the War Between the States ended, he was laid in his grave.

Captain Sutter (1803–1880)

Johann A. Sutter (1803–1880)

Captain Sutter and His Fort. At the time when Professor Morse sent his first message by telegraph from Washington to Baltimore (1844), Captain Johann Augustus Sutter, an emigrant from Switzerland, was living near the Sacramento River in California. California then belonged to Mexico. The governor of that part of the country had given Captain J. A. Sutter a large piece of land. The captain had built a fort at a point where a stream that he named the American River joins the Sacramento River. People then called the place Sutter's Fort, but today it is known as Sacramento, the capital of the great and rich state of California.

In his fort, Captain Sutter lived like a king. He owned land enough to make 1,000 fair-sized farms. He had 12,000 head of cattle, more than 10,000 sheep, and over 2,000 horses and mules. Hundreds of laborers worked for him in his wheatfields, and fifty well-armed soldiers guarded his fort. Many Americans had built houses near the fort. They thought that the time was coming when all that country would become part of the United States.

Captain Sutter Builds a Sawmill. About forty miles up the American River was a place the Mexicans called Coloma, or the beautiful valley. There was a good waterfall there and plenty of big trees to saw into boards, so Captain Sutter sent a man named James Wilson Marshall to build a sawmill at that place. The captain needed a sawmill to produce lumber to build with, and to fence his fields.

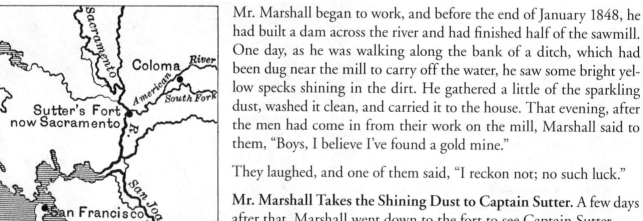

Map of Sutter's Fort

Mr. Marshall began to work, and before the end of January 1848, he had built a dam across the river and had finished half of the sawmill. One day, as he was walking along the bank of a ditch, which had been dug near the mill to carry off the water, he saw some bright yellow specks shining in the dirt. He gathered a little of the sparkling dust, washed it clean, and carried it to the house. That evening, after the men had come in from their work on the mill, Marshall said to them, "Boys, I believe I've found a gold mine."

They laughed, and one of them said, "I reckon not; no such luck."

Mr. Marshall Takes the Shining Dust to Captain Sutter. A few days after that, Marshall went down to the fort to see Captain Sutter.

"Are you alone?" he asked when he saw the captain.

"Yes," he answered.

"Well, would you please do me a favor and lock the door; I've something I want to show you."

The captain locked the door, and Mr. Marshall took a little bag out of his pocket, opened it, and poured some glittering dust on a paper he had spread out.

"See here," said he, "I believe this is gold; but the people at the mill laugh at me and call me crazy."

Captain Sutter examined it carefully. He weighed it; he pounded it flat; he poured some strong acid on it. There are three very interesting things about gold. In the first place, it is very heavy, heavier even than lead. Next, gold is very tough. If you hammer a piece of iron long enough, it will break to pieces; but you can hammer a piece of gold until it is thinner than the thinnest tissue paper. Last of all, if you pour strong acids on gold, they will have no more effect on it than an acid like vinegar has on a piece of glass.

For these and other reasons, most people think that gold is a very valuable metal; and the more they see of it, especially if it is their own, the better they are pleased with it.

Well, the shining dust stood all these tests. It was very heavy, it was very tough, and the sharp acid did not hurt it. Captain Sutter and Mr. Marshall both felt sure that it was gold.

But, strange to say, the captain was not pleased. He wished to build up an American settlement and have it called by his name. Captain Sutter did not care about a gold mine. He did not need riches, for he had everything he wanted without it. He was afraid, too, that if gold should be found in any quantity, thousands of people would rush in; they would dig up his land and probably take it all away from him. We shall see very soon whether he was right or not.

Sutter's Mill

How California Was Settled. While these things were happening, the United States had been at war with Mexico for two years (1846–1848) because Texas and Mexico could not agree about the western boundary line of the new state. Texas wanted to push that line as far west as possible, so as to have more land; Mexico wanted to push it as far east as possible, so as to give up as little land as possible. This dispute soon brought on a war between the United States and Mexico. Soon after gold was discovered at Coloma, the war ended (1848); and the United States obtained not only

Washing Gold out of Dirt

all the land the people of Texas had asked for, but a great deal more; for it obtained the great territory of California and New Mexico, out of which several states have since been made.

In May 1848, a man came to San Francisco holding up a bottle full of gold dust in one hand and swinging his hat with the other. As he walked through the streets, he shouted with all his might, "Gold! gold! gold! from the American River!"

Then the rush for Coloma began. Every man had a shovel and pickax. In a short time, the beautiful valley was dug so full of holes that it looked like an empty honeycomb. In 1845, 100,000 people poured into California from all parts of the United States. The discovery of gold filled that part of the country with emigrants years before they would have gone if no gold had been found there.

Captain Sutter lost all his property. He would have died poor if the people of California had not given him money to live on. Mr. Marshall was still more to be pitied. He received nothing for his discovery. Years after he had found the shining dust, someone wrote to him and asked him for his photograph. He refused to send it. He said, "My likeness … is, in fact, all I have that I can call my own; I want something for myself."

The United States Buys More Land. Long before Captain Sutter died, the United States bought from Mexico another great piece of land (1853), marked on the map by the name of the Gadsden Purchase. Many years later (1867), the United States bought the territory of Alaska from Russia. Alaska became a state in 1959.

This map shows the extent of the United States in 1853 after we had added the land called the Gadsden Purchase, bought from Mexico; the land is marked on the map, 1853.

The War for American Independence ended over 200 years ago. If you look on the map, you will see how the United States has grown during that time. Then there were only thirteen states. They stretched along the Atlantic Ocean, and with the country west of them, extended as far as the Mississippi River. If you add up the additions that have been made of new territory on the North American continent, you will see that, beginning with the Louisiana Purchase in 1803 and ending with Alaska in 1867, they number seven in all. The United States, with its fifty states, now stretches from the Atlantic Ocean into the Pacific Ocean. It also controls a few islands far away.

Summary. In 1790, Captain Robert Gray of Rhode Island first carried the American flag around the world. In 1792, he entered and named the Columbia River. Because he did that, the United States claimed the country, known as the Oregon Country, through which that river runs. In 1846, the United States added the Oregon Country to its possession; it now forms the three great states of Oregon, Washington, and Idaho.

General Sam Houston of Tennessee led the people of Texas in their war against Mexico. The Texans gained the victory and made their country an independent state with General Houston as its president. After a time, Texas was added to the United States. The United States then had a war with Mexico and added a great deal more land in the West. General Houston died during the war between the North and the South in the 1860s.

In January 1848, gold was discovered at Captain Sutter's sawmill at Coloma, California. Soon after that, the United States acquired California and New Mexico from Mexico. Thousands of people, from all parts of the country, hurried to California to dig gold; and so that state grew more rapidly in population than any other new part of the United States ever had.

Campaigns of the Mexican-American War

Comprehension Questions

1. What items did Captain Gray buy from the Pacific coast Indians?

2. What name did Captain Gray give to the large river he found in the Oregon Country?

3. In what year did the United States acquire the Oregon Territory?

4. What was Davy Crockett's motto?

5. What happened at Fort Alamo?

6. When was Texas added to the United States?

7. Who owned the territory of California in 1844?

8. What country went to war with the United States during the years 1846–1848?

9. What valuable item did Mr. Marshall find near Coloma, California?

10. Why did so many people move out to California in 1849?

Chapter 30
Abraham Lincoln (1809–1865)

Abraham Lincoln (1809–1865)

Not many days before gold was found at Sutter's sawmill in California (1848), a tall, awkward-looking man from Illinois was making his first speech in Congress. At that time, he generally wrote his name "A. Lincoln," but after he had become President of the United States, he often wrote it out in full: Abraham Lincoln. The plain country people of Illinois, who knew all about him, liked best to call him by the title they had first given him: "Honest Abe Lincoln," or "Honest Abe" for short. Let us see how he received that name.

Abraham Lincoln's Early Life. Abraham "Abe" Lincoln was born on February 12, 1809, in a log cabin on a lonely little farm in Kentucky. When Abe, as he was called, was seven years old, his father, Thomas Lincoln, moved to Indiana. There they built a new home in the woods. That new home was not as good or as comfortable as some of the barns that cows sleep in. It was simply a hut made of rough logs and tree limbs. It had no door or any windows. One side of it was left entirely open; and if a traveling Indian or a bear wanted to walk in for dinner, there was nothing whatsoever to stop him. In winter, Abe's mother often hung up some buffalo skins before this wide entrance to keep out the cold; during the summer, the skins were taken down, so that living in such a cabin was not much better than living outdoors.

The end of the War of 1812 signaled the defeat of the British and the Indians who sided with them. By treaties with the United States, the Indians exchanged their land for land in the Louisiana Territory; this opened the old Northwest Territory to settlement. Pioneers emigrated rapidly to this new area and began clearing the forests and cultivating the land. One such pioneer was Thomas Lincoln, who settled with his family in present-day Spencer County, Indiana.

The Lincoln family stayed in that shed for about a year, while they were building a new log cabin that had four sides to it. They also made a new set of furniture for the new house. To make a table, Abe's father split a large log in two, smoothed off the flat side, bored holes in the underside, and drove in four stout sticks for legs. They had no chairs, for it would have been too much trouble to make the backs; they did, however, have three-legged stools, which Thomas Lincoln made with an ax just as he did the table. Perhaps Abe helped him push in the legs.

In one corner of the loft of this cabin, the boy had a big bag of dry leaves for his bed. Whenever he felt like having a new bed, all he had to do was go out into the woods and gather more leaves.

He worked around the cabin during the day, helping his father and mother. For his supper, he had a piece of cornbread. After he had eaten it, he climbed up to his loft in the dark, by a ladder of wooden pins driven into the logs. Five minutes after that, he was fast asleep on his bed of sweet-smelling leaves and dreaming of hunting, or of building big bonfires out of sticks.

Abe's mother was not strong, and before they had been in their new log cabin a year, she became sick and died. She was buried on the farm. Abe often went out and sat by her lonely grave in the forest and cried. It was the first great sorrow that had ever touched the boy's heart.

After he had grown to be a man, he said with eyes full of tears, to a friend with whom he was talking, "God bless my mother; all that I am or ever hope to be, I owe to her."

After a year, Thomas Lincoln married again. The new wife that he brought home was a kind-hearted and excellent woman. She did all she could to make the poor, ragged, barefooted boy happy. After he had grown up and become famous, she said, "Abe never gave me a bad word or look, and never refused to do anything I asked him. Abe was the best boy I ever saw."

Lincoln's Education. There was a log schoolhouse in the woods quite a distance off where Abe went for a short time. At the school, he learned to read and write a little, but after a while he found a new teacher—that was himself. When the rest of the family had gone to bed, he would sit up and read his favorite books by the light of the great blazing logs heaped up on the open fire. He had not more than half a dozen books in all. They were *Robinson Crusoe, Pilgrim's Progress, Aesop's Fables*, the Bible, a *Life of Washington*, and a small *History of the United States*. The boy read these books over until he knew many of them by heart and could repeat whole pages from them.

Part of his evenings he spent writing and doing math. Thomas Lincoln was so poor that he could seldom afford to buy paper and pens for his son, so the boy had to manage without them. He often took the back of the broad, wooden fire shovel to write on and a piece of charcoal for a pencil. When he had covered the shovel with words or with sums in arithmetic, he would shave it clean and begin again. If Abe's father complained that the shovel was getting thin, the boy would go out into the woods, cut down a tree, and make a new one; while the woods lasted, fire shovels and furniture were cheap.

Young Abe and the Fire Shovel

By the time Abe was seventeen, he could write well, do hard examples in long division, and spell better than anyone else in his area. Sometimes he wrote a little piece of his own about something that interested him; when he read it to the neighbors, they would say, "The world can't beat it."

At nineteen, Abraham Lincoln had reached his full height. Barefooted, he stood nearly six feet four inches. He was a good-natured giant. No one in the neighborhood could strike an ax as deep into a tree as he could, and few, if any, were equal to him in strength. It takes a powerful man to put a barrel of flour into a wagon without help, and there is not one in a hundred who can lift a barrel of cider off the ground. But, it is said that young Lincoln could stoop down, lift a barrel onto his knees, and drink from the bunghole.

Lincoln on a Flatboat

At this time, a neighbor hired Abraham Lincoln to travel with his son to New Orleans. The two young men were to take a flatboat loaded with corn and other produce down the Ohio River and the Mississippi. It was a voyage of about 1,800 miles, and it would take three or four weeks.

Young Lincoln was greatly pleased with the thought of making such a trip. He had never been any distance away from home, and, as he told his father, he felt that he wanted to see something more of the world. His father made no objection, but as he told his son good-bye he said, "Take care that in trying to see the world you don't see the bottom of the Mississippi."

The two young men managed to get the boat through safely. But one night, a gang of robbers came on board, intending to steal part of their cargo. Lincoln soon showed the robbers he could handle a club as well as he could an axe. The rascals, bruised and bleeding, were glad to get off with their lives.

The Lincolns Move to Illinois. Not long after young Lincoln's return, his father moved to Illinois. It was a two weeks' journey through the woods with ox teams. Abraham helped his father build a comfortable log cabin. Then he and a man named John Hanks split walnut rails and fenced in fifteen acres of land for a cornfield.

The Log Cabin in Illinois that Lincoln Helped His Father Build

That part of the country had but few settlers, and it was still full of wild beasts. When the men became tired of work and wanted some fun, they had a grand wolf hunt. First, a tall pole was put up in a clearing; next, the hunters in the woods formed a big circle ten miles around. Then they began to move nearer and nearer together, beating the bushes and yelling with all their might. The frightened deer and other wild creatures within the circle of hunters were driven to the pole in the clearing; there they were shot down.

Young Lincoln was not much of a hunter, but he always tried to do his part. Yet, after all, he liked the ax better than he did the rifle. He would start off before light in the morning and walk to his work in the woods, five or six miles away. There he would chop steadily all day. The neighbors knew when they hired him that he would not sit down on the first log he came to and fall asleep. Once when he needed a new pair of trousers, he made a bargain for them with a Mrs. Nancy Miller. She agreed to make him a certain number of yards of cloth, and dye it brown with walnut bark. For every yard she made, Lincoln agreed to split 400 good fence rails for her. In this way, he made his ax pay for his clothes.

The year after young Lincoln came of age, in 1831, he moved out on his own. Lincoln made a second trip by flatboat on the Mississippi River to take goods from Illinois to New Orleans. After he got back, he decided to work at a grocery store in New Salem, Illinois. There was a gang of foolish teens in that neighborhood who made it a point to pick a fight with every stranger. Sometimes they beat him black and blue; sometimes they amused themselves with rolling him down a hill. The leader of this gang was a fellow named Jack Armstrong. He made up his mind that he would try his hand on "Tall Abe," as Lincoln was called. He attacked Lincoln, and he was so astonished at what happened to him that he never wanted to try it again. From that time on, Abraham Lincoln had no better friends than young Armstrong and the Armstrong family.

Denton Offutt's store in New Salem, Illinois, where Lincoln was employed as a clerk from 1831 to 1832.

"Honest Abe." Through his work in the store, Lincoln soon won everybody's respect and confidence. He was faithful in little things, and in that way, he made himself able to deal with large ones. Once a woman made a mistake in paying for something she had bought and gave the young man six cents too much. He did not notice it then, but after his customer had gone, he realized she had overpaid him. That night after the store was closed, Lincoln walked to the woman's house, some five or six miles out of the village, and paid her back the six cents. It was such things as this that caused people to call him "Honest Abe."

The next year, Lincoln went to fight the Indians in what was called the Black Hawk War. The people in that part of the country had been expecting the war. Some time before, an Indian had walked up to a settler's cabin and said, "Too much white man." He then threw a handful of dry leaves into the air, to show how he and his warriors were coming to scatter the white men. He never came, but a noted chief named Black Hawk, who had been a friend of Tecumseh's, made an attempt to drive out the settlers and get back the lands that certain Indians had sold them. Lincoln said that the only battles he fought in this war were with the mosquitoes. He did not kill a single Indian, but allegedly he saved the life of one old warrior.

Statue of Chief Blackhawk

The Black Hawk War of 1832 resulted in the deaths of about seventy settlers and soldiers, and hundreds of Black Hawk's men. Abraham Lincoln served in Illinois Governor John Reynolds's militia during the time of the Black Hawk War, but Abe never saw any action.

After Lincoln returned from the war, he was made postmaster of New Salem. He also found time to do some surveying and to begin the study of law. On hot summer mornings, he might be seen lying on his back, on the grass, under a big tree, reading a law book; as the shade moved around, Lincoln would move with it, so that, by sundown, he had traveled nearly around the tree.

In 1837, when Lincoln began to practice law in Springfield, everybody who knew him had confidence in him. Other men might be admired because they were smart, but he was respected because he was honest. When he said a thing, people knew that it was because he believed it. They also knew that he could not be hired to say what he did not believe. That gave him great influence.

State of
Illinois

Mason County

Beardstown   New Salem
          Springfield

Abraham Lincoln was as keen as he was truthful and honest—or maybe it would be better to say that he was keen because he was truthful and honest. A man was killed in a fight near where Lincoln had lived, and the son of one of his friends, William "Duff" Armstrong, was charged with the murder in Mason County. Everybody thought that he was guilty and felt sure that he would be hanged. Lincoln made some inquiry about the case and became convinced that Duff Armstrong had not killed the man. Mrs. Hannah Armstrong was too poor to hire a lawyer to defend her son, but Lincoln wrote to her that he would gladly defend him for nothing.

In Beardstown, when the day of the trial came, the chief witness, Charles Allen, testified that he saw young Armstrong strike the man dead. Lincoln questioned him closely. He asked Allen when it was that he saw the murder committed. The witness said it was in the evening, at a certain hour, and that he saw it all clearly because there was a bright moon.

"Are you sure?" asked Lincoln.

"Yes," replied the witness.

"Do you swear to it?"

"I do," answered the witness.

Then Lincoln took an almanac out of his pocket, turned to the day of the month on which the murder had been committed, and said to the court, "The almanac shows that there was no moon shining at the time at which the witness says he saw the murder." The jury was convinced that the witness had not spoken the truth; they declared the prisoner "Not guilty," and he was immediately set free.

Lincoln was a man who always paid his debts. Hannah Armstrong had been very kind to him when he was poor and friendless. Now he had paid that debt.

Some men have hearts big enough to be kind to their fellow men when they are in trouble, but not to a dumb animal. Lincoln's heart was big enough for both.

Lincoln and the Pig. One morning, just after he had bought a new suit of clothes, he started to drive to the courthouse, many miles away. On the way, he saw a pig that was making desperate efforts to climb out of a deep mud hole. The creature would get part way up the slippery bank, and then slide back again over his head in mire and water. Lincoln said to himself: "I suppose that I should get out and help that pig"; if he's left there, he'll smother in the mud. Then he remembered his fine new clothes. He felt that he really could not afford to spoil them for the sake of any pig, so he whipped up his horse and drove on. But the pig was in his mind, and he could think of nothing else. After he had gone about two miles, he said to himself, "I've no right to leave that poor creature there to die in the mud, and what is more, I won't leave him." Turning his horse, he drove back to

the spot. He carried half a dozen fence rails to the edge of the hole, and placed them so that he could reach into the mud without falling in himself. Then he bent down, seized the pig firmly by the forelegs, and pulled him up onto the solid ground, where he was safe. The pig grunted out his best thanks, and Lincoln, plastered with mud, but with a light heart, drove on to the courthouse in his carriage.

Lincoln Enters Politics. Many people in Illinois thought that they would like to see such a man as Abraham Lincoln in the state legislature, helping to make their laws. They knew they could trust him. They first elected him in 1834; and, as he was too poor at that time to pay for a train ride, he walked from New Salem, a distance of over 100 miles, to Vandalia, which was then the capital of the state. Lincoln was elected to the Illinois legislature four times. During his time in the legislature, Lincoln moved to Springfield, Illinois, and made that place his home for the rest of his life. He also helped make Springfield the capital city of Illinois.

Mary Ann Todd Lincoln (1818–1882)

After finishing four terms in the legislature, Abraham Lincoln took some time off from politics to establish a family. He married Mary Todd in 1842, and the next year, the first of his four sons—Robert Todd Lincoln—was born. A few years later, however, the people elected him to a new office. This time they sent him to Washington to help make laws as a representative in Congress, not for his state only, but for the whole country. He had come a long way up since the time when he worked with John Hanks fencing the cornfield around his father's cabin; but he was going higher still—he was going to the top.

Abraham Lincoln served two years in Congress and, afterwards, came back to Springfield. He practiced law in Illinois for a few years, but renewed controversy over slavery and its possible spread into the territories brought him back into politics. He ran for the United States Senate in 1858 and, even though he lost the election, he became well-known for his participation in a series of debates that focused on the issue of slavery.

Lincoln Becomes President. Abraham Lincoln was elected President of the United States in 1860. In the spring of 1860, a great convention, or meeting, was held in Illinois. Lincoln was present at that convention. The object of the people who had gathered there was to choose a candidate that they would like to see elected President of the United States. Several speeches had already been made when Lincoln's old friend, John Hanks, and one of his neighbors brought in two old fence rails and a banner with these words painted on it:

```
                ABRAHAM LINCOLN,
   THE RAIL CANDIDATE FOR THE PRESIDENCY
                    IN 1860.
        TWO RAILS FROM A LOT OF 3000
                  MADE IN 1830
       BY JOHN HANKS AND ABE LINCOLN.
```

The rails were received with cheer after cheer; and Lincoln was chosen candidate. About a week after that, a much greater meeting was held in Chicago, and he was chosen there in the same way. The next November, Abraham Lincoln, "the Illinois rail-splitter," was elected President of the United States. He had little time to rejoice, however, because the nation was experiencing numerous political problems at that time.

The Country Splits Apart. Within just a few weeks after Lincoln's election as President, and before he had even taken office, the United States began to break up between the North and the South. South Carolina seceded in December and was followed within the next two months by the states of Georgia, Florida, Alabama, Mississippi, Louisiana, and Texas. These Southern states felt that they would not receive fair treatment if Lincoln were their President; thus they decided to establish their own country. They set up an independent government, called the Confederate States of America, and made Jefferson Davis its president.

What had caused this split between North and South? The main reason why so many of the people of the South wished to withdraw from the United States was that, little by little, the North and the South had become like two different countries. Their economies were very different. The South had little industry and depended upon just a few crops—especially cotton—grown on large farms, called plantations, for its wealth. The North had a far more varied economy, with both significant farming and industrial sectors. The northeastern states had the fastest growing large industrial sector in the world by 1860.

The above statue of Lincoln portrays him writing the Emancipation Proclamation, which gave slaves their freedom. This statue is located in Fairmount Park, Philadelphia.

This difference in the economies of the North and South resulted in other distinctions between the two regions. The North had a far more extensive and effective rail system than the South, connecting the manufacturing regions of the East with the agricultural areas further west, while much of the South's rail system was designed to link its plantation regions to the seaports so that the crops could be easily exported. In addition, most new immigrants were moving into the North rather than the South because of greater opportunities for work in the cities of the North or farming in the free states and territories further west.

The diverging economies caused political conflicts between the North and South. Many Northerners wanted the federal government to establish high tariffs to protect their industries, while Southerners usually wanted low tariffs because they were more interested in selling their crops to other countries. Northerners also wanted the federal government to give away or sell cheaply federal land to people who wanted to establish farms in the West, while Southerners tended to oppose such efforts. Finally, Northerners often supported the federal government helping to build railroads and canals, while Southerners usually opposed federal assistance, preferring to depend upon assistance from their states if government help was needed for such projects.

The main reason why so many of the people of the South wished to withdraw from the United States, however, had to do with slavery. Alexander Stephens, vice president of the Confederate States, made that point clear in a speech in Savannah, Georgia, in March 1861 about the new Southern government. "The new [Confederate] constitution has put at rest, *forever*, all the agitating questions relating to our peculiar institution—African slavery as it exists among us—the proper *status* of the negro in our form of civilization. This was the immediate cause of the late rupture and present revolution."

At the time of the War for American Independence, when the American colonies broke away from the rule of England, every one of the states held slaves from Africa; but, in the course of many years, a great change had taken place. The states of the North gradually abolished slavery, and the slaves in the North were either set free or sold to the South by the early 1800s. The Southern states, however, kept their slaves. In the course of time, all labor in the North had come to be done by free men, while black slaves did nearly all the hard work in the South. This difference in the way of doing work made it impossible for the North and the South to agree about many things.

In the South, most of the people thought that slavery was right and that it helped the whole country; in the North, the greater part of the people were convinced that it was wrong and that it did harm to the whole country. The slaveholders in the South wanted to add to the number. They hoped

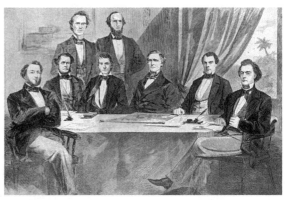

The Confederate Cabinet

From Left to Right:
Judah P. Benjamin, Stephen Mallory, Christopher Memminger, Alexander Stephens, LeRoy Pope Walker, Jefferson Davis, John H. Reagan, and Robert Toombs.

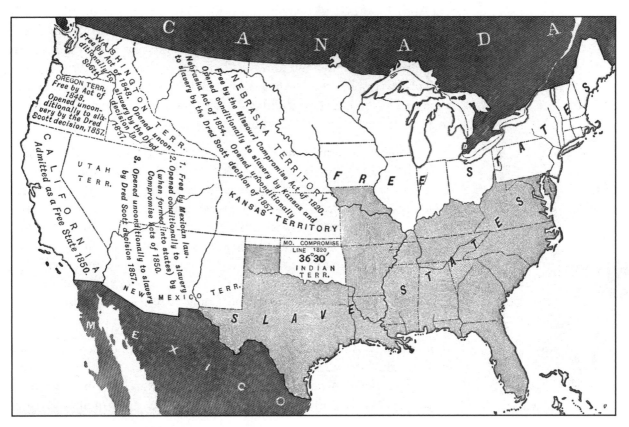

to get more of the new country west of the Mississippi River for slave states, so that there might always be at least as many slave states in the Union as there were free states. But Abraham Lincoln, like most of the people in the North, believed that slavery did no good to anyone. He and his party were fully determined that no slaves whatsoever should be taken into the territories west of the Mississippi River, and that every new state that would be added should be entirely free.

For this reason, it happened, that when Lincoln was elected President, seven of the slave states resolved to leave the Union, and, if necessary, fight rather than be compelled to stay in it. The North and South had come to be like two boys in a boat who want to go in opposite directions. One pulls one way with his oars, the other pulls another way, and subsequently, the boat does not get ahead.

The War Between the States. Abraham Lincoln became President on March 4, 1861. At that time, an uneasy peace existed between the North and South, but it did not last very long. The Confederate States had already taken over most of the federal government property in their states, but a few forts were still controlled by United States forces. The most important of these was Fort Sumter in the harbor of Charleston, South Carolina. The Confederate government wanted the United States to give up these forts, but Abraham Lincoln would not do so. As a result, fighting began on April 12, 1861, when Confederate forces in Charleston opened fire on Fort Sumter to prevent it from being replenished. Two days later, the fort surrendered.

On April 15, President Lincoln called for 75,000 troops to be raised from the militia of the states to fight against the seceded states. This action caused four more states—Virginia, North Carolina, Tennessee, and Arkansas—to secede from the Union and join the Confederate States. This brought to a total of eleven states that formed the Confederate States. Twenty-two states remained in the Union, including the four border slave states of Delaware, Maryland, Kentucky, and Missouri.

The four new seceding states did so because they, along with most Southerners, believed that states had the right to leave the Union if they wanted to do so. For example, Jefferson Davis, in his last speech to the United States Senate in 1861, said, "... I have for many years advocated, as an essential attribute of State sovereignty, the right of a State to secede from the Union." On the other hand, most Northerners believed that secession was unconstitutional. In his first inaugural address, President Lincoln argued that "... the Union of these States is perpetual." These views of the nature of the Union could not be reconciled; it would only be settled by fighting.

In less than six weeks after Lincoln became President, in the spring of 1861, a terrible war broke out between the North and the South. This war is often called the Civil War, or the War Between the States. A civil war means that people who live in the same country are fighting with each other. The North had the most fighting men, the most money, and the

Jefferson Finis Davis (1808–1889)

most factories; but the people of the South had the advantage of being able to stay at home and fight on their own ground. Also, the South had several skilled and brave generals such as General Thomas "Stonewall" Jackson, General Robert E. Lee, and General J.E.B. Stuart.

The war lasted four years (1861–1865). Many terrible battles were fought, and thousands of brave men were killed on both sides. During the war, President Lincoln made an important proclamation known as the Emancipation Proclamation, which gave the slaves their freedom in all the states that were fighting against the Union. The rest of the slaves received their freedom soon after the war with the passage of the Thirteenth Amendment.

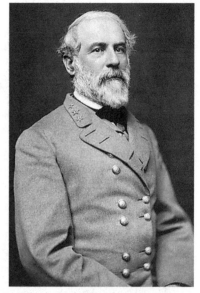

Robert Edward Lee (1807–1870)

After a time, the command of all the armies of the North was given to General Ulysses S. Grant. General Lee became the chief defender of the South. Although the Southern armies frequently won the various battles during the war, the South was slowly forced to retreat because they were consistently forced to fight against much larger Northern armies.

During the first two years of the War Between the States, it looked as if the South might be victorious; they won many of the early battles. However, in July 1863, the Confederates lost two key battles that eventually led to their defeat. General Lee lost a battle at Gettysburg, Pennsylvania, when the last major Confederate invasion of the North was defeated. At the same time, General Grant forced the Confederates to surrender the city of Vicksburg, Mississippi. General Grant's victory split the Confederacy in two between East and West and gave the Union control over the Mississippi River.

Ulysses S. Grant (1822–1885)

The war lasted almost two more years, but the defeat of the Confederate States was inevitable. The last major battles were fought around Richmond, Virginia. When the Southern soldiers saw that it was useless to attempt to fight longer, they laid down their arms, and peace was made—a peace honorable to both sides. General Lee surrendered to General Grant on April 9, 1865, and the remaining Confederate armies surrendered soon afterwards. The success of the North in the war preserved the Union; and as all black slaves were now free, there was no longer any political dispute about slavery. The North and the South could now begin to pull in the same direction again.

The saddest occurrence at the close of the war was the murder of President Lincoln by a man named John Wilkes Booth. Not only the people of the North, but many of those in the South, shed tears at his death. Lincoln loved all of America, just as any American should love his whole country.

The Murder of Abraham Lincoln

Summary. Abraham Lincoln, of Illinois, became President of the United States in 1861. He was elected by a party in the North that was determined that slaves should not be taken into the territories, and that no more slave states should be made. Most of the slave-holding states of the South resolved to withdraw from the Union. A great war followed, and President

Harriet Beecher Stowe (1811–1896)

Abolitionism

The abolitionist movement was dedicated to ending slavery in the United States. It took advantage of the emotion stirred up by religious revivals by directing the converted people towards the goal of making America a purer nation. Harriet Beecher Stowe was likely the most influential abolitionist through her book *Uncle Tom's Cabin*.

According to legend, when Abraham Lincoln met Harriet Beecher Stowe shortly after the Civil War began, he said to her, "So you're the little lady who made this big war." Stowe had written *Uncle Tom's Cabin* in 1852 because of her firm belief that slavery was preventing America from being the Christian nation it could be. The book was enormously popular, selling over 300,000 copies in its first year, and it provoked extreme reactions. Many people in the North joined the abolitionist cause because of it, and it was largely banned in the South. In short, there is no question that *Uncle Tom's Cabin* poured gasoline on the fire that was destroying the Union between the North and the South, helping speed up the momentum toward the War Between the States.

Lincoln did everything in his power to preserve the Union. President Lincoln gave the slaves their freedom during the war. The North succeeded in the war, and the Union was made stronger than ever because the North and the South could no longer have any dispute over slavery. Both sides now shook hands and became friends. President Lincoln was murdered just a few days after the Union armies achieved victory in the Civil War.

Comprehension Questions

1. What did Abraham Lincoln and John Hanks do?

2. How did Lincoln get the name of "Honest Abe"?

3. Tell why so many people in the South wished to leave the Union.

4. How long did the Civil War last?

5. What did President Lincoln do for the slaves?

6. What was the saddest thing that happened at the close of the war?

The Angel of Marye's Heights

In December 1862, the major Confederate and Union armies in the East clashed in the area of Fredericksburg, Virginia. The Union army suffered a serious defeat, incurring over 12,600 casualties. Among those casualties were approximately 9,600 wounded. Many thousands of wounded lay on the battlefield overnight and into the next day because they were unable to retreat. The plight of the wounded was terrible; many were crying for water. One soldier decided to do what he could. Sergeant Richard Kirkland (1843–1863) of South Carolina was given permission to bring water to the wounded Union soldiers in front of his position on Marye's Heights. In spite of the danger of being shot as he went to help the wounded, he bravely and compassionately went about his mission of mercy. For over an hour and a half, Kirkland brought water to all the Union wounded he could. It is for that reason that he is called "The Angel of Marye's Heights."

Chapter 31
America Grows Again (1865–1925)

The time immediately following the War Between the States was difficult for the states of the defeated Confederacy. Parts of the South suffered tremendous damage because the Northern armies that invaded the South often inflicted as much punishment as possible upon the Southern people. Many farms and some cities were destroyed during the final months of the war, and this left many people in the South homeless and hungry. To make matters worse, almost a quarter of the men of military age in the states of the old Confederacy were killed during the war. The governments of most of the Southern states had collapsed and had to be rebuilt.

How the United States Grew. A difficult period of reconstruction began in the South. Because of the destruction of the war, the people of the South were forced to patiently endure a period of suffering and humiliation. It took several years before the South began to recover from all the death and destruction. After the time of reconstruction was over, the united North and South began to grow again and prospered as never before. In the South, many new and flourishing towns and cities were established. Mines of coal and iron were opened, hundreds of factories were built, and the railroads were rebuilt and expanded.

In the West, even greater changes took place. Cities and towns were established where there were none before the Civil War, silver and gold mines were opened, and immense farms and cattle ranches were established that helped to provide food to feed America and the world. Several great railroad lines were built across the West to connect with railroads in the East. This connected the continent by rail from the Atlantic to the Pacific. Into that vast country beyond the Mississippi, millions of industrious people moved from all parts of the earth and built homes for themselves and for their children.

More than 500 years have passed since Columbus crossed the ocean and discovered this new world that we call America. In 1893, we celebrated that discovery made by

In 1893, Chicago hosted the World's Columbian Exposition, which was one of the largest displays of industry in the nineteenth century.

Columbus, not only in the schools throughout the country, but also with a great fair called the "World's Columbian Exposition" held in Chicago. There, on the low shores of Lake Michigan, on what was once a swamp, the people of the Midwest had built a great city. They had built it where a United States government engineer had said that it was simply impossible to do such a thing. Large groups of people from every state in the Union visited the exposition, and many came from all parts of the globe to join them in Chicago.

Booker T. Washington. One of the greatest failures of Southern reconstruction was the desperate relationship between blacks and whites. Congress attempted to impose racial equality on the South—at times with the help of the United States Army—but its efforts ultimately failed. Laws were passed in many places that had the effect of making blacks second-class citizens. They were often segregated from whites in forms of transportation, social gatherings, and work places.

During this period, there arose one of the greatest Americans of the late 1800s and early 1900s—Booker T. Washington. Mr. Washington was born in 1856 into slavery on a Virginia plantation. After the Civil War, he worked in a coal mine while he attended night school to further his education. Washington worked his way through the Hampton Institute as a janitor, attended a seminary, and returned to Hampton as an instructor. A few years later, Mr. Washington began his greatest work in helping to found a college in Alabama known as the Tuskegee Institute. With tireless effort, he overcame the difficulties of poverty and racial bigotry to build a truly successful college with more than forty buildings and a large staff. Many gifted students graduated from this college.

Booker Taliaferro Washington
(1856–1915)

Professor Washington taught his students that the best way for black Americans to improve themselves economically and politically was by developing a better level of job and educational skills. He advised his fellow citizens to live peaceably within the system, to learn new skills, and to reform American society by working hard and honestly. Professor Washington was wise enough to realize that the best way for any American to obtain access to his legitimate civil or constitutional rights is by developing economic power through self-improvement, hard work, and persistence.

President Theodore Roosevelt thought highly of Booker T. Washington. Roosevelt once wrote the following to a friend about his dinner, which was controversial at the time, with Mr. Washington at the White House, "I respect him greatly and believe in the work he has done. I have consulted so much with him it seemed to me that it was natural to ask him to dinner to talk over this work...."

George Washington Carver. *Time* magazine carried an article (1941) about scientist George Washington Carver, calling him the "Black Leonardo," comparing him to the great Italian Renaissance scientist Leonardo da Vinci. George Washington Carver was one of America's greatest scientists. Carver was born into slavery in Missouri and orphaned early in life. His

George Washington Carver
(1864–1943)

former owners raised him as part of their family—including teaching him the basics of reading and writing—after slavery was abolished. Carver had to struggle against anti-black prejudice throughout his life, yet he never let such

Tuskegee Institute, 1916

attitudes hold him back. When he was rejected by one college simply because he was African-American, he went elsewhere. Carver graduated from Iowa State Agricultural College (now Iowa State University)—where he became the first black student and later the first black faculty member—earning both a bachelors and masters degree. While at Iowa State, Carver began his experiments in botany that later led to worldwide fame.

Carver went to teach at the Tuskegee Institute in 1896, founded only five years earlier by Booker T. Washington, to lead its Agriculture Department, where he served for forty-seven years. One of his goals was to improve Southern agriculture and, in particular, help former slaves become better farmers. Carver eventually developed approximately 300 applications for peanuts and 118 for sweet potatoes. He eventually became very well known, undermining the belief of many whites at the time that blacks were intellectually inferior. Carver met three Presidents (Theodore Roosevelt, Calvin Coolidge, and Franklin Roosevelt), testified before Congress on his work with peanuts, and won many awards. Carver used his fame to promote racial reconciliation, speaking at numerous white colleges in the South between 1923 and 1933.

The 1940 Junior Class in Farm Management at the Tuskegee Institute

Carver was, however, more than simply a great scientist. He was also a man of faith. Carver was sickly as a child and was not expected to live past twenty-one, yet he trusted God from his youth—deepening his faith as God enabled him to live a long, useful life. The *New York Times* criticized Carver in 1924 for saying that God guided his research. With regard to the relationship between God and nature, Carver wrote: "I love to think of nature as an unlimited broadcasting system, through which God speaks to us every hour, if we will only tune in." Carver was also concerned about the development of his students' character and taught a Bible study class to Tuskegee students every Sunday.

Carver at Work in His Laboratory

The Invention of the Telephone. Long after the telegraph had come into use, Professor Alexander Graham Bell of Boston began to make experiments with the human voice. His friends thought that he was wasting his time, but he said, "Professor Morse made an electric wire write, while I hope to do still better, for I believe I can make an electric wire talk."

After many disappointments, he succeeded in sending a faint sound over a wire that passed from one room to another. Next, he stretched one from

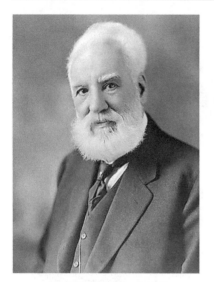

Alexander Graham Bell
(1847–1922)

the basement of a building in Boston up to the third floor. One day when he was at work, he called down through this wire to his assistant, "Mr. Watson, come up here; I want you." Mr. Watson rushed upstairs greatly excited, crying out, "Mr. Bell, I can hear your words!" Then Mr. Bell knew that he had made the wire speak.

That was in the spring of 1876. In the summer, the Centennial Exposition was held in Philadelphia to celebrate the remarkable things that had been done in the United States since the Declaration of Independence 100 years before. Mr. Bell took his Speaking Wire, or "Talking Telegraph," to exhibit at this World's Fair. Nobody seemed to pay much attention to it. Nevertheless, one evening the emperor of Brazil came in and said, "Professor Bell, I am delighted to meet you again; I want to see your new machine." Mr. Bell went to the end of the long hall and took up the mouthpiece of the wire while the emperor, standing where Mr. Bell had left him, picked up the other end and put it to his ear. He listened a moment, and then, suddenly throwing his head back, he exclaimed, "Why, it talks!"

Yes, it did talk, and it has been talking ever since. At first, the telephone, as it was finally named, could only be used for very short distances. But now, after many years of improvement, it will talk all across the United States, from the Atlantic to the Pacific, and even around the world. Today a boy in New York can speak to a boy in San Francisco and hear what he says in reply. The telephone makes the two boys just as near to each other, so far as talking is concerned, as though they lived in the same house. This was done by using an electric wire over 3,000 miles long. But now people can speak to each other without using any wire at all—using wireless telephones—just as they can now telegraph one another without a wire. In both cases, they send their messages along the electrical particles in the air. In addition, FAX machines and computers make it possible to transmit written images from one device to another. People can use the phone to send letters and other written documents to people all over the world.

Mr. Edison and His Work. Thomas A. Edison began earning his living by selling newspapers on a railroad train in Michigan. He was then a boy of twelve. A few years later, he began printing a small weekly paper of his own in the baggage car of the train. After he had grown to manhood, he invented the record player, or phonograph (1877). That machine makes a recording of what is said to it and can repeat the words years afterward. It can also repeat music in the same way. Once people would have declared such a thing impossible, but Mr. Edison found a way of doing it. His phonograph became so popular that almost everyone wanted to hear it talk or sing. Besides being used for amusement, it was used by many businesses and schools.

Next Mr. Edison invented the electric light (1879), which we see in every house and store. The next year (1880), he built an electric railroad car, which he used for a while at Menlo Park, New Jersey, where he lived at the time. That started people thinking how convenient it would be to have electric cars in which to travel. Now people are using cars, though no longer primarily electric, to rush in all directions across America and around the world.

Later, Mr. Edison took up a small toy that showed a few pictures, the size of postage stamps, in motion. He greatly improved that toy, and out of it, in 1895, he produced the motion pictures we know so well.

The Flying Machine. Eight years after Edison began to astonish people with his marvelous pictures, two brothers, Orville and Wilbur Wright, of Dayton, Ohio, did something remarkable that no one had done before. The Wright brothers decided to learn to fly, but instead of making wings, they made a flying machine. It was simply a long, light frame of wood covered with cotton cloth that they called a "glider." They would take it to the top of a hill, and when the wind blew strong and steadily, one of them would mount the glider and slide downhill on the air. It was good fun unless the wind happened to die and let the rider down with a bump. However, this was not flying as a bird flies, so the Wrights decided to do something different.

They made a very light engine, like the engine of an automobile, and fastened it on the glider. The engine drove an air-wheel that somewhat pushed the glider forward, as paddle wheels push a steamboat forward. They practiced awhile with this and at last, in 1903, their "Flying Machine" (for it was now more than a glider) flew against the wind, for fifty-nine seconds! They tried hard to stay in the air for a whole minute, but could not.

After awhile, they succeeded, one at a time, in staying up for several minutes. They nearly always had to fly in a straight line because, if they tried to turn corners, they were in great danger of crashing.

However, they were not the kind of men to quit. They were determined that their machine should turn and twist like a letter "S"; so they watched the hawks and gulls to see how they managed. These big birds spread their wings and fly swiftly round and round as though they enjoy the game. Finally, the two brothers found out how the birds did it, and the next year they made two circular flights of three miles each in their new airplane.

In 1909, they went to Fort Myer, Virginia (across the Potomac River from Washington, D.C.), to show some officers of the United States government what they could do. The government offered to give a prize of $25,000 to any man who could accomplish these three things:

1. He must fly a whole hour without coming down.
2. He must take a passenger with him in his flight.
3. He must fly at the rate of not less than forty miles an hour.

Edison-Swan Light Bulb

Who Really Invented the Light Bulb?

In 1860, Sir Joseph W. Swan invented a working light bulb for which he received a patent in Britain. However, he was unable to produce a good vacuum and an adequate source of electricity; thus his bulb produced poor light and did not last very long.

By 1875, Mr. Swan created a better vacuum and a carbonized thread for his filament; three years later he received a British patent for these improvements. In 1879, he began installing his light bulbs in homes and buildings throughout Britain. Edison secured patents in America that were based on Swan's patents and allegedly started promoting himself as the real inventor.

Another British lamp maker tried to sue Swan but failed, so Edison decided not to take legal action against Swan in England. In 1883, Edison and Swan resolved their differences and formed a joint venture called the Edison & Swan United Electric Light Company, known as "Ediswan," to market the light bulb. Eventually, Ediswan was purchased by Associated Electrical Industries (1929), which later was acquired by the General Electric Company (1967) and renamed the Marconi Corporation in 2003.

Dwight Lyman Moody (1837–1899)

The Refined Revivalist

Dwight L. Moody redefined American revivalism. Before he became popular in the late nineteenth century, revivals were mostly energetic and raucous affairs. Moody did not believe that Americans needed to be scared into their senses. Instead, he argued that Americans just needed to be reasoned with since Christianity was a moralizing and stabilizing force in American society. Thus, his revivals were very organized and calm, using popular songs, written and performed by the musician Ira Sankey, and a calm preaching style. All his revivals presented the same basic message, which was summarized with the three R's: *Ruin* by sin, *Redemption* by Christ, and *Regeneration* by the Holy Spirit.

Moody's methods proved to be very effective, and by the end of the century, Moody was arguably the most influential evangelical preacher in America. It is not for his preaching that he remains famous, however. He is more famous today for the institutions he helped start, including the Moody Bible Institute located in downtown Chicago.

One of the Wrights did all these things, and better, too. He went up in his airplane, as it is now generally called, and flew with a passenger for more than an hour. Next, he flew at the rate of a little more than forty-two miles an hour. Thousands watched him as he glided like a bird through the sky and then landed on the grass as easily and gracefully as a bird lands.

The great crowd cheered and shouted like mad. The United States government was entirely satisfied. It not only paid the Wright brothers $25,000 for their airplane, but it gave them $5,000 more because they had made greater speed than was demanded. These two men, by years of patient and persistent effort, had won the victory. They had taught the world how to travel through the air. Some of their friends asked them if it was very hard work finding out how to do it. They answered, "Yes, it was." But they also said, "After all, it is easier for a man to learn to fly than for a child to learn to walk."

While the Wright brothers were growing up and while they were learning to travel through the air, two more remarkable machines came into use. One of these was the typewriter. It was exhibited at the Centennial Exposition in Philadelphia in 1876, and was used worldwide until the development of the word processor and, later, computer programs. The other machine was the "Horseless Carriage," now called the automobile, which began to attract a good deal of attention about 1900. It did not move very rapidly at first, but now it enables people to move through the country at a rate of speed that beats even the railway trains of America.

An automobile manufacturer named Henry Ford taught the world how to make cars quickly. He revolutionized automobile production during the early 1900s by introducing the concept of an assembly line for producing cars. His assembly line utilized teams of workers who each contributed certain parts to each car until it was ready to roll.

Summary. The North and South began to become one nation again as the nation recovered from the War Between the States. American inventors began to create wonderful new machines about the turn of the century. These inventors gave the world the telephone, phonograph, electric light, motion pictures, airplane, and automobile.

Comprehension Questions

1. Where was the World's Columbian Exposition held?
2. Who founded the Tuskegee Institute?
3. Name one of George Washington Carver's goals while at Tuskegee Institute.
4. Who invented the telephone?
5. Who invented the phonograph?
6. What machine did the Wright brothers invent?
7. What concept did Henry Ford introduce for producing cars?

Unit 5

Maturing of America

Chapter 32
Theodore Roosevelt (1858–1919)

President Theodore Roosevelt was the twenty-sixth President of the United States. He served from 1901 until the year 1909, and was largely responsible for strengthening America's military and establishing a system of national parks. Roosevelt was an avid hunter and loved the outdoors. He loved God's creation and used his presidential power to encourage the federal government to take an active role in conserving America's natural resources. President Roosevelt was a man of action. He loved to confront problems in a straightforward manner. As a young boy, Theodore was often sick and in a weakened condition. However, his mother taught him to trust in God and work hard to overcome problems. As an older man, President Roosevelt would often credit his mother for giving him a strong character and godly convictions. Mr. Roosevelt was grateful for the Christian training that he received at home. He often said that "a thorough knowledge of the Bible is worth more than a college education."

Roosevelt became a Badlands hunter and rancher from 1884 to 1886. But he moved back East after the devastating winter of 1886–87.

Trouble in Cuba. A few years before Roosevelt became President, the United States had some trouble with Spain over Cuba. A little less than five years after the opening of the Columbian Exposition, the United States declared war against Spain. The Spanish-American War was the first time Americans had crossed swords with any European nation since General Jackson defeated the British army at the famous Battle of New Orleans in the War of 1812.

When William McKinley became President in 1897, the United States had no expectation of fighting Spain. The contest came suddenly, and Cuba was the cause of it. Spain once owned not only all the large islands in the West Indies that Columbus had discovered, but also most of South America, Mexico, Florida, and the greater part of that vast country west of the Mississippi River, which now belongs to the United States, as well as the Philippine Islands and Guam in the Pacific. Piece by piece Spain lost control of all these great lands, until, eventually, she had nothing left but the two islands of Cuba and Puerto Rico in the West Indies and the Pacific territories of Guam and the Philippine Islands.

Many Cubans hated Spanish rule, and with good reason. They made several attempts to rid themselves of it and fought for ten years (1868–1878), but without success. Finally, in the spring of 1895, they took up arms again, and with the battle cry of "Independence or death!" they set to work in grim earnest to drive out the Spaniards. Spain was determined to crush the rebellion. She sent over thousands of soldiers to accomplish it. The desperate fight continued to go on year after year, until it looked as though the whole island, which Columbus said was the most beautiful he

José Martí (1853–1895)

At the end of the Ten Years' War, the Spanish government had defeated the freedom fighters and made promises of economic reform. During the 1890s, however, Spain began to impose restrictions on Cuban trade and to further oppress the people. In April 1895, José Martí declared a new war for independence, which he had planned during his ten-year exile (1885–1895) in the United States. Martí was killed, however, at Dos Rios (Two Rivers) shortly after landing in Cuba, for which he became a martyr and national hero.

had ever seen, would be converted into a wilderness covered with graves and ruins. During the war great numbers of peaceful Cuban farmers were driven from their homes and starved to death; and many Americans who had bought sugar and tobacco plantations saw all their valuable property completely destroyed.

Cuba is about the size of the state of Pennsylvania. It is our nearest island neighbor on the south, and is very close to Key West, Florida. The people of the United States could not look on the war without sadness. While they were sending shiploads of food to feed the starving Cubans, it was both natural and right that they should hope that the terrible war might be quickly brought to an end.

The United States government first urged, and then demanded, that Spain try to make peace in the island. Spain did try, tried honestly so far as America could see, but failed. The Cuban revolutionaries had no faith in Spanish promises; they flatly refused to accept anything short of separation and independence. Spain was poor and proud; she replied that come what may, she would not give up Cuba.

While America was waiting to see what should be done, a terrible event happened. Captain Charles D. Sigsbee, in command of the battleship *Maine*, had been sent to visit Havana. On the night of February 15, 1898, the *Maine* exploded in the harbor at Havana. Out of 353 officers and men on board the vessel, 266 were instantly killed, or were so badly hurt that they died soon after. The United States appointed a Court of Inquiry, composed of naval officers, to examine the wreck. After a long and careful investigation of all the facts, they reported that the *Maine* was blown up by a mine planted in the harbor or placed under her hull. Whether the mine was exploded by accident or by design, or who did the evil deed, was more than the court could say.

Above, the USS *Maine* is shown entering Havana Harbor on January 25, 1898. Three weeks later, more than five tons of power exploded in its hull, destroying the front third of the ship. As a result of the explosion, 266 men lost their lives, and eight more died later from injuries. In 1950, the Navy ruled that the *Maine* had been sunk by a faulty boiler.

The Spanish-American War. President McKinley sent a special message to Congress in which he said, "The war in Cuba must stop." Soon afterward Congress decided that the people of Cuba "are, and of a right ought to be, free and independent." They also resolved that if Spain did not proceed at once to withdraw her soldiers from the island, they would take measures to make her do it. Spain refused to withdraw her army, and war was promptly declared by both nations in April 1898.

The first battle was far away from Cuba. In the Pacific, Spain owned the group of islands called the Philippines. Many of the people of those islands had long been discontented with their government, and when the Cubans rose in revolt against Spain, it stirred the people of the Philippines to begin a struggle for liberty. They, too, were fighting for independence.

William McKinley, Jr. (1843–1901)

President McKinley resolved to strike two blows at once. He decided that the Army would hit Spain in Cuba, and at the same time attack Manila, the capital of the Philippines. The United States had a fleet of six ships under the command of Commodore George Dewey stationed at Hong Kong, China. Assistant Secretary of the Navy Theodore Roosevelt had the foresight to send orders to Commodore Dewey before the war started that if war with Spain was declared, he should go immediately to Manila and "capture or destroy" the Spanish fleet that guarded that port. The Spaniards there were brave men who were determined to hold Manila against all attack; they had forts to help them, and they had twice as many vessels as Commodore Dewey. On the other hand, the American vessels were larger and better armed, and the American soldiers were better trained.

Commodore Dewey carried out his orders very well. On May 1, 1898, he sent a letter to the President, saying that he had just fought a battle and destroyed every Spanish warship without losing a single man in the fight. The victorious Americans took good care of the wounded Spaniards.

President McKinley immediately sent General Wesley Merritt from San Francisco with many soldiers to join Commodore Dewey. Congress voted the "Hero of Manila" a sword of honor; and the President, with the consent of the Senate of the United States, made him Rear Admiral, and later Admiral. This honor gave Admiral Dewey the highest rank to which he could be promoted in the U.S. Navy.

Spain had lost one fleet in the Philippines, but she still had another and a far more powerful one under the command of Admiral Pascual Cervera. Where Admiral Cervera was the Americans did not know. For all they knew, he might be coming across the Atlantic Ocean to suddenly attack New York or Boston or some other city on the Atlantic coast.

The President had already sent Rear Admiral William T. Sampson with a fleet of warships to blockade Havana and other Cuban ports, so that the Spaniards could not get help from Spain to carry on the war. He next put Commodore Winfield Scott Schley in command of a "Flying Squadron" of fast war vessels, so that he might stand ready to act when called upon. President McKinley sent Commodore Schley with his "Flying Squadron" to find the Spanish fleet. After a long search, the Commodore found that the Spanish warships had secretly moved into the harbor of Santiago on the southeastern coast of Cuba.

A day or two afterward, Rear Admiral Sampson went to Santiago with several war vessels and took command of the combined fleet in front of that port. One of Admiral Sampson's vessels was the famous battleship *Oregon*, which had come from San Francisco around South America, a voyage of about 13,000 miles, in order to join in the coming fight.

The entrance to the harbor of Santiago is by a long, narrow, crooked channel guarded by forts. The fleet could not enter it without great risk of losing their ships. It was plain enough that they had "bottled up" Cervera's fleet, and so long as Cervera remained there he could do no harm. But there was a chance, despite their watching the entrance to the harbor as a cat watches

Commodore George Dewey
(1837–1917)

On May 1, 1898, Commodore Dewey led his squadron to victory in the Battle of Manila Bay, sinking or capturing the entire Spanish Pacific fleet in only six hours.

Rear Admiral William T. Sampson

Rear Admiral Sampson ordered the USS *Merrimac* to be sunk at the opening of the harbor of Santiago in hope of preventing the Spanish fleet from escaping.

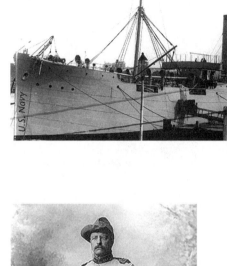

a mouse-hole, that the Spanish commander might slip out of his hiding place and, under cover of darkness or fog, escape Sampson's guns.

Admiral Sampson believed that he saw a way by which he could effectually cork the bottle and make Cervera's escape impossible. By permission of Admiral Sampson, Lieutenant Richmond P. Hobson proceeded to carry out his daring scheme. With the help of seven sailors, who were eager to go with him at the risk of almost certain death, Lt. Hobson ran the coal ship USS *Merrimac* into the narrow channel and, by exploding torpedoes, sank the vessel part way across it. Then he and his men jumped into the water to save themselves as best they could—a very brave deed that was long remembered. Shortly, the Spaniards captured Lt. Hobson and his men, but they treated them well, and after a time sent all of them back to the United States in exchange for Spanish prisoners of war.

The Battle of Santiago. A few weeks later, General William Rufus Shafter landed a large number of American soldiers on the coast of Cuba near Santiago to fight with pro-independence Cuban rebels. The force included General Joseph Wheeler's cavalry, and among them were the "Rough Riders," who formerly had been Western "cowboys." Colonel Roosevelt, who had resigned as assistant secretary of the U.S. Navy, was one of their leaders. On horseback or on foot, these men were a force to be dealt with.

The Americans immediately set out to find the enemy. The Spaniards had hidden in the underbrush, where they could fire on the Americans without being seen. They opened the battle, and as they used smokeless powder, it was difficult for the men to tell where the bullets came from or how to reply to them. But in the end, after fairly sharp fighting, the Americans gained possession of some high ground from which they could plainly see Santiago, where Admiral Cervera's fleet lay hidden behind the hills.

Colonel Roosevelt

A week later the U.S. regular soldiers, with the Rough Riders and other volunteers, stormed up the steep heights, drove the Spaniards into Santiago, and forced them to take refuge behind the earthworks that protected the town.

Meanwhile, Rear Admiral Sampson had gone to consult with General Shafter. While he was absent, Commodore Schley and the other commanders of the fleet maintained a sharp lookout for Admiral Cervera, who was anxious to escape.

On Sunday morning, July 3, 1898, a great shout was sent up from the flagship *Brooklyn*, and another from Captain Robley Dunglison Evans's ship, the *Iowa*: "The Spaniards are coming out of the harbor!" It was true, for the sunken *Merrimac* had only half-corked the bottle after all, and Cervera was making a dash out, hoping to reach the broad Atlantic.

This is an 1898 photograph of Roosevelt and his Rough Riders on top of San Juan Heights.

Then all was excitement. "Open fire!" shouted Commodore Schley. The Americans opened fire. The Spanish admiral was a brave man; he did the best he could, but it was of no use. In less than three hours all of the enemy's ships were helpless, blazing wrecks. Admiral Cervera himself barely escaped with his life. The crew of the *Gloucester* rescued him; as he came on board that ship, Commander Richard Wainwright said to him, "I congratulate you, sir, on having made a most gallant fight." When not long afterward the American cruisers reached Portsmouth, New Hampshire, with Cervera and more than 1,000 other prisoners of war taken in the battle, the people sent up cheer after cheer for the Spanish admiral who had treated Lieutenant Hobson and his men so kindly.

The End of the War. Soon after this crushing defeat the Spaniards surrendered Santiago. Puerto Rico surrendered to General Nelson Appleton Miles soon afterwards, and Guam had already surrendered. By that time, Spain had given up the struggle and begged for peace. An armistice was signed between Spain and the United States on August 12, 1898, to stop the fighting until a peace treaty could be signed between the two countries. The United States government immediately sent a letter to the forces at the Philippines ordering them to stop fighting. Before the message could get there, Rear Admiral Dewey and General Merritt had taken Manila.

The war was not without its bright sides. The war showed that the North and South had truly come back together again as soldiers from all of the states fought bravely together. Former Confederate general Joseph Wheeler commanded the United States cavalry forces in Cuba. Black soldiers fought well as part of segregated Army regiments.

The American Red Cross Society under Clara Barton did a noble work during the Spanish-American War. They labored on battlefields and in hospitals to help the wounded and the sick of both armies, and to soothe the last moments of the dying. Many a poor fellow who was called to lay

Public Domain

Above is an artist's conception of the Spanish torpedo boat *Furor* being attacked by the battleships *Iowa*, *Indiana*, and *New York*. The *Furor* sank before reaching land.

Clara Barton is one of the greatest American humanitarians of the nineteenth century. She did much to help wounded soldiers during the War Between the States and afterwards. Early in the war, she started an organization to provide needed supplies to wounded Union soldiers. She was later given permission to travel behind the Union army lines to provide help to the wounded. General Benjamin Butler even put her in charge of the nurses at his army's hospitals. In 1865, President Lincoln asked her to help find out about the soldiers who were considered missing.

A few years later, Clara Barton went to Europe, where she learned about the work of the International Committee of the Red Cross. She was so impressed with their work, especially during the Franco-Prussian War, that when she came home, she began to organize the American Red Cross and became its first president. Her idea was that the American Red Cross would provide help in times of natural disasters, as well as during wartime. The American Red Cross continues to carry out her original ideals.

Clara Barton (1821–1912)

down his life for the American cause, and many others who fell fighting for Spain, blessed the kind hands that did everything that human power could do to relieve their suffering; for the Red Cross helpers and nurses treated all alike. They did not ask under what flag a man served or what language he spoke; it was enough for them to know that he needed their aid. So, too, it is pleasant to find that the Spanish prisoners of war were so well treated by the American people that when they sailed for Spain they cheered heartily for America and the Americans.

While the war was going on, the United States peacefully annexed the Hawaiian Islands, on July 7, 1898. Before the end of the contest with Spain the U.S. flag waved above those islands, as a sign that they had become part of the territory of the United States. Many years later, in 1959, Hawaii became America's fiftieth state.

The United States and Spain signed a peace treaty to end the war on December 10, 1898, although fighting had already ended in August. Spain gave up its colony of Cuba and gave the islands of Guam and Puerto Rico to the United States. In addition, the United States bought the Philippine Islands from Spain for $20 million.

The U.S. Senate ratified the treaty with Spain on February 6, 1899. On New Year's Day, 1899, the Spanish colors were hauled down at Havana, and the Stars and Stripes took their place, as the sign of guardianship of Cuba. It should be remembered that Havana is the city in which Columbus was believed to be buried. By order of the queen of Spain, his remains were sent back after the war (December 12, 1898) to Valladolid, his old home in Spain. Today the Spaniards have nothing left on this side of the Atlantic to call their own, not even the corpse of the great navigator who rediscovered the New World—unless by chance Columbus's body still rests in an old church in Santo Domingo, as some claim.

Results of the War. Many of the American people desired to keep all of the islands that were conquered from Spain. They believed that by so doing the United States would open new markets for American goods in the East and in China, and that by having possessions in various parts of the globe the United States would become a great world power—the greatest, perhaps, that had ever existed in history. Some also realized that acquiring these territories would give American missionaries greater opportunities to spread the gospel.

Many other Americans, who were equally patriotic and equally proud of their country, believed that it would be a mistake for the United States to keep all of these islands. They said that distant possessions would make the U.S. weaker instead of stronger; they would be likely to get America into quarrels with other nations, and the government would have to spend large sums of the people's money to defend these new territories.

The United States did not keep every territory gained from Spain. America never intended to make Cuba a U.S. colony. The Teller Resolution, which Congress passed before going to war with Spain, stated "that the United States disclaims any intention of control over said island except for the pacification thereof, and asserts its determination, when that is accomplished, to leave the government and the control of the island to its people." America followed through on this commitment by withdrawing from Cuba in 1902 after the first president of Cuba was installed in office.

American troops remained in the Philippines for many years. Not all of the Filipinos wanted the United States to occupy their country; many had already been fighting the Spanish for their independence. Therefore, America had to put down a revolt against its authority right after assuming control over the territory. After their victory in the Philippines, Americans soon set about to prepare the Philippines for independence. It eventually became an independent republic in 1946, after Allied forces liberated these islands from Japanese occupation during the Second World War.

General Emilio Aguinaldo (1869–1964) played a crucial role in the Philippine revolt against Spain (1896). In 1899, Aguinaldo became president of the First Philippine Republic. During the Philippine-American War (1899–1902), President Aguinaldo resisted American occupation but eventually pledged his allegiance to the United States on April 1, 1901.

Puerto Rico and Guam still remain under American control. However, the residents of these islands were awarded American citizenship many years ago. They each have internal self-government, electing their own legislatures and governors, and each also has a non-voting representative in the U.S. Congress.

Theodore Roosevelt Becomes President. In the autumn of 1900, William McKinley was reelected President of the United States with Colonel Theodore Roosevelt as Vice President.

In the spring of 1901, a grand exhibition called the Pan-American Exposition was opened at Buffalo, New York. In the autumn, President McKinley attended a public reception at the Exposition on September 6. On this occasion, great numbers of people came forward to shake hands with him. Among these was a young man named Leon Czolgosz—a radical who thought American society was unjust. At the moment the President was reaching out his hand to Czolgosz, he shot McKinley twice with a gun hidden in his handkerchief. The President fell back fatally wounded and died about a week later on September 14. His last words to his friends were: "Good-bye, all; good-bye. It is God's way. His will be done."

By law, Vice President Roosevelt then became President. Five days later, the body of the dead President was laid in its last earthly resting place at his former home in Canton, Ohio. President Roosevelt appointed that day for mourning and prayer. Not only did the people of the United States solemnly keep it, but also great numbers of the people of Europe joined with America in her sorrow.

Throughout America, a great silence fell upon the people when the body of the murdered President was laid in the grave. In New York, and in many other chief cities, cars and steamboats ceased to run for a time; the ever-busy telegraph ceased to click its messages, and thousands of people

The Pan-American Exposition featured many magnificent buildings like the Temple of Music (a concert hall and auditorium) shown above at night. Nikola Tesla's recent invention of a system of alternating current allowed architects and builders to light the Exposition using power generated twenty-five miles away at Niagara Falls.

stood reverently in the streets as though they felt that they were present at the burial ground in Ohio. None who took part in this somber event soon forgot it.

Theodore Roosevelt (1858–1919)

USS *Oregon* (BB-3)

The Panama Canal. Theodore Roosevelt considered the building of a canal across Panama to be one of his greatest achievements as President. While he was President, the United States hired a strip of land on the Isthmus of Panama, which was kept until full control over the canal was given to the Republic of Panama on December 31, 1999. The strip is ten miles wide, and it extends clear across the Isthmus from the Atlantic Ocean to the Pacific Ocean, a distance of nearly fifty miles (see map on page 185). Not far from there, Columbus had attempted to build a town on the Atlantic coast, but it came to nothing. On the other side Balboa, the Spanish explorer, climbed a mountain from which he discovered the largest ocean on the globe. The United States paid tens of millions of dollars for the right to use that narrow piece of land, named the Canal Zone; yet, it seemed to be worthless. Farmers would pay very little for it because most of the land consists of rocks, hills, and swamps. Then again, very few Americans would care to stay long in a climate that is either extremely hot and dry or beastly hot and humid.

Why, then, was the United States so eager to get possession of such a small territory? It was due to the fact that, when the battleship *Oregon* had to sail around the whole continent of South America to get from California to Cuba during the Spanish-American War, the Americans made up their minds that they must construct a canal across the Isthmus of Panama. Then American steamships and warships could pass through both ways, from New York to San Francisco or from San Francisco to New York, and save thousands of miles in distance and several weeks in time. During the 1850s, America had already made some use of the Isthmus; after gold was discovered in California, an American company built the Panama Railway across that neck of land, which proved to be a complete success. Then a French company tried to construct a canal alongside of the railway, but they wasted so much money and lost so many men from malaria and yellow fever that they were glad to sell out their rights to the United States. Everybody expected that when the Americans began to build the canal in 1905 they would "make the dirt fly," but it was slow business; and for several years they did not seem to get ahead much. Finally, in 1907, President Roosevelt appointed Colonel George W. Goethals to see what he could do about it. Colonel Goethals was an engineer in the United States Army, and he knew just how to push the work to completion.

He saw that the first thing to be done was to make the Canal Zone so clean and healthful that forty or fifty thousand men could labor there all day in the hot sun and still keep well and strong. Perhaps his greatest enemies were mosquitoes—not common mosquitoes, but certain dangerous kinds that abound in that climate and whose bite means sickness and sometimes death. In his fight against these winged pests the new chief engineer was entirely successful. He barred the mosquitoes out of the houses with wire screens, and then killed them off by the millions by pouring kerosene in their breeding places. That battle never stopped even for a day, and never can stop.

Next, Colonel Goethals, the "Great Digger," whose motto was "to dig the most dirt for the least money," set to work to tame the Chagres River. It was a very difficult stream with which to deal. At that time it flowed across the line of the canal he had set out to dig, and in the rainy season it became a raging torrent. The colonel found a cure for this. He took the earth he had dug out and built a dam over 100 feet high and nearly a mile and a half long. This dam held the troublesome river in check and converted it into a peaceful lake thirty miles long and deep enough for the largest ships to pass through. That lake is many feet above the level of the sea, but Colonel Goethals built some immense locks, or water-stairs, by which vessels entering the canal can ascend to the lake and can go down from it when they pass out at the other end.

A Steam Shovel at Work on the Panama Canal

But, hard as it was to tame the Chagres River, there was a harder job to come. The line of the canal was blocked by the Culebra Hills. The highest of these hills are about 500 feet above the canal. They form part of that great Pacific coast mountain range that begins in Alaska and extends down through the western part of the United States, then across the Isthmus of Panama, and then down the western coast of South America to Cape Horn. Get your atlas and you will see that these mountains are the "backbone" of the American continents. In order to construct the canal, a ditch nearly nine miles long had to be dug directly through that "backbone." At first, that seemed an easy thing for the steam shovels to do, for each shovel could scoop up a huge bucket of earth and stone at a time. But here came an unexpected difficulty: as fast as they dug the stuff out, the rock above kept crumbling to pieces, sliding down, and filling up the ditch. Heaps as big as a whole row of houses would come roaring down and would cover up everything in a moment. Then all the wearisome labor of scooping it out had to be done over again. This happened time after time and month after month. Some of the workmen began to feel discouraged and to think they must give it up. The young officer who had charge of this particular work never lost heart, but he became so worn out with this enormous task that all the strength went out of him and he died. Still the battle went on, day by day, and after seven years of toil the cut was made so wide that it was believed the sliding rocks could not fall into the ditch. Then Colonel Goethals spoke the word, and President Woodrow Wilson, sitting in his office at the White House in Washington, D.C., pressed an electric button; the water rushed in, and the great Panama Canal across the Isthmus of Panama was practically finished.

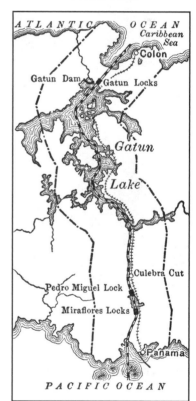

The Gatun Locks on the Panama Canal

U.S. Navy Photo

The photograph above shows the USS *Missouri* passing through one of the locks in the Panama Canal.

In 1904, Thomas Nast created a cartoon depicting President Roosevelt as a character from *Gulliver's Travels*. He is carrying a "big stick" (the United States Navy) in the Caribbean.

One reason why it was finished was that during all the seven years Colonel Goethals made a practice of setting apart one day of every week to meet his men. He would see them at his office and talk with them in a sensible and friendly way about what they were doing, and would find out what he could do for them. In this way they all worked together like a great family, each one of whom meant to do his "level best."

The Panama Canal opened in 1914, and ships are going through it all the time. Although the United States and other nations frequently sent warships through the Panama Canal during World War I and World War II, the canal has most often been used by non-military ships to transport commercial goods throughout the world.

When the eminent French engineer began his unsuccessful attempt to cut his canal through the Isthmus in 1882, the company set up a statue of him there. Colonel Goethals, however, has no monument or statue on the Isthmus. He would not want one. He liked it best to keep in the background and let you look at what he had done. The success of the Panama Canal is enough of a monument for Colonel Goethals.

An Active President. Theodore Roosevelt was the youngest man ever to be elevated to President (following McKinley's assassination), although John F. Kennedy was the youngest one elected to office. Roosevelt was an energetic man who sought to use the government to improve conditions within the country and to make the United States a great power. Theodore Roosevelt described his foreign policy ideas in a motto he gave at the Minnesota state fair in 1901, before he even became President: "Speak softly and carry a big stick." We have already read about Roosevelt's work in Panama, but he also acted to prevent intervention by European countries in Venezuela and the Dominican Republic. Roosevelt helped Japan and Russia to end their war in Asia, earning him the Nobel Peace Prize for his efforts. Later, toward the end of his time as President, Roosevelt sent many of the ships of the United States Navy—known as the Great White Fleet because the ships' hulls were painted white—on a very successful worldwide tour. They visited many parts of the world on a voyage that lasted longer than a year, impressing many people with the strength of the U.S. Navy.

Theodore Roosevelt is often best known for his efforts at conserving America's natural resources. He worked with Congress to establish the United States Forest Service. He created five additional national parks and sixteen national monuments, as well as adding millions of acres to the national forests. Roosevelt believed, as he wrote in his autobiography, "… that the rights of the public to the natural resources outweigh private rights, and must be given its first consideration."

Theodore Roosevelt was very popular with the people. He won the 1904 presidential election and could probably have been reelected in 1908 if he had wanted. However, he decided to return to private life and afterwards went on a couple of extensive exploration tours. Soon after leaving office, he went on an African safari to collect samples for scientific study. A few years later, he went on a similar journey into the Brazilian jungle, where he almost died from disease. Many years after his death, Theodore Roosevelt was one of four Presidents—along with George Washington, Thomas Jefferson, and Abraham Lincoln—to be memorialized as part of the sculptures on Mount Rushmore in South Dakota.

The Discovery of the North Pole. While the laborers on the Isthmus were digging the canal, and while Howard Taft was President, a remarkable piece of work was done at the North. For many years explorers had tried to make their way to the North Pole, but had always failed to get there. It was a terrible journey over ice and snow, and not a few who started on it perished miserably of cold and starvation. But in the spring of 1909 Commander Robert E. Peary of the United States Navy succeeded in getting to the Pole, and he put up an American flag there. Later Captain Amundsen of Norway discovered the South Pole; so we can now say we have seen the top and the bottom of the world.

Summary. America enjoyed peace for over thirty years after the War Between the States ended. However, in 1898, the United States declared war against Spain for the purpose of helping to free the people of Cuba from Spanish rule. Thankfully, this war only lasted several months. America was successful in freeing the people of Cuba from Spanish rule. The new century began with the tragic murder of President McKinley in September 1901. Vice President Theodore Roosevelt assumed the office of President of the United States in 1901. The Panama Canal was opened in 1914 to connect the Atlantic and Pacific oceans.

Comprehension Questions

1. How long has it been since Columbus discovered America?
2. Who were the "Rough Riders"?
3. What happened to Cervera's fleet?
4. What did the Red Cross do in Cuba?
5. What happened to the remains of Columbus?
6. What terrible event happened at Buffalo in the autumn of 1901?
7. Who built the Panama Canal? When did it open?

Chapter 33
America and the Great War (1914–1921)

The twentieth century was one of the most deadly in human history. The two most devastating wars ever to occur—World War I and World War II—happened during that century. The United States entered both wars after they had begun, but it began to fight particularly late in World War I. World War I was often called the Great War before World War II.

America Stays Out of War. In the summer of 1914, after Woodrow Wilson became President, one of the greatest wars ever known began in Europe. On June 28, 1914, Serbian nationalists murdered Franz Ferdinand (heir to the Austro-Hungarian throne) and his wife in Sarajevo, the capital city in the Austro-Hungarian province of Bosnia. Their murder led to the beginning of World War I in less than two months. The war soon involved Russia, Serbia, Montenegro, Austria-Hungary, Germany, Belgium, France, the Ottoman Empire, and Great Britain. Several other countries eventually became participants in the Great War.

The people of the United States resolved not to take any part in it if they could avoid it, but to do everything they could to hasten the coming of peace. To show good will towards all, the Americans sent a ship to Europe loaded with Christmas presents for thousands of poor children whose fathers had left their homes to go and fight.

While the war raged in Europe, the people of San Francisco had opened a World's Fair, called the Panama-Pacific International Exposition, in 1915. It celebrated two things: first, Balboa's discovery of the Pacific Ocean, about 400 years earlier; and second, Colonel Goethals' completion of the Panama Canal, which united the waters of the Atlantic and the Pacific.

Thomas Woodrow Wilson
(1856–1924)

The Palace of Fine Arts at the Panama-Pacific International Exposition, 1915

The largest building in the Fair was Machinery Palace. There, and elsewhere, many laborsaving inventions made by Americans were exhibited. One of these inventions was a little machine that would add up a long column of figures in less than half the time that you or I could do it. Another interesting thing was a model of one of the big steam shovels used in digging the Panama Canal. Those big steam shovels did more hard work in an hour than 600 men could do with hand shovels in that amount of time. A third invention was a press that could print more than 1,000 newspapers in a minute, fold them, and pile them up. Looking at these things, people could understand why American machines were sold and used throughout the world.

America Goes to War. After a time, the United States decided that it must enter the Great War, called the "War to End All Wars." This happened because the German submarines, which had destroyed many English vessels, began to blow up American merchant ships trading with England. President Wilson told Germany the destruction must stop. Unfortunately, it did not stop. When the Americans found that Germany meant to keep on making war with them by destroying their ships, they saw that they must declare war against her, and Congress made that declaration in the spring of 1917.

During the Great War, the *Lusitania* was torpedoed by a German submarine on May 7, 1915. This British ocean liner sank in only eighteen minutes, killing nearly 1,200 passengers—including 128 Americans. The sinking of the *Lusitania* turned public opinion against Germany.

Later on, President Wilson ordered Admiral William Sims to begin the fight. He accordingly went, as speedily as possible, to command the American warships that were to help the English fleet hunt down and destroy the terrible German submarines, which were enemies to both countries.

The battle with the submarines was long and hard, for these vessels could quickly sink out of sight, could stay under water for many hours, or could slyly travel miles away without being seen or heard. In the end, however, the American and English sailors managed, by working together, to get the better of these slippery craft so that fewer and fewer escaped.

But the United States soon discovered that it would need many more warships and must also have a great number of transport ships to carry fighting men across the ocean. Nor was that all, for America needed a whole fleet of other ships to carry over food and clothing and powder and guns for the men. It took America a great while to get ready to build these new vessels. But after the builders really set to work, no country in the world ever completed so many ships in the same number of days.

Americans then had to meet a still greater difficulty. They found that money was running short, because it always costs far more to carry on war, even for a single year, than it does to pay the expenses of many years of peace. The people, however, did not shrink back frightened and declare

William Sowden Sims (1858–1936)

THAT LIBERTY SHALL NOT
PERISH FROM THE EARTH
BUY LIBERTY BONDS
FOURTH   LIBERTY   LOAN

Citizens of the United States were encouraged to buy Liberty Bonds, War Savings Stamps, and Thrift Stamps to help the war effort.

General John "Black Jack" Pershing
(1860–1948)

that they never could raise all the dollars that the government in Washington wanted. On the contrary, they met the case bravely and declared that they stood ready to give money in taxes and to lend money to the government to use as it saw fit. This was done because the Americans felt that they must push the war forward—no matter what it might cost—until a victory was won that would make them safe in every way. They wanted also to make the friendly nations of Europe, that were fighting along with them, as safe as possible, on land and sea.

This feeling explains why so many people so willingly paid their taxes and also bought Liberty Bonds. Also, later on, thousands of boys used to go to the post offices and buy War Savings Stamps, or, if they did not have enough money for that, they would buy Thrift Stamps. Thousands of girls did the same thing. They also set to work at home and knit great piles of woolen sweaters and socks to send abroad to their soldiers. Then, for fear that they had not done enough, they made up little boxes of good things to add to what they had sent.

While these preparations were going on, the President dispatched General John "Black Jack" Pershing to command the American troops that would be going to fight in Europe. A small American force of regular troops went along with General Pershing to France. They went there to help the people in their desperate fight against the powerful German armies that had entered their country. The enemy was rapidly marching forward to capture the great city of Paris, the capital of the French Republic, which means as much to every true Frenchman as the city of Washington does to every American.

The people over there swung their hats and cheered with all their might when they saw the men landing from the vessels. They had good reason for giving such a rousing welcome, for these were the first American soldiers that had ever been sent to fight anywhere on the continent of Europe. The soldiers went there because France, England, and the United States had joined hands to beat back Germany, whose emperor was determined not to let any free country rest in peace unless it would give in to him and do whatever he ordered. That would have made the American people, and those of England and France as well, no better than slaves.

The Army Gets Into the Fight. The American Army was not ready for a major war in 1917; it was too small to do much good in Europe. Therefore, before the regular troops had gone abroad, America had begun getting ready to raise a new and much stronger army to follow them. The Americans resolved that this should be the largest army that they had ever collected, much bigger than the Union army during the War Between the States or the number of American troops sent to Cuba during the Spanish-American War.

It is interesting to see how the United States started to raise such an army. It was done in this way: President Wilson commanded all the young men in the whole country to write their names and the names of the places where they lived on cards that were to be sent to Washington. These cards were then numbered and put in small drawers so that they could be easily examined when needed.

When this task had been accomplished, the government officer who had charge of the cards gave notice that on July 20, 1917, he would proceed to select those young men who would enter the new fighting force. The selection was made in the fairest possible manner so that all might be treated alike, and no one could say that his name had been picked out on purpose. The method employed used many slips of paper, each of which had a number printed on it. These were then deposited in a large glass jar. The officer in charge of the draft closed his eyes, bound his handkerchief over them, and drew out one of the slips from the jar. The slip was then opened, and the number on it decided who should first have the privilege of entering the new American Army of Liberty, as it was called.

All of the young men chosen were examined to see if they were strong enough to go to war; if they were, and were not excused on some other account, they went to military camps in different states to be trained as soldiers. A good many of them had never in their lives held a gun in their hands, and some had never seen a gun fired. But they showed themselves quick to learn, prompt to act, and eager to do their part in the Great War.

When the American men were ready, they sailed for France—many thousands going over at a time. The Germans, knowing that they were coming, ordered the captains of their submarines to be on the watch and to sink every Yankee transport ship with all on board. But the Americans were also on the watch, and American or British naval ships always crossed the Atlantic along with them to guard them from attack. No American transport ship was ever sunk on its way to Europe.

These steamers also carried over to France great numbers of Red Cross nurses and Salvation Army Lassies, as the girls called themselves. They went to look after the comfort and welfare of the "boys." The Salvation Army Lassies kept near the firing line, and in their huts they always held themselves ready to serve the tired fighters with hot coffee and hot doughnuts. The Red Cross nurses took good care of those who fell sick or who were wounded in battle. Red Cross dogs, that were trained to go out and search for missing soldiers who had been so badly hurt that they could neither move nor call for help, assisted these faithful nurses. When the dogs found such cases, they would trot back and get someone to go with them and bring the poor fellows to the hospital.

Now let us see how the American soldiers lived and what they did. You might think that the first thing they would do would be to use their guns. No, the first thing they did was to use their shovels. They dug long lines of deep trenches or ditches, and they also hollowed out rude rooms and pas-

Alvin York (1887–1964)

One of the bravest American soldiers of World War I was also one of the most reluctant. Alvin York of Tennessee won the Congressional Medal of Honor, as well as medals from three other countries, for his bravery against the Germans while fighting in France. On October 8, 1918, York led an attack on a German machine gun position. His actions led to the capture of 32 machine guns and the capture of 132 German soldiers. York himself killed 28 Germans.

York was not a natural warrior. As a young man, he lived a wild life gambling, drinking, and fighting, in spite of his parents' instructions. He was converted to faith in Christ, however, and lived a changed life. When the United States entered World War I, he faced a question: Should he go into the Army and fight? After being drafted into the Army, York eventually decided after a time of prayer and reflection that he could in good conscience go to France to fight in the war. As he wrote in his diary: "… if a man can make peace by fighting he is a peacemaker." In his famous fight, York credited the Lord for not being injured. "So I am a witness to the fact that God did help me out of that hard battle; for the bushes were shot up all around me and I never got a scratch."

sages underground. These were for shelter and for defense against attack. Additionally, they built strong fences and entanglements of barbed wire to keep the enemy at a distance. It is safe to say that no one likes to stand very long in a ditch, but the soldiers had to do it, and when it rained they often stood in mud and water a foot deep or more.

In these trenches and underground "dugouts," the men did something more than fight, for many of them ate and slept there. They lived there because oftentimes "dugouts" were the only safe places where they could live. What did they see when they looked out? In front of them, not very far away, they saw long stretches of barbed wire. In back of those cruel-looking entanglements they saw trenches like their own, but those swarmed with German soldiers. These soldiers always fired at them when they had a good chance, just as the American men fired at the Germans. That was what they were there for. There would be days, however, when the soldiers in the trenches, on both sides, would suddenly climb out and engage in fierce hand-to-hand fights in "No Man's Land," as the strip that separated the combatants from each other was called.

The various armies developed new technologies and tactics to win the war. Both sides used the same kinds of weapons, such as guns and machine guns, each one of which could shoot hundreds of bullets in a minute. Both sides also threw many thousands of cast-iron explosive shells, known as grenades, which were about as big as an orange. Those who worked the cannon fired huge shells, sometimes weighing a ton or more, which rushed screaming through the sky, bursting with a terrific crash when they struck, and tearing everything to pieces around them.

In July 1917, Germany introduced mustard gas into the war. The Allied forces on the Western Front protected themselves against such gases as shown above. Members of the 45th Battalion of the Australian Imperial Force stand guard wearing gas masks in a trench near Ypres, Belgium, in the fall of 1917.

Sadly, on the Eastern Front, the Russians were less prepared and suffered nearly 420,000 casualties and more than 55,000 deaths. After the war ended, people were so horrified and outraged by the use of poison gases, such deadly weapons were outlawed in 1925.

The Germans tried some new techniques to overcome the Allied defenses on the Western Front, but with little success. They invented poison gas, a horrible new weapon that caused painful deaths or injuries to soldiers but did not enable the Germans to defeat the British and French, who soon began using poison gas as well. The Germans also introduced the flamethrower, a weapon that spread fire by shooting burning fuel toward the enemy. As with poison gas, flamethrowers had some initial success but had little long-term effect on the war and were soon copied by the Allies.

While this fighting was taking place on the ground, desperate battles would often be going on overhead. Airplanes had changed dramatically since the days of the Wright brothers. Airplanes were first used to spot enemy soldiers; however, they soon began to be used to attack troops on the ground, bomb enemy locations, and to attack each other. All of the major countries, including the United States, used airplanes in the war. All sides used observation balloons, and the Germans even used large airships known as Zeppelins as long-range bombers and scouts.

The Tank. Trench warfare made it very difficult for armies to break through enemy lines to victory. Instead, large numbers of soldiers were killed in futile attacks. The British had an idea about how to overcome the extensive German defenses on the Western Front. They wanted to invent a vehicle that could cross trenches, crush barbed wire, and be armored enough so that it would not be affected by machine gun fire.

In the beginning, this new armored vehicle had nothing at all that was warlike about it. It was a big, strong automobile invented by an American and manufactured in one of the Western states. It was built to do certain kinds of farm work on rough ground where neither horses nor oxen could be used. Because it had enormous pulling power, it was called a tractor, and as it crept along very slowly, it got the name of the "Caterpillar Tractor." It could easily force its way over stones and through brush and up and down steep places where an ordinary automobile would have been upset and knocked to pieces. In doing this, the tractor could drag gangs of heavy plows that would break up the hardest soil and prepare it for raising crops of wheat and corn.

An English military officer happened to see this go-ahead machine. He gazed at it in silence and then exclaimed, "This is just the sort of thing we want in the war against the Germans, for this thing can be made to fight!" He bought several of these tractors before the parts were put together, and had the parts boxed up and shipped to England. There some alterations were made in the strange machines, and they were covered over with plates of steel. All work on them was done secretly, in order that the Germans might not find out what they were. Luckily, a report got abroad that they were water-carriers, though in reality they were forts on wheels, made to carry men and guns. When they were finished, they were sent off by night to the battlefields of France. As soon as the English soldiers over there caught sight of them, they laughed outright at the awkward way in which these new water-carriers stumbled along. They nicknamed them "tanks" and predicted that they would speedily get wrecked. But the tanks astonished everybody by beating down and breaking through German barbed-wire entanglements and utterly destroying the enemy's nests of machine guns. Besides, what harm could their showers of bullets do to these slow-moving monsters, protected by walls of steel, which stopped at nothing, but went straight across trenches or down into them and out again without tipping over?

From that time on, it was plain that, however odd the tanks might look or act, they would certainly "do their bit." The Allied armies were able to make effective use of this new technology; the new tanks helped them gain some hard-fought battles that might have been lost without them. The Germans, on the other hand, only produced a few tanks that never accomplished very much. It would not be until World War

U.K. Government

Benjamin Holt invented one of the first caterpillar track vehicles that was originally used for farming on the West Coast. Holt's design was based on the work of David Roberts of England. One year after Hornsby & Sons of Britain sold Roberts's design to Holt, the British Army ordered over 440 of Holt's caterpillar tracked vehicles, as shown above (hauling an 8-inch Howitzer). These tracked vehicles were actually built under license by the British manufacturer Ruston, which merged with Hornsby & Sons in the fall of 1918. In 1925, Holt Manufacturing merged with the C. L. Best Tractor to form the now famous Caterpillar Tractor Company of Peoria, Illinois.

U.K. Government

British Mark I Tank in the Battle of Thiepval Ridge, France

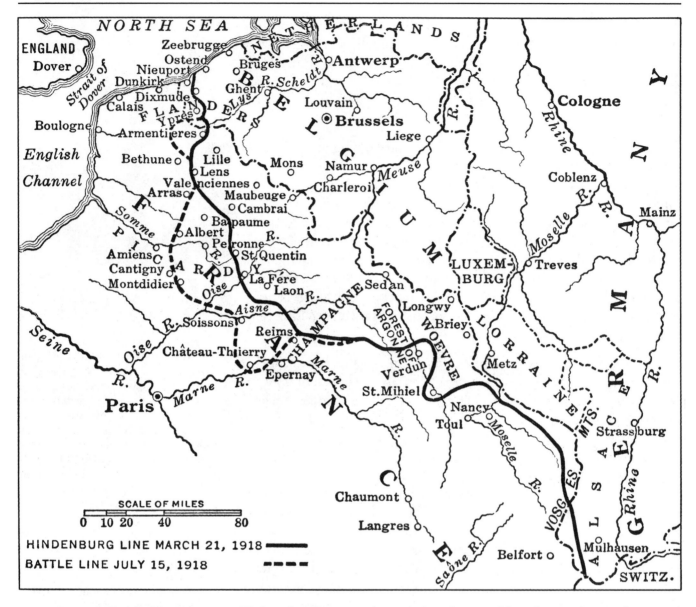

**German Battle Lines
(March 21–July 15, 1918)**

The Hindenburg Line was a broad belt of defense, which extended from the North Sea across Belgium and France to Switzerland, or nearly 470 miles. Its width varied from three to twelve miles. It consisted of an immense number of trenches, dugouts, tunnels, and underground rooms, defended by machine guns, artillary, and great masses of barbed-wire entanglements.

II that the Germans showed that they could make good use of armored vehicles.

The End of the Great War. But the war itself was now changing. American men were no longer standing in muddy trenches week after week, since the armies on both sides had begun to move. Little by little, General Pershing's great American army in the east of France was gaining ground from the enemy. Also, the Americans who were acting with the French and English armies on the west were gaining. All of them working together were steadily pushing the Germans out of France and Belgium and compelling them to move back toward Germany.

Still, the German troops, even while they were retreating, continued their terrible work of destruction. Often when they left a city or a country village that they had captured and held, they left it a mass of smoking ruins. The officers accomplished this by ordering a certain number of men to remain behind long enough to burn down buildings, blow up bridges, destroy roads, fill up wells, and saw down fruit trees. So far as it was practical, they seemed determined to leave nothing that could be of use or value to the French or Belgian people who had made these places their homes.

Notwithstanding this far-reaching destruction, the time had at last arrived when everyone could see that the end of the Great War was near. The American men had not been fighting long, but they had fought bravely and well. Their reward came on November 11, 1918, when the fighting ended and the Germans gave up and signed an armistice (a peace agreement), and solemnly bound themselves to do what France, England, America, and Italy demanded. Then the last gun was fired, and the fighting stopped. After that memorable day, November 11 became known as "Armistice Day," although it is now called Veterans Day in the United States and Remembrance Day in the Commonwealth of Nations (fifty-three sovereign nations, most of which are former British colonies).

The American soldiers began to return, full of joy at the thought of setting foot on American soil again. General Pershing came back and marched at the head of a division of his victorious soldiers through Washington. Peace treaties were signed between the Allies and the enemy nations in 1919 and 1920. Congress declared an end to the war between the United States and Germany by joint resolution in 1921.

Pershing's Victorious Army in Washington, D.C.

Summary. The first of the great wars of the twentieth century—known as the Great War or World War I—began in 1914. The United States attempted to stay out of the war but eventually was compelled to join in 1917 because of German submarine attacks on American ships. A great many new technologies were introduced during the war. The fighting ended on November 11, 1918, when the Germans gave up and signed an armistice.

Comprehension Questions

1. What event helped to start World War I?

2. When and why did the United States enter the Great War?

3. Who commanded the American Army in Europe?

4. Who assisted the American soldiers near the front lines?

5. What did soldiers first learn to use and why?

6. What new vehicle did the British develop to overcome the German defenses?

Chapter 34
J. Gresham Machen (1881–1937)

Harry Emerson Fosdick (1878–1969)

On May 22, 1922, a minister named Harry Emerson Fosdick delivered a sermon in New York City at the First Presbyterian Church. While this does not seem to be an earth-shattering event at first glance, it quickly became one of the more famous sermons ever preached in American history. The sermon was titled "Shall the Fundamentalists Win?" In the sermon, Fosdick claimed that certain people in the church were being too strict about what people had to believe. Those certain people were the fundamentalists, and those strict beliefs included the virgin birth, resurrection, and miracles of Jesus Christ. Fosdick argued that it was all right if you believed those things, but you didn't have to believe them to be a Christian.

After Fosdick's sermon was sent to 130,000 preachers by a wealthy friend, the church had to respond to the attack made against the truth of the Bible. One of the most energetic defenders of truth was J. Gresham Machen. Machen was a professor at Princeton Theological Seminary at the time, and he almost gave up everything he had in order to defend God's Word. In fact, Machen was willing to stand up to Fosdick because of his belief that God's truth can never change.

This 1870s cartoon embodies the evolutionary myth by depicting Charles Darwin as an ape. According to Genesis, God created man in His image—thus evolution is an affront to God and His Word.

Science Challenges Christianity. To be honest, all Fosdick really wanted was to make God appear more acceptable to modern-day listeners. As man grew in his understanding of how the world worked, it seemed as if God was no longer necessary to explain the mysteries of the world. Many scientists believed God was completely unnecessary because of Charles Darwin's theory of evolution. In a nutshell, Darwin argued that all living organisms in the world had come from one tiny living organism over the course of millions (or even billions!) of years through a large number of large changes. Basically, instead of trusting that God created the world, the scientists argued that the world was always there.

The theory of evolution became increasingly popular as time progressed from the late nineteenth century to the early twentieth century. One reason it became more popular was because Darwin presented the theory in the midst of the Industrial Revolution. The Industrial Revolution was a time period when many technological advances were made, such as the steam engine, the telephone, the car, and the airplane. Basically, it seemed like humans were getting very close to controlling the world by using inventions created through modern science. It was science that was giving man an unhealthily high opinion of himself. Soon many people began to believe anything the scientists had to say; and when many scientists accepted the theory of evolution and promoted their belief in it, those people just followed them.

Of course, many people in the church were impressed with all that the scientists were accomplishing. Even the preachers were impressed, and they felt a lot of pressure to accept the new discoveries unearthed by scientists. Thus, some preachers began to dismiss anything in the Bible that science revealed was impossible, including Jesus being born of a virgin, His rising from the dead, and any other miracle the Bible recorded. By the time Fosdick preached his sermon in 1922, he was simply defending beliefs held by many leaders in the church.

Fosdick did not care for the fundamentalists. The fundamentalists were a group of church leaders who opposed man's blind belief in science. Instead of doubting the Bible, they argued that the Bible was completely trustworthy since it was the Word of God. They defended all of the "fundamental," or core, beliefs of Christianity. These fundamental beliefs included Jesus being fully God and fully man, His being born of a virgin, and the fact that He *actually* died on the cross for His people's sins and then *actually* rose from the dead. Machen was definitely on the side of the fundamentalists in this battle.

Machen Responds to the Challenge. Not long after Fosdick preached his famous sermon, Machen wrote a book he titled *Christianity and Liberalism*. In the book, Machen clearly laid out the differences between those who believed in the Bible (the Christians) and those who believed more in science (the liberals). Machen's conclusion was that the liberals had replaced the true religion of God with a false religion of man. In other words, the liberals thought it was unnecessary to put one's faith in God to save them when mankind had the ability to save himself.

J. Gresham Machen (1881–1937)

Liberals did not like Machen's book. They believed Machen was being insensitive to those who had different opinions about God than he did. The liberals wanted to avoid talking about specific points of belief in God because they were afraid that someone would be offended. They wanted to be as accepting as possible when it came to other opinions about God. Ironically, while they were very tolerant of most opinions, they were not tolerant at all of Machen.

Because the liberals did not like Machen's book, they tried to prevent him from spreading its message to the church. One of the first things they did was take over the school where he worked to train ministers (Princeton Theological Seminary). Machen knew he would have to leave to continue teaching what he knew was the truth. So he and a few other professors started Westminster Theological Seminary in 1929. The new seminary was committed to training pastors who believed and defended the core beliefs of Christianity. There was no room for pastors who did not believe in the God of the Bible at Westminster.

CHRISTIANITY
BIBLE NOT INFALLIBLE
MAN NOT MADE IN GODS IMAGE
NO MIRACLES
NO VIRGIN BIRTH
NO. DEITY
NO ATONEMENT
NO RESURRECTION
AGNOSTICISM
ATHEISM

THE DESCENT OF THE MODERNISTS

The Rise of Modernism & The Social Gospel

In the early twentieth century, a movement was undertaken to help Christianity become a more influential world force. To reach that goal, many believed that it was necessary to downplay Christianity's traditional beliefs and emphasize its ability to make a social impact. In other words, some argued that Christians should focus more on helping the poor than on teaching others about Christ's death and resurrection. A movement known as the Social Gospel argued that basic point.

The most important defender of the Social Gospel was Walter Rauschenbusch (1861-1918). He wrote a number of important books and gained a loyal following of 'disciples.' Even though Rauschenbusch and his followers did not reject the traditional teachings of the Bible, by deemphasizing them the Social Gospel helped open the door for the blatant attacks made against Christianity by the liberals in the 1920s.

Machen Runs into More Problems. But the problems were just beginning for Machen. Soon he found himself in the middle of another battle. This time the battle was over the best way to do missionary work. A book titled *Re-Thinking Missions* by William Ernest Hocking was published in 1932. The book tried to convince people that missionaries who tried to convert people in other countries with the teaching that the God of the Bible was the only true God were not doing missions the right way. Instead, the book stated that missionaries should help to create a new religion that the whole world could accept. Obviously, this new religion would have to reject anything that other people would find offensive, including the claim that Jesus is God.

When Machen's church, the Presbyterian Church in the United States of America (PCUSA), refused to affirm that the missionaries' main job was to preach the Word of God, Machen helped create a missionary organization that would send out Bible-believing missionaries. Just like when Machen had created his own seminary, the church did not appreciate Machen's actions. Machen and his supporters in the church (which included many ministers and missionaries) were commanded to break up their group and support the missionaries who believed the message taught by *Re-Thinking Missions*. Machen refused, of course, and he was kicked out of his church for his decision.

It was clear that the PCUSA wanted to have influence in the world more than it wanted to please God. It had studied the advances made by science and decided to adjust what it believed about God in light of them. Machen tried to explain to people in the church that God never changes, but not enough people listened to him. Soon after he was kicked out of the PCUSA, Machen and his few remaining friends created a new church that became known as the Orthodox Presbyterian Church (OPC). Machen claimed that he and his friends had "become members, at last, of a true Presbyterian church." Not long after the OPC was created in 1936, Machen passed away.

Machen's Failure? From a human point of view, it seems like Machen was a failure. Even though he fought against the attempt by those both outside and inside the church to place science above God, Machen was able to convince fewer and fewer people he was right as his life progressed. But Machen cared more about pleasing God than he did about pleasing man. Machen gave up a lot in his quest to defend God's name, including fame and many friends. In Machen's mind, however, all the treasures on earth could not replace the knowledge that God loved him and was pleased with him. In other words, while many people believe that Machen was a failure, God considers him a huge success because there is nothing more important than believing and defending God. Machen definitely understood that to be the truth.

Summary. In the early 1920s, Rev. Harry Emerson Fosdick shocked the Christian world by attacking the orthodox teachings of the Bible (the virgin birth, death, and resurrection of Christ) from the pulpit. He tried to water down biblical truth to make it acceptable to modern-day listeners, who were being swayed by Darwin's theory of evolution. People began to put their trust in man and the technological advances of the Industrial Revolution and to reject God and His Word. All was not lost, though. God raised up J. Gresham Machen to defend the truth by writing a landmark book entitled *Christianity and Liberalism*. The liberals did not like what Machen wrote and forced him out of Princeton Theological Seminary, where Machen had taught. In response, Machen and a few others established Westminster Theological Seminary, where pastors could be trained according to God's Word and learn to defend the core beliefs of Christianity. Liberals also attacked the preaching of the gospel to other people groups, so Machen stepped up to defend the Great Commission. In the end, the Presbyterian Church USA drove Machen and his followers from that mainline denomination; thus, in 1936, the Orthodox Presbyterian Church was formed as a true Bible-centered church. In spite of Machen's shortcomings, he understood the truth and, by God's grace, defended it well. Today, all of Evangelical Christianity is truly indebted to Machen's faithfulness to God and service to the Church.

"The Bible is the center and core of that with which Westminster has to do."

J. Gresham Machen, Founder of Westminster Theological Seminary, spoke these words at the opening convocation of this school on September 25, 1929.

Comprehension Questions

1. What did Fosdick argue in his sermon "Shall the Fundamentalists Win?"

2. Why was Machen willing to stand up to Fosdick?

3. How did the Industrial Revolution give man a high opinion of himself?

4. What did Machen argue in *Christianity and Liberalism*?

5. Of what did the book *Rethinking Missions* try to convince people?

6. Do you think that Machen was a failure?

Chapter 35
Franklin D. Roosevelt (1882–1945)

Warren Gamaliel Harding
(1865–1923)

John Calvin Coolidge, Jr.
(1872–1933)

Return to Normalcy. America was doing well during most of the 1920s. In 1921, Warren G. Harding became President and Calvin Coolidge Vice President. They were elected in 1920 on a policy of reestablishing normalcy after the crisis of World War I. During the time between the end of World War I and the beginning of the Great Depression, the United States was generally in good spirits. By 1920, America had established itself as a great industrial power in the eyes of the world. The United States had developed into a busy and prosperous nation because it produced new and better products in its factories. After a brief business decline soon after the end of World War I, the United States economy grew rapidly. Home ownership and automobile sales increased significantly during the 1920s. Movie production, commercial radio broadcasting, and sales of radios became big business during this decade.

Even though the United States never joined the League of Nations, President Harding maintained an active foreign policy. He sought peaceful relations with other countries, improving ties with Colombia and promoting peace in the Pacific region. Between November 1921 and February 1922, the United States met with Great Britain, France, Italy, and Japan in Washington, D.C., to stop a naval arms race. Each of these countries agreed not to build another battleship for ten years.

Warren G. Harding's presidency ended suddenly, however, when he died on August 2, 1923. Calvin Coolidge, who later went on to win the 1924 presidential election, succeeded Harding. President Coolidge largely followed the policies of Warren Harding. Coolidge was opposed to government intervention in the economy. His economic policy can be summed up by one of his most famous statements: "The business of America is business." He also generally followed Harding's foreign policy. In 1928, the United States participated in a conference in London to limit the construction of smaller warships.

President Coolidge signed into law the Immigration Act of 1924, limiting the number of immigrants who could be admitted from any country to 2% of the number of people from that country who were already living in the United States in 1890. However, in an appendix to the bill, the President stated his displeasure that the bill specifically excluded Japanese immigrants. Note that General Pershing is standing to the right of President Coolidge.

The airplane had gone through many changes and improvements in the few short years since it had been introduced to the world by the Wright brothers. A daring young pilot named Charles Lindbergh flew his single engine plane

across the Atlantic Ocean in 1927. This was the first solo, non-stop flight from the United States to Europe. The plane Lindbergh flew was called the *Spirit of St. Louis.* This great event opened up a new era in world travel and further established America as a world leader.

Charles Lindbergh (1902–1974)

The Great Depression. Herbert Hoover was elected President of the United States after Coolidge. During the first few months that Hoover was in office, the United States still seemed to be a prosperous nation, but not all was well with America. There were problems in the economy that would lead to serious trouble. The economy was becoming weaker and, soon, the "good times" of the 1920s came to an end. In one month, the stock market lost $16 billion, with the worst decline occurring on October 29, 1929, which became known as "Black Tuesday."

A great depression soon began; the stock market in the United States went down as fast as the confidence of the American people in the national economy. Thousands of banks closed and many factories shut down. Many people lost their savings, and millions of workers lost their jobs. Unemployment rose dramatically, going from a rate of 3.2% to a high of 24.9% in 1933. During the Great Depression's worst days, one out of every four American workers was without a job. This was a time of extreme hardship in America—as well as in much of the world—that lasted from late 1929 through 1941. Many people were devastated by their financial losses and were looking for help.

Herbert Clark Hoover (1874–1964)

Most Americans were desperate for assistance, and Franklin D. Roosevelt offered them hope during the 1932 presidential campaign. Franklin Roosevelt overwhelmingly defeated President Hoover and won the election. After Roosevelt assumed office in 1933, he began a series of government programs—collectively known as the New Deal—to combat the effects of the Great Depression. He sought to raise the people's spirits, promising in his first inaugural address that the United States would revive and "… that the only thing we have to fear is fear itself…." He continued with a series of radio broadcasts to the American people, known as "fireside chats," where he explained his programs and the issues of the day. Yet, for all of President Roosevelt's programs and encouragement, he was never able to actually overcome the Depression.

Roosevelt's Life at a Glance. Franklin Roosevelt was one of the most important Presidents in American history. He was born into a wealthy and influential New York family. He was a fifth cousin to President Theodore Roosevelt and married a niece of Theodore Roosevelt. Most of his career was in government service and politics. Before becoming President, he was

Franklin Delano Roosevelt
(1882–1945)

Roosevelt with Ruthie Bie, 1941

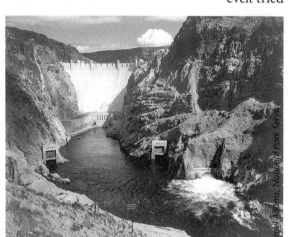

This photograph of the Hoover (Boulder) Dam was taken by Ansel Adams for the National Park Service in 1941.

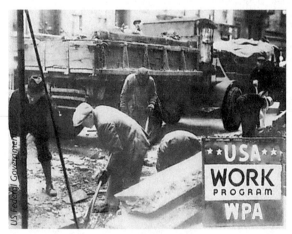

The Works Progress Administration (WPA) employed millions of unemployed and unskilled workers, especially in the rural and Western mountain areas.

elected to the New York legislature, served in the Navy Department during the Woodrow Wilson administration, and ran for Vice President in 1920 but lost to the presidential ticket of Harding and Coolidge. In 1921, Franklin Roosevelt was struck with a disease that left him permanently paralyzed from the waist down. Roosevelt learned to walk again for short distances using braces and resumed his political career. He was elected governor of New York and then went on to become President, serving longer than anyone in American history by winning the presidential elections of 1932, 1936, 1940, and 1944. During Roosevelt's presidency, he led the United States during its two most critical periods in the twentieth century—the Great Depression and World War II.

The New Deal. Both Herbert Hoover and his successor Franklin Roosevelt tried to fix the nation's economic problems. They each used the power of the federal government in an effort to combat the effects of the depression. They each used deficit spending to try to get more money into the economy. Many public works projects were constructed during the depression, such as the Hoover Dam (begun during the Hoover administration and completed during the Roosevelt administration). As one of his first New Deal programs, President Roosevelt also established a construction program known as the Civilian Conservation Corps (CCC). The popular CCC program provided employment for young men by having them do such outdoor work as planting trees, creating parks, and building roads. These construction programs by both the Hoover and Roosevelt administrations put people to work and built useful projects.

President Roosevelt, however, went further than public works activities. Roosevelt was willing to go beyond traditional constitutional limits to try to fix the economy. Some of his New Deal programs significantly intervened in the American economy. Roosevelt thought that the only way for America to get out of her economic problems was through a government-planned economy. In addition, the President established for the first time in American history permanent, national social welfare programs. Although Congress supported much of President Roosevelt's New Deal legislation, others began to question them. The United States Supreme Court declared some of his programs to be unconstitutional in 1935 and 1936.

In spite of all of the programs of Hoover and Roosevelt, they contributed little to a permanent improvement in the American economy and may have even helped make things worse. It took almost ten years for industrial production to get back to the level of 1929. In spite of the fact that Franklin Roosevelt said in his first inaugural address that his most important job was "… to put people to work," millions of people remained unemployed throughout the 1930s. The unemployment rate never fell below 10% until 1941 and was as high as almost 20% as late as 1938. Certainly many people were helped, but at the cost of a great change in the system of government. It was not, however, until World War II and the economic expansion after the war that America truly recovered from the Great Depression.

New Leaders in the World. The world saw the rise of several dictatorships during the 1920s and 1930s. Russia was the first country to be taken over by an oppressive regime. It had not done well during World War I, losing many battles to the Germans and Austrians after some initial success in 1914. At the same time, the Russian economy became steadily worse. In addition, the Russian imperial government was both clumsy in its conduct of the war and repressive against its critics. Many Russians could no longer support the Russian emperor (also known as the tsar), and strikes and uprisings occurred throughout the country. Finally, Tsar Nicholas II had to step down from his position on March 15, 1917, because he could no longer control the country.

Nicholas II of Russia (1868–1918)

A new, more democratic government took over but could do no better. Russia continued to do badly in the war, and the economy continued to get worse. As disorder increased, a revolutionary group called Bolsheviks (now commonly called Communists) led by Vladimir Lenin seized power in the Russian capital of Petrograd (now known as St. Petersburg) on November 7, 1917. The Bolsheviks made peace with Germany and Austria in 1918, and attempted to gain complete control over Russia, but were only able to do so after winning a bloody civil war against anti-communist Russians. Many Russians were killed in the war, including the tsar and his family.

By 1921, the Communist party won the Russian Civil War and gained complete control over most of the old Russian Empire, changing the name of Russia to the Union of Soviet Socialist Republics (also known as the Soviet Union). Lenin died in 1924, and one of his followers, Joseph Stalin, came to power in 1928. Both of these men claimed to act on the behalf of workers and peasants, but were tyrants who chose to win political power through murder and deceit. Many millions of the Soviet people were killed or imprisoned during the 1920s and 1930s for daring to speak out against the communist system of government or resisting communist policies.

Vladimir Ilyich Lenin (1870–1924)

Joseph Stalin was even worse than Lenin. The killing and imprisonment of Russians became even more common during his time as the ruler of the Soviet Union. He became so concerned to keep his own power that he even had many of the older supporters of Lenin put on trial, and then imprisoned or executed, to protect his own position.

From the beginning, the Communists attempted to expand their influence and control throughout the world as they had opportunity to do so. Communist uprisings took place in Germany and Hungary right after World War I. In the 1920s, Communists took power in Mongolia and were involved in a civil war against the Nationalists in China, which did not end until a Communist victory in 1949.

Joseph Stalin (1878–1953)

Benito Mussolini (1883–1945)

Adolf Hitler (1889–1945)

Under communism, the Russians enjoyed even less freedom than they did under the tsar. The people were not allowed to freely worship God; the Communists often oppressed the Christians. The government forced the people to live as the government wished. The people did not even have the right to vote for the leaders of their choice. They were only allowed to vote for Communists as their rulers.

In many respects, the Russian people living under Communist rule were like slaves. The government owned all property—allowing the people to use only as much as it thought best—as well as all the means of business and industry. For example, under Joseph Stalin in 1928, the Soviet Union began a series of five-year economic plans, in which the Communist government set goals and plans for the entire economy. Millions of people were put into labor camps and provided free work on major construction projects. Millions of people died of starvation during the early 1930s when the Soviet government forced peasants to combine their farms into large, government-run collectives.

Dictators Arise Around the World. In 1922, Benito Mussolini came to power as the dictator in Italy. Many claimed that Mussolini would make the economy of Italy work better. For example, some said that he made the trains run on time. However, economic improvements came at the expense of the Italian people's freedoms.

As the 1930s began to unfold, many countries throughout the world were experiencing economic trouble and social turmoil. In Germany, people began to turn to leaders they thought could get them out of their economic trouble. In 1933 the National Socialist (Nazi) party, led by Adolf Hitler, came to power in the country of Germany. Hitler promised the German people economic revival and revenge against those who had defeated them in the Great War. Germany and Italy became friends with each other during the 1930s. Hitler promised the German people a thousand-year long empire, but, after only twelve years of rule, he provided only war and death in Germany and the rest of Europe.

Dictatorship spread to Spain in the late 1930s. War broke out between the Nationalist movement and the Republican government during the Spanish Civil War. During the war, both sides received support from other countries. The Germans and Italians sent thousands of troops, airplanes, tanks, and military supplies to the Nationalists, while the Soviet Union sent some soldiers and sold military equipment to the Republican government. It was almost as if the Spanish Civil War was practice for the upcoming World War II in Europe. The Nationalists won the war in 1939 and established a new dictatorship in Spain under the leadership of Francisco Franco.

On the other side of the world, a series of military-dominated governments came to power in Japan during the 1930s, which led Japan into a policy of territorial expansion against neighboring countries in the 1930s and 1940s. The trend toward military governments in Japan culminated in the appointment of a strong Japanese military leader, General Hideki Tojo, who was appointed Minister of War in 1940 and Premier in 1941. It was General Tojo who led Japan into war with the United States.

The aggressiveness of these dictatorships led the world into another world war. In the 1930s, Japan attacked China, killing many people in their quest for land and power, and fought a border war with the Soviet Union. Italy conquered Albania and Ethiopia during this same decade. Germany peacefully took over Austria, Czechoslovakia, and part of Lithuania during this time. Japan joined in friendship with Germany and Italy, and these countries—known as the Axis powers—tried to help each other during World War II.

World War II. America tried to stay out of these troubles during the 1930s. Congress passed neutrality laws to prevent the sale of weapons to warring nations. Most people did not want the United States to get involved in another war. However, Roosevelt understood that the American defenses needed to be improved and began, therefore, a rearmament program in 1938.

However, opinion began to change after the Japanese renewed their attacks on China in 1937 and the Germans invaded Poland on September 1, 1939. Congress passed a "Cash and Carry" law two months later, which allowed countries to buy military supplies if they could pay cash and carry them on their own ships. Research on a possible atomic bomb—in what later became known as the Manhattan Project—was begun soon after World War II began in Europe.

After the Germans conquered Denmark, Norway, Belgium, the Netherlands, and France between April and June 1940, and began bombing Britain, President Roosevelt realized that more was needed to help countries fighting against the Axis powers. Several weeks after he won the 1940 election, President Roosevelt gave one of his "fireside chats." In this radio address to the nation, he told Americans that the United States "… must be the great arsenal of democracy." America must build the weapons it needed to defend itself and to provide support for those fighting against the Germans, Italians, and Japanese. President Roosevelt's promise of America being an "arsenal for democracy" was put into effect in early 1941, when Congress passed his lend-lease proposal, which provided military supplies to countries fighting the Axis powers. Through the lend-lease program, the United States gave over $50 billion worth of military supplies to Great Britain, the Soviet Union, China, France, and other countries between 1941 and 1945.

Roosevelt also began to take steps to improve America's defenses and more directly oppose the Axis powers. He convinced Congress to approve America's first peacetime draft to provide men for the Army and Navy in 1940. In September of the same year, the United States agreed to trade fifty destroyers to the British for naval and air bases in British colonial territories near the United States. In 1941, American warships began to protect supply ships going to Britain and were authorized to fire on any Ger-

Hideki Tojo (1884–1948)

Jack Aeby, US Department of Energy

Photograph of First Nuclear Test Explosion by the Manhattan Project

Roosevelt gave his fireside chats to encourage people to put their faith in the banks and to support his New Deal programs.

U.S. Army Center of Military History

Go For Broke

After the Japanese attack on Pearl Harbor, many in the government and military distrusted Japanese residents and Japanese-American citizens. Would these people be loyal to the United States? The members of the 442nd Regimental Combat Team proved that they were. The 442nd was primarily made up of Nisei, the sons of Japanese immigrants to the United States, from Hawaii and the mainland. The soldiers from the mainland of the United States were largely recruited from the internment camps, where they and their families had been sent from their West coast homes. This unit became the most highly decorated unit of its size—including 21 men earning the Medal of Honor—with over 9,000 gaining Purple Heart awards for being wounded in combat, and winning seven Presidential Unit Citations. One part of the regiment had so many wounded that it became known as the Purple Heart Battalion.

The 442nd Regiment's motto was "Go For Broke," which was taken from a Hawaiian phrase referring to a willingness to "risk it all" to gain a desired end. After training, it was sent to Italy, where it spent most of its time in Europe. The 442nd's most famous action, however, was in southern France during 1944. In a grueling fight over five days, the 442nd *went for broke* to rescue the "Lost Battalion," about 210 soldiers from a different unit who had been surrounded by the Germans. These brave Japanese-American soldiers suffered several hundred wounded and 121 dead, proving their sacrificial loyalty to the United States.

man ships or submarines that attacked ships under their protection. The United States Navy also began to provide help to British ships at American naval bases. After the Japanese occupied the entire French colony of Indochina—now Vietnam, Cambodia, and Laos—Roosevelt cut off sales of oil to Japan. Additional military forces were sent to the Philippines to help protect the islands from a possible Japanese attack.

War came to the United States on December 7, 1941, when the Japanese attacked American bases in Hawaii before Japan actually declared war on the United States. The Japanese attack was very successful—eighteen ships were sunk (including five battleships) and several others were damaged, 2,386 Americans were killed and 1,139 were wounded, and almost 190 American aircraft were destroyed or damaged. Soon afterwards, the Japanese attacked American bases in the Philippines, Guam, and other Pacific islands, as well as the British colonies of Hong Kong and Malaya. President Roosevelt spoke to Congress the next day, calling for a declaration of war and declaring that December 7 would be "… a date which will live in infamy…." Three days later, on December 11, Germany and Italy declared war on the United States. The United States was now at war with all of the Axis powers.

Roosevelt believed that Germany was more dangerous than Japan. Therefore, he decided to focus American resources on the war in Europe. American forces worked with the British to defeat the Germans in the Mediterranean area and northwestern Europe. At the same time, American forces, after suffering defeats by the Japanese during the first six months of the war, went on the offensive, pushing the Japanese back across the Pacific toward the Japanese home islands. During the war, Roosevelt met several times with important foreign leaders to coordinate strategy for the war and afterwards. A few months before the war ended, Franklin Roosevelt died on April 12, 1945.

Although Roosevelt provided effective leadership during the war, it was not without controversy. President Roosevelt approved the removal of approximately 120,000 Japanese and Japanese-American residents—over 60% of which were American citizens—of California, Oregon, and Washington State to camps in the interior of the nation. Although aliens of other enemy countries—such as Germany and Italy—were also interned, no citizens of German or Italian ancestry were placed under custody; only Japanese-American citizens were placed in camps. Some people were concerned that they would be loyal to Japan, not the United States, but the FBI never found any evidence of espionage by Japanese-American citizens.

President Roosevelt has also been accused of being naïve in his dealings with Joseph Stalin and the Soviet Union. This concern has been particularly raised regarding the Yalta Conference. In February 1945, Roosevelt met with Stalin and Winston Churchill (the prime minister of Great Britain) at Yalta, on the Black Sea in the Soviet Union, to discuss the end of the war and the condition of Europe after the war. Roosevelt was willing to make concessions to Stalin to ensure that the Soviet Union became part of the new United Nations and entered the war against Japan. In addition, he accepted Stalin's assurances that free elections would be held in Eastern Europe—especially with regard to Poland—none of which came true. Of course, the fact that the Soviet army occupied the countries of Eastern Europe made it impossible to compel the Russians to allow free governments without another war, but Roosevelt was unwilling to support even peaceful actions to encourage free elections.

Summary. For most of the 1920s, America was doing very well. Its economy was the envy of much of the world, and many did very well during the 1920s. However, the United States' economy went into a serious depression in 1929. President Franklin D. Roosevelt greatly increased the size and power of the federal government in an effort to combat the effects of the Great Depression. Roosevelt went on to lead the United States during the Second World War.

The "Big Three"—Winston Churchill, Franklin Roosevelt, and Joseph Stalin—at the Yalta Conference, 1945

The 1920s and 1930s saw the rise of several dictatorships around the world. The Communists gained complete control of Russia in 1921 and began a reign of terror. Dictators also came to power in Italy, Germany, and Japan as people looked for strong leaders to bring an end to their troubles. These aggressive dictatorships led the world into World War II, the most devastating war ever known in human history.

Comprehension Questions

1. Who made the first solo, non-stop airplane flight from the United States to Europe?

2. During what year did the Great Depression begin in America?

3. How successful were the New Deal programs in ending the Great Depression?

4. Who were the two most important leaders in Russia during the 1920s and 1930s?

5. In what year did Adolf Hitler come to power in Germany?

6. Who was Hideki Tojo?

7. How did the United States enter World War II?

8. What country did President Roosevelt believe was the most dangerous enemy during World War II?

Chapter 36
Douglas MacArthur (1880–1964)

Douglas MacArthur (1880–1964)

General Arthur MacArthur, Jr.
(1845–1912)
Father of Douglas MacArthur

Douglas MacArthur was one of America's greatest soldiers. He led men in three wars, attained the highest rank in the United States Army, helped to transform the nation of Japan, and prevented South Korea from being overrun by communist North Korea. General Matthew Ridgeway, who served with MacArthur in Korea and later replaced him as the commander of American forces in the Far East, remarked, "[W]hen Fate suddenly decided that I would serve directly under him in Korea, I welcomed the chance to associate once again with one of the few geniuses it has been my privilege to know."

Douglas MacArthur Was Born to Be a Soldier. In 1880, Douglas MacArthur was born in Little Rock, Arkansas, into a military family. His father, Arthur MacArthur, earned the Congressional Medal of Honor for his service during the War Between the States, or the American Civil War. Arthur MacArthur became a career soldier and had a varied career. He served on the frontier in the West and fought in the Philippines during and after the Spanish-American War. He retired as a lieutenant general.

Douglas MacArthur followed in his father's footsteps. He went to school at home as a young boy and then went to a military preparatory school in Texas. MacArthur attended the United States Military Academy at West Point, where he graduated first in his class in 1900. He became a second lieutenant in the United States Army Corps of Engineers and was initially sent to the Philippines, where he served with his father. Douglas MacArthur, like his father, was a brave soldier. He was first recommended for a Medal of Honor for personal bravery during the Vera Cruz Expedition in Mexico in 1914. Although he did not receive the Medal of Honor then, he would later be awarded several different medals, including the Medal of Honor, during World War II.

MacArthur left the engineers for the infantry in early 1917—shortly before the United States entered World War I and after being promoted to the rank of colonel. After the United States entered the war, he went to France with the 42nd Infantry Division. During his time in France, MacArthur was promoted to brigadier general and later, just before the war ended, commanded the division for a short period of time.

MacArthur's practice was to lead his men from the front. He earned a reputation during the war for being one of the Army's greatest fighting men and was the most decorated American officer of the war. Among his many medals were two Purple Hearts for being wounded in action. MacArthur often refused to wear a gas mask—even when his men used their masks— which contributed to breathing problems the rest of his life.

Between the World Wars. After World War I, MacArthur was appointed superintendent of the United States Military Academy at West Point in 1919. During his time at West Point, MacArthur made many improvements to the military academy. After finishing his time at West Point, MacArthur was assigned several important positions, including two tours of duty in the Philippines. In 1925, he was promoted to the rank of major general, the youngest officer of that rank at the time. In 1930, Douglas MacArthur was appointed Chief of Staff of the Army, giving him command of the entire Army.

One of Douglas MacArthur's most controversial actions occurred while he was chief of staff. In 1932, during one of the worst periods of the Great Depression, up to 20,000 World War I veterans and their families went to Washington, D.C., to demand an early payment of a bonus that Congress had promised to give them in 1945. They began arriving in May and started calling themselves the "Bonus Army." They camped in city parks, occupied abandoned buildings, and established a "shantytown" in Washington, D.C.

Congress failed to give the bonus early, and several thousand disappointed veterans took the government's offer of free transportation home. However, most still remained in Washington. Tensions rose during the summer as the remaining veterans became frustrated with the lack of action on their concerns. To make matters worse, the American Communist party took advantage of this situation by trying to cause trouble. Very few of the veterans and their supporters were actually Communists, but those that were there did help create problems in Washington.

On July 28, the police were ordered to clear out the veterans occupying some abandoned buildings. A fight broke out, and some of the police were threatened with serious injury. They fired in response, killing two veterans. The police could not handle the situation; therefore, the Army was called out to evict the veterans. The soldiers exceeded their orders and forced all of the Bonus Army out of Washington. This was accomplished without any shootings and with few casualties; however, the public did not like to see the Army using cavalry, tanks, tear gas, and bayonets against veterans and their families. To make things even worse for General MacArthur, he was directing the attack against the Bonus Army.

After MacArthur's time as chief of staff ended in 1935, he returned to the Philippines to become the military advisor to the president of the new commonwealth government of the Philippines. MacArthur's job was to assist the Philippines in developing an army as it prepared for independence from the United States. In 1937, MacArthur retired from the Army and remained in the Philippines to continue to help develop its defenses.

Guy Gabaldon (1926–2006)

Pied Piper of Saipan

During World War II, the Japanese were very reluctant to surrender to American forces. The Japanese would often kill themselves rather than surrender because they usually thought it was dishonorable to give up rather than die for their emperor. For example, on the island of Saipan in the Pacific, approximately 22,000 Japanese civilians and 30,000 Japanese soldiers died during June and July 1944 rather than surrender to an American invasion force. One man, however, was able to persuade many Japanese soldiers and civilians to surrender to American military forces. Guy Gabaldon, a young Mexican-American Marine from Los Angeles who had lived for a time with a Japanese-American family, became known as the Pied Piper of Saipan because of his ability to convince approximately 1,500 Japanese to give themselves up. Gabaldon, who was part of the American invasion force, used his knowledge of the Japanese language to talk many into surrendering. On one occasion, he brought back 800 prisoners. Although Galbadon was later wounded in battle, he survived and was awarded the Navy Cross—the second highest medal that could be given to servicemen in the Navy and Marines—for his bravery.

America Enters World War II. The world went to war again in 1939. World War II officially began on September 1, 1939, when Germany invaded Poland. Later, the armies from the Soviet Union (Russia) also invaded the country of Poland. Poland was quickly taken over by these two countries. On September 3, 1939, Britain and France declared war on Germany—Europe was at war again. By June 1941, just before Germany invaded the Soviet Union, the Germans and their allies had conquered almost all of Europe. The United States, however, was still at peace.

This is a photograph of the USS *West Virginia*, one of eight battleships that were severely damaged during the Japanese attack on Pearl Harbor.

It was Japan that forced the United States into World War II. Japan had already been at war with China, and America had been trying to peacefully help the Chinese. Japan decided to attack the American naval and air bases in and near Pearl Harbor, Hawaii. This was to keep the United States from interfering with its plans to invade other lands in Southeast Asia and the East Indies. Without warning, on December 7, 1941, Japanese planes from aircraft carriers attacked American naval and air forces stationed in the Hawaiian Islands. The attack resulted in the deaths of thousands of American sailors and soldiers and severe damage to their ships and airplanes. In response, the Congress of the United States declared war against Japan on December 8, 1941. Germany and Italy then declared war on the United States on December 11, 1941. America was now a full-fledged participant in the war.

When war with Japan seemed likely in 1941, President Roosevelt called Douglas MacArthur back into service with the United States Army to command the combined United States and Filipino armed forces in the Philippines. After the Japanese attacked America at Pearl Harbor, they captured American, British, and Dutch possessions throughout the Pacific region during the following six months.

War came to the Philippines on December 8. The Japanese achieved surprise in their initial air attacks on American air and naval bases—in spite of the warning of war with Japan due to the attack on Pearl Harbor—heavily damaging these bases and destroying up to half of the U.S. Air Force in the area. Soon afterwards, Japanese troops began to land in the Philippines. American and Filipino forces retreated to the Bataan Peninsula but were forced to surrender on April 9, 1942. The remaining American and Filipino forces in the rest of the Philippines surrendered on May 6, 1942.

General MacArthur reluctantly left the Philippines for Australia on March 11, 1942, after being ordered to do so by President Roosevelt. Soon after arriving in Australia, MacArthur said the following to reporters:

> The President of the United States ordered me to break through the Japanese lines and proceed from Corregidor [in the Philippines] to Australia for the purpose, as I understand it, of organizing the American offensive against Japan, a primary objective of which is the relief of the Philippines. I came through and I shall return.

"I shall return" became MacArthur's motto for the Filipinos. For his bravery and leadership in the defense of the Philippines, General MacArthur was awarded the Congressional Medal of Honor.

On October 20, 1944, General MacArthur—covered by aircraft from the U.S. Third Fleet under the command of Admiral William "Bull" Halsey—landed at Leyte Island, keeping his promise to return to the Philippines.

Victory over Japan. After arriving in Australia in 1942, General MacArthur was given command of all Allied forces in the Southwest Pacific region. He was unable to immediately return to the Philippines because of the advance of the Japanese. Instead, he helped to organize the offensive against the Japanese conquests. American and Australian forces stopped the Japanese advance in New Guinea and then pushed them back in a fight that lasted throughout the rest of the war. On October 20, 1944, General MacArthur fulfilled his promise to return to the Philippines when the United States Army landed on the island of Leyte. Manila, the capital of the Philippines, was liberated in March 1945 after a devastating month-long battle. In December 1944, Douglas MacArthur was promoted to the rank of General of the Army, becoming one of only five generals to become a five-star general.

Navajo Code Talkers

Code Talkers

One of the most important, yet least known, secrets of the Pacific campaign of World War II is the use of Navajo code talkers with the Marine Corps. Most code talkers were Navajo Indians who served as part of the Marines and served as part of communication units. They would translate military terms and words into a Navajo code and then back into English. Because few non-natives understood Navajo and few books were printed in Navajo, it was a useful language to use as a code. The Marines developed a code based on Navajo letters and words so that even Navajos who did not know the code would find it hard to break. For example, the Navajo word for "potato" was the code for hand grenade and the Navajo word for "tortoise" was the code for tank. This was important because many Japanese had studied in the United States and knew English well. The Japanese never broke the Navajo code, even after they had captured a Navajo soldier who did not know the code. The Navajo code talkers played an important role in the victory over Japan; high-ranking officers have said that they do not think the Americans would have won the Battle of Iwo Jima without the work of the code talkers. The Marine Corps also used Navajo code talkers during the Korean War, but stopped doing so early in the Vietnam War. The role of the code talkers was kept secret until 1968, and official recognition was delayed until 1982.

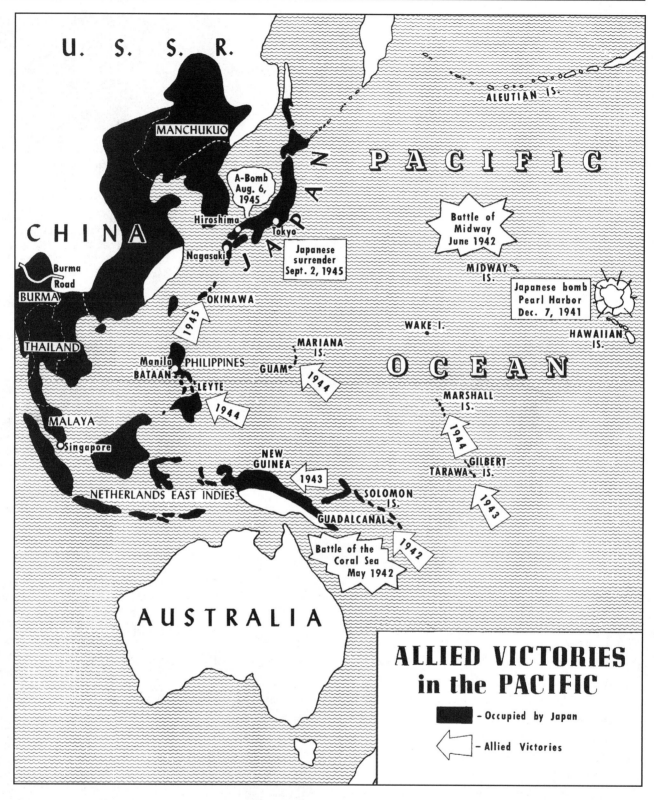

Even as General MacArthur was leading an offensive against the Japanese in the southwest Pacific, other Allied forces were fighting the Japanese. The United States Navy won an important naval battle against the Japanese at the Battle of Midway in June 1942 (*see map above*), seriously weakening the Japanese Navy. Later that same year, American forces began a long offensive against the Japanese in the Pacific. They practiced an "island hopping" strategy, capturing important Japanese-held islands while isolating others to let them "wither on the vine." By early 1945, American forces had advanced far enough toward Japan that they were able to capture the Japanese islands of Iwo Jima and Okinawa, helping to prepare the way for an invasion of the Japanese main islands. Even as the Americans were advancing in the Pacific, the British defeated a Japanese invasion of India and then went on to recapture their colony of Burma.

The fighting with Japan dragged on until August 1945. Even though it was clear that the Japanese were losing, they continued to fight. American planes severely bombed several Japanese cities, and U.S. submarines continued to sink Japanese ships. MacArthur was given command of all United States Army forces in the Pacific and began to help prepare for a possible invasion of Japan. However, an invasion was not needed. Japan stopped fighting after the United States dropped atomic bombs on two Japanese cities on August 6 and 8, 1945, and the Soviet Union declared war on Japan and attacked Japanese forces in China and Korea. President Harry S. Truman, who had become President after Franklin Roosevelt died of a heart attack, decided to drop these bombs on Japan after it seemed that both the Americans and Japanese would suffer terrible casualties if Japan were invaded. The atomic age had begun in a dreadful manner.

The atomic bomb that was dropped on Nagasaki, Japan, caused about 35,000 deaths and horrible, extensive devastation.

World War II officially ended on September 2, 1945, after Japan signed the surrender agreements on board the American battleship USS *Missouri*. General MacArthur was at the Japanese surrender, along with representatives of the other victorious countries. The world could at last rejoice in the fact that World War II was over. This war was the most destructive and horrible war that the world has ever known. Let us hope, by God's grace, that there will never be such a terrible war again.

General MacArthur went on to command the American occupation forces in Japan and was responsible for the reconstruction of Japan. MacArthur was appointed the Supreme Commander of Allied Powers for the occupation of Japan. He held this position until General Matthew Ridgeway replaced him in 1951. As Supreme Commander, MacArthur and his staff made arrangements for Japanese war crimes trials, helped

On September 2, 1945, the Japanese surrendered to General Douglas MacArthur aboard USS *Missouri*. The unconditional surrender of the Japanese to the Allies officially ended the Second World War.

write a new constitution for Japan, and reformed the Japanese economy. By the time Japan regained its independence in 1952, it had been transformed by Allied occupation, much of the work having been done at the direction of General MacArthur.

One of the first major international crises of the Cold War was the Berlin Blockade (June 1948–May 1949), in which the Soviet Union blocked railroads and highways into the portions of West Berlin that were controlled by the United States, the United Kingdom, and France. In response, the Western Allies formed the Berlin Airlift to supply the city. Above, West Berliners watch as a Douglas C-54 Skymaster lands at Tempelhof Airport with needed resources.

The Korean War. After World War II was over, a new threat to the nations of the world arose. The armed forces of the Soviet Union (Russia) had taken over most of Eastern Europe and the northern part of Korea during World War II. They did not want to give up their control of these countries. Communist governments were established in most of the areas that had been occupied by the armies of the Soviet Union during the Second World War. Communist forces in China won a civil war and took over the mainland of the country in 1949, while the Nationalist Chinese government was forced to retreat to the island of Taiwan.

A type of "Cold War" began to develop. A cold war is mostly a war of words between countries that do not agree with each other; however, it can include military and economic support for threatened areas. In 1949, the countries of Western Europe, Canada, and the United States established a military alliance known as the North Atlantic Treaty Organization (NATO) to oppose Soviet moves in Europe. The United States would later establish alliances with countries around the world to help fight against the spread of Communist forces.

In 1950, the Cold War became hot in Korea. On June 25, 1950, Soviet-equipped Communist forces of North Korea launched a surprise invasion of the non-communist country of South Korea to bring the entire peninsula under Communist control. This act led to the Korean War.

In spite of the surprise attack, world reaction was swift. The United Nations, an organization that had been developed just before the end of World War II in the hope that nations could meet together on a regular basis and solve their problems without war, decided the same day as the North Korean invasion to help the South Koreans. Soldiers and supplies from fifteen other countries were sent to help the South Koreans defend themselves. General Douglas MacArthur was chosen as Supreme Commander of the United Nations' forces. However, most of the soldiers who fought under MacArthur in Korea were Americans and South Koreans.

American Soldiers in the Korean War

The Korean War lasted for three years. The North Koreans were very successful at first and almost captured the entire peninsula of Korea. However, their advance was finally halted and then defeated after General MacArthur led a successful landing of troops behind North Korean lines. United Nations troops went on to invade North Korea and almost captured the entire country before the Communist government in China decided to send soldiers to help the North Koreans. The UN forces were surprised by the Chinese attack and had to retreat from North Korea, but were able to successfully

After Japan surrendered in 1945, the 38th parallel was established as the boundary between North and South Korea. During the Korean War, South Korean and UN troops were forced to withdraw behind this line.

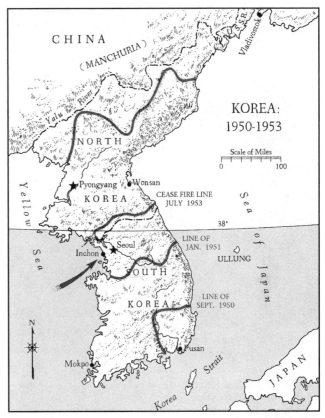

defeat further Chinese and North Korean attempts to conquer South Korea.

The fighting finally ended after both sides signed a truce on March 5, 1953, but no final peace treaty was ever agreed upon. General MacArthur was not part of this peace because he had been relieved of duty by President Truman on April 11, 1951, due to disagreements on how the war should be fought. The United States has maintained forces in South Korea ever since the war to help defend the country against another possible attack by North Korea.

Summary. One of America's greatest soldiers in the twentieth century was General MacArthur. He bravely led soldiers in France during World War I, helped lead the fight against Japan during World War II, reformed Japan, and saved South Korea during the early part of the Korean War. This military hero often reminded the American people that in war there is no substitute for victory.

In September 1950, U.S. Marines fought North Koreans in the streets of Seoul, Korea.

Comprehension Questions

1. Where did Douglas MacArthur study to be a soldier?

2. What branch of the Army did MacArthur join when he first became an officer? What branch did he join shortly before the United States entered World War I?

3. What did the veterans who went to Washington, D.C., in 1932 call themselves?

4. What did MacArthur do before World War II to help the Philippines?

5. What was MacArthur's motto for the Philippines after he was forced to leave the islands?

6. Why did the Japanese finally stop fighting?

7. List two ways MacArthur helped Japan after World War II.

8. Which countries attempted to conquer south Korea?

Chapter 37
Dwight D. Eisenhower (1890–1969)

Dwight David "Ike" Eisenhower
(1890–1969)

On July 1, 1916, Dwight Eisenhower married Mamie Geneva Doud at the home of her parents in Denver. They are shown above at St. Mary's University of San Antonio, Texas, where he was the football coach.

An Unlikely Soldier. World War II saw the rise of many important American commanders. We have already learned about Douglas MacArthur and his work in the Pacific. Another great general of World War II was Dwight Eisenhower. The two men were very different from one another, yet each in his own way was crucial to the winning of the war.

Dwight Eisenhower did not seem destined for the Army. As a child, he wanted to be a professional baseball player, not a soldier. His mother's various religious affiliations were anti-military. She grew up in a branch of the Mennonites and later joined the Jehovah Witness sect when Eisenhower was a young child. For several years, Jehovah Witness meetings were held in the Eisenhower home in Kansas.

In spite of his mother's religious influence and his desire to be a baseball player, Dwight Eisenhower went to the United States Military Academy at West Point, New York, in 1911. He graduated in 1915 and was commissioned an infantry officer in the United States Army. Eisenhower served at a variety of bases in the United States, Panama, and the Philippines before World War II. He never led men in combat but was recognized as one of the Army's best staff officers, excelling in planning, organizing, and training. He served under several of the Army's top generals in the 1920s and 1930s, including General Pershing and General MacArthur. From 1935 to 1939, Eisenhower served in the Philippines with General MacArthur as assistant military advisor to the Philippine government. One of his more important experiences was working with tanks for a time during and after World War I.

World War II Begins. World War II officially began on September 1, 1939, when Germany invaded Poland. The armies from the Soviet Union later invaded the country of Poland. Poland was quickly taken over by these two countries. On September 3, 1939, Britain and France declared war on Germany, and the whole of Europe was soon at war.

In less than three months (April–June 1940), Germany conquered Denmark, Norway, Belgium, the Netherlands, Luxembourg, and France, and forced the British Army off of the continent of Europe. German airplanes inflicted a lot of damage with bombing attacks on British cities in what is known as the Battle of Britain. In 1941, Germany turned toward North Africa and Eastern Europe. Yugoslavia and Greece were defeated, and German troops were sent to Hungary, Bulgaria, and Rumania. On June 22, 1941, Germany invaded the Soviet Union and was very successful at first. Still, America refused to enter the war at that time. It would take the country of Japan to force the United States into World War II.

America entered the war on December 7, 1941, after its naval and air forces stationed at Pearl Harbor in the Hawaiian Islands were attacked by Japanese airplanes. The attack resulted in the deaths of thousands of American sailors and soldiers, and severe damage to the ships and airplanes at the base. In response, the Congress of the United States declared war against Japan on December 8, 1941. Germany and Italy then declared war on the United States on December 11, 1941.

Early on December 7, 1941, Japanese aircraft and submarines began a surprise attack on the U.S. naval base at Pearl Harbor, Hawaii. The battleship *Arizona* (shown above) was hit with a bomb that penetrated one of its ammunition compartments—the ship blew up and sank within seconds. All together, nine U.S. ships were sunk and twenty-one were severely damaged; over 2,000 armed servicemen and nearly seventy civilians were killed.

America was now a full-fledged participant in the war. Soon after the Japanese attacked Pearl Harbor, they invaded several of Britain's colonies in Asia and the Pacific, as well as the Dutch East Indies and the American territory of the Philippine Islands. These actions turned what had been two separate wars—the war in Europe and Japan's war of conquest in China—into a war that was truly worldwide.

The Tide Turns. German and Italian armed forces continued their winning ways for a while in 1942. German submarines sank many American and British ships in the Atlantic Ocean. Although the Soviets had been able to push the German armies back from their capital city of Moscow, the Germans launched a new offensive in the summer that conquered much of southern Russia. German and Italian armies advanced deep into Egypt in 1942.

However, the success of the Germans and Italians soon ended. The British had already conquered the Italian holdings in East Africa (including Ethiopia) in 1941 and were able to stop the German and Italian offensive in Egypt by the summer of 1942. In October, the British armies in Egypt began an offensive of their own that forced the German and Italian armies out of Egypt and Libya and into French Tunisia. American and British forces invaded French North Africa in November 1942 and, with the British army attacking from Libya, forced the Germans and Italians in Tunisia to surrender in May 1943.

During the First Battle of El Alamein (July 1942), the British infantry stopped the Germans and Italians from advancing further into Egypt. During the Second Battle of El Alamein, Britain's Field Marshal Montgomery led Allied forces in attacking and defeating the German Afrika Korps led by Field Marshal Rommel. This battle was considered the turning point of World War II—Winston Churchill wrote, "Before Alamein we had no victory, and after it we had no defeats."

In the East, the Germans were defeated in late 1942 and early 1943 at the Battle of Stalingrad, losing an entire army in the process. The Soviets also defeated the Germans' summer offensive in 1943. While much hard fighting remained in the East, the Soviets began to drive the German armies from their territory. In 1943, the British and American navies were finally able to get the German submarines under control. The American and British air forces began a bombing campaign on German targets, which would continue and grow throughout the rest of the war. By September 1943, American and British forces were able to force Italy to surrender after capturing the island of Sicily and invading the Italian mainland.

Eisenhower played an important role in turning the tide against the Germans and Italians in the Mediterranean region. He commanded the forces

During the first days of the Invasion of Normandy, Allied troops and supplies were unloaded on Omaha Beach at low tide (mid-June 1944).

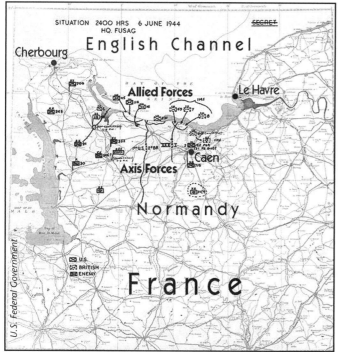

This official U.S. 12th Army map shows the exact positions of the landing operations set for midnight, launching D-Day (June 6, 1944).

that invaded French North Africa. Eisenhower was also in charge of the invasion of the Italian island of Sicily and the following invasion of the Italian mainland. He gained experience working with allied British and French forces and came to know a number of the commanders who would later be involved in the invasion of France.

Germany Is Defeated. By the middle of 1944, Germany still held considerable territory but was in a dangerous position. The Soviets were advancing in the East, and the Allies (the United States, Great Britain, France, and Canada) were fighting in Italy and getting ready to attack the Germans in France. General Eisenhower had already been appointed Supreme Allied Commander in Europe and had gone to England to prepare for the invasion of France. On June 6, 1944, British, Canadian, and American forces invaded northern France from Britain, on what is now known as D-Day; and French and American troops attacked southern France on August 15, 1944. The Soviets also began massive offensives during the summer of 1944.

Much hard fighting remained; the Germans were not willing to simply give up. Even after they were forced out of most of France and Belgium, they launched an attack against American forces in December 1944 in what is now known as the Battle of the Bulge. The German attack was

Willie and Joe

"You blokes leave an awfully messy battlefield."

"Willie and Joe" were characters in a series of cartoons drawn by Bill Mauldin (1921–2003) for various military newspapers—most importantly *Stars and Stripes*, which was distributed to American soldiers in Europe—and reprinted in newspapers in the United States. Mauldin was himself a soldier who had participated in the invasions of Sicily and Italy before being assigned to a full-time position as a cartoonist for *Stars and Stripes*. "Willie and Joe" represented the average American combat soldier and were based on soldiers Bill Mauldin knew. Enlisted soldiers enjoyed Mauldin's cartoons, although some officers—including General Patton—took offense at the way officers were often portrayed in the cartoons.

In this picture, a British soldier is commenting to Willie and Joe as they are leaving the battlefield about how messy they had left things. This cartoon contrasts how Americans were prone to litter the field with equipment, while the British were much thriftier and neater, even in war. This cartoon is based on action in Anzio, Italy, where British and American troops fought together against the Germans.

Department of Defense

"You blokes leave an awfully messy battlefield."

defeated, however, and the Allied armies under the command of General Eisenhower invaded Germany the next spring. The Soviets also invaded Germany and captured the German capital of Berlin on May 2, 1945. American and Soviet forces met each other on April 25, 1945, thus cutting Germany in two. Germany finally surrendered on May 8, 1945. In less than a year after the D-Day invasion, the people of Europe had been freed from Hitler's control, and Germany had been crushed.

Shortly before the final defeat of Germany, the leaders of the United States, Italy, and Germany died. President Roosevelt died of a heart attack on April 12, 1945. On April 28, 1945, Italians who were opposed to the Germans killed Mussolini. Hitler killed himself on April 30, 1945, before he could be captured by the Soviets.

Each nation had brave and skillful commanders. Marshal Georgy Zhukov, who was the Soviet Union's most decorated soldier, led Soviet forces to several victories, including the successful defense of Moscow and the destruction of the German army at Stalingrad. Generals George S. Patton and Omar Bradley led the American armies to victory against the Germans and Italians. Britain's best-known general was Bernard Montgomery. Dwight Eisenhower was recognized for

CLOSING IN ON GERMANY

his successful command of Allied forces in Europe by being promoted to General of the Army (five-star general) in December 1944, the same rank to which Douglas MacArthur had been promoted.

The Cold War Begins. After World War II was over, most people wanted peace. There was great hope that the new United Nations would be able to keep the peace between the nations. The troops wanted to come home and return to civilian life. Dwight Eisenhower was promoted to the position of Chief of Staff of the Army in 1945, and much of his work was to oversee an orderly reduction of the Army. The United States armed forces—Army, Navy, and Marines—went from 12 million in June 1945 to about 1.5 million in June 1947. In 1948, Eisenhower himself retired, becoming the president of Columbia University in New York City.

However, a new threat to the nations of the world arose. The forces of communism in the Soviet Union had taken over most of Eastern Europe and the northern part of Korea during World War II and did not want to give up their control of these countries. Communist governments were established in most of the areas that had been occupied by the armies of the Soviet Union during the Second World War. Communists completed their

Prime Minister Winston Churchill greets crowds in London on Victory in Europe Day—May 8, 1945. This is the day that the Nazis surrendered in a suburb of Berlin, Germany.

take-over of Eastern Europe with the overthrow of a democratic government in Czechoslovakia in 1948. The Soviets blockaded the land routes to the city of Berlin in the same year; and, for several months, the British and American air forces had to send supplies to the city by air. Yugoslavia and Albania were taken over by local Communist forces. Communists in Greece and China were engaged in rebellions against the governments of their countries. Although Greece was able to remain outside of Communist control, the Communist Chinese movement under the leadership of Mao Tse-tung took over Mainland China in 1949. The Nationalist Chinese government was forced to retreat to the island of Taiwan.

A type of "Cold War" began to develop after World War II between the United States and the Soviet Union. There was concern that Joseph Stalin, who was still the leader in the Soviet Union, was looking for more power in Europe and Asia. It was a time of competition and tension between these two countries and their allies in a wide variety of areas, but especially in international politics, development of military strength, and economics. The United States and Soviet Union never fought a war against each other, but each provided military and economic support for what they considered threatened areas.

The United States began to provide financial and military assistance to many countries. The first step was to establish an economic recovery plan for Western Europe called the Marshall Plan—named after Secretary of State George Marshall, who promoted it—which began in 1947 and lasted for four years. The Soviet Union and Eastern European countries were invited to participate, but they rejected the offer.

The United States also established alliances with countries around the world to help fight against the spread of Communist forces. America's most important alliance was established in 1949. The countries of Western Europe, Canada, and the United States established an alliance known as the North Atlantic Treaty Organization (NATO) to oppose Soviet moves in Europe. At first, NATO did not have a military organization; it was largely a political alliance. However, with the invasion of South Korea in 1950 by the Communist North Korea, it was believed necessary that NATO become a more effective military alliance.

In December 1950, President Harry Truman recalled Dwight Eisenhower to military service and sent him to Europe to become the first Supreme Allied Commander for NATO. During his time as commander, he directed the buildup of military forces to defend against a possible Soviet invasion of Western Europe. In the spring of 1952, Eisenhower resigned his position and returned to the United States.

"I Like Ike." Eisenhower was persuaded to run for President of the United States in 1952. One of his most effective campaign slogans was "I like Ike." He was greatly respected and admired by many people and was overwhelmingly elected as the thirty-fourth President of the United States. Eisenhower held the office of President for eight years, winning reelection in 1956.

Mao Tse-tung (1893–1976)

Joseph Stalin (1878–1953)

General Dwight D. Eisenhower
First Supreme Allied Commander
of NATO

On February 7, 1954, Rev. George MacPherson Docherty (*left*) spoke on the principle of a nation "under God." President Eisenhower (*second from left*) was so moved that he decided that the pledge needed to be amended.

Pledge of Allegiance

I pledge allegiance to the flag of the United States of America, and to the Republic for which it stands: one Nation under God, indivisible, With Liberty and Justice for all.

On February 7, 1954—Lincoln Sunday—Eisenhower declared:

"These words [*under God*] will remind Americans that despite our great physical strength we must remain humble. They will help us to keep constantly in our minds and hearts the spiritual and moral principles which alone give dignity to man, and upon which our way of life is founded."

On February 8, 1954, Congressman Charles Oakman of Michigan introduced the bill to the House of Representatives that would add the words "under God" to the Pledge of Allegiance. Senator Homer S. Ferguson, also of Michigan, introduced the bill to the Senate. President Eisenhower signed the bill into law on Flag Day, June 14, 1954.

The Eisenhower Interstate System was authorized by the Federal-Aid Highway Act of 1956.

Shortly after Eisenhower was inaugurated President in 1953, he joined a Christian church for the first time. He was baptized and became a communicant member of the Presbyterian church. He continued his membership after retirement, joining a local Presbyterian congregation after moving to Gettysburg, Pennsylvania.

Eisenhower's presidency was a period of relative peace, and the American people turned their attention to solving problems within their own land. One of the greatest problems in America at this time was racial discrimination. Many people in America who had black, brown, yellow, or red skin were denied the basic rights granted to all Americans under the Bill of Rights. President Eisenhower, along with the United States Congress and the federal courts, began to deal with this problem during the late 1950s. However, it would take several more years before the constitutional rights of all American citizens would be clearly protected.

The federal government continued to grow steadily under President Eisenhower, although at a slower rate than during the administrations of Franklin Roosevelt and Harry Truman. Gradually, the government began to spend great sums of money in an effort to provide jobs, food, clothing, education, and housing for millions of people. One of the major programs started by President Eisenhower in 1956 was the Federal-Aid Highway Act. This act was responsible for starting the largest road building project in American history. These new roads were called interstate highways. The federal government felt that this was a good project, for it would help to unite the entire country and help with the movement of troops and equipment during a time of emergency. The building of the interstate highways also provided jobs for many Americans.

During President Eisenhower's time as President, the Cold War was quiet and stable enough that most American soldiers could remain at home. The death of Joseph Stalin in 1953 helped to calm world affairs. Eisenhower was able to obtain a truce in the Korean War. In spite of this relative peace, America did not withdraw from actively participating in the world. The United States kept soldiers in South Korea and Europe to protect these areas from attack. Agreements were made with other countries around the world to help protect them against Communist aggression and revolution. The people of East Germany, Poland, and Hungary tried to free themselves from Communist oppression, but these uprisings were brutally defeated.

Toward the end of his time in office, Eisenhower supported the creation of the National Aeronautics and Space Administration (NASA). The number of states grew during Eisenhower's administration. In 1959, the states of Hawaii and Alaska were added to the Union. The United States now has a total of fifty states.

The National Aeronautics and Space Act (NASA) was passed shortly after the Soviet Union launched the robotic spacecraft, called *Sputnik I.* President Eisenhower signed this act into law on July 29, 1958.

After Eisenhower's term as President ended in 1961, he retired to Gettysburg, Pennsylvania. Even in his retirement, he was willing to be an informal advisor to his successors, Presidents Kennedy and Johnson, when requested. When Eisenhower died in 1969, he was greatly appreciated by the nation.

Summary. In Dwight Eisenhower's early life, he seemed to be an unlikely heroic figure, yet he became one of America's most popular generals and presidents. He led Allied forces to victory in Europe during World War II and helped strengthen NATO defenses in the early days of the Cold War. He went on serve a successful eight years as President of the United States.

Comprehension Questions

1. Why was Dwight Eisenhower an unlikely soldier?

2. In what year did World War II begin?

3. When did the United States enter World War II?

4. Where did the D-Day invasion occur?

5. Why did President Truman recall Eisenhower to military service?

6. What project was begun in 1956 that was designed to unite the country and help with the movement of troops and equipment during an emergency?

7. What states joined the United States while Eisenhower was President?

Chapter 38
The United States Changes (1960–1980)

John Fitzgerald "Jack" Kennedy
(1917–1963)

On August 2, 1943, Lt. Kennedy was on patrol in the Solomon Islands. Suddenly, his Motor Torpedo Boat (PT-109) was rammed by a Japanese destroyer. He was injured but swam to safety, pulling a wounded man with him. Kennedy received the Navy and Marine Corps Medal for his heroic conduct.

A New Generation Takes Over. A new generation came to political power after President Eisenhower. With the election of John F. Kennedy in 1960 to become the thirty-fifth President, the World War II generation took power in the United States. Each President from John F. Kennedy through George H. W. Bush was of this generation. Many changes occurred in America with the increasing influence of the World War II generation and their children.

John F. Kennedy came from a prominent Irish Catholic family in Massachusetts. During World War II, Kennedy served in the United States Navy against the Japanese in the Pacific. He received a medal for bravery for rescuing one of his crewmen after his boat, PT-109, was sunk by a Japanese ship. After the war, Kennedy entered politics, serving in the United States House of Representatives and then the Senate, prior to his election as President.

John F. Kennedy presented a popular, idealistic image to the nation. In his inaugural address on January 20, 1961, he called Americans to action when he stated: "And so, my fellow Americans: ask not what your country can do for you—ask what you can do for your country." In many ways, however, he continued and expanded upon some of the same policies of previous Presidents.

President Kennedy had to spend much time dealing with foreign problems. He continued the policies of Presidents Truman and Eisenhower to oppose Communist forces in Vietnam and surrounding countries. Kennedy, in fact, even expanded the number of American troops in South Vietnam from 800 to 16,000.

One of the early major foreign policy problems that Kennedy faced was in Europe. Trouble arose in August 1961 over the building of the Berlin Wall by the East German Communists. The East German government built the wall to severely limit the ability of East Germans to travel in and immigrate to West Berlin. During the years following 1961, the Berlin Wall was strengthened and improved. It has been estimated by some that over 200 people were killed trying to cross the wall into West Berlin before it was finally destroyed in 1989. In June 1963, President Kennedy traveled to West Berlin and gave a famous speech, denouncing the wall as an example of the failure of communism and illustrating his support for West Berlin by saying that he was a Berliner.

The Cuban Missile Crisis. President Kennedy's most dangerous problem was with the island of Cuba. This nation was taken over by the Communists in 1959, and a violent dictator named Fidel Castro came to power. The United States tried to work with Castro at first but soon came to understand the communistic character of his government. In 1960, President Eisenhower authorized the Central Intelligence Agency to begin planning for an invasion of Cuba by anti-communist Cubans to overthrow Castro's government. President Kennedy continued the plan, and anti-communist Cubans were landed at the Bay of Pigs in Cuba in April 1961. However, insufficient help was given to the invaders, and the anti-communist Cubans were defeated. Over 1,000 anti-communist Cubans were captured, most of whom were later ransomed by the United States. The failure of this invasion had the effect of strengthening the Communist movement in Cuba.

The Soviets began to send weapons to Cuba in 1962. The Cubans and Soviets claimed that these were just conventional weapons that all countries have, but, in fact, they were also secretly sending nuclear weapons. Since Cuba is located just a few miles from the state of Florida, many people in America became concerned. Late in 1962, it was confirmed that Cuba had nuclear missiles that could destroy American cities. President Kennedy told the Soviets and the Cubans that all missiles and nuclear weapons must be removed from Cuba. To show that he meant business, the United States established a naval blockade around Cuba during October and November 1962 to keep the Soviets from bringing any more weapons into the country. The Cubans and Soviets agreed to remove the missiles, provided that America would not invade Cuba with American soldiers. This problem, commonly referred to as the Cuban Missile Crisis, was settled without a war being fought.

President Kennedy also sought to fight communism by helping poor and undeveloped countries. He sent foreign aid to troubled lands in Latin America. President Kennedy also established the Peace Corps. The Peace Corps would send Americans to live in poor countries and help them to develop their economies and societies in such areas as health care, education, construction, and farming.

Expansion of Civil Rights. One of the great issues in America during this time was that of civil rights. African-Americans in much of America had for decades been denied the full expression of their human and civil rights. After World War II, the federal government began to address these issues. President Truman integrated the armed forces, and President Eisenhower supported new civil rights laws passed by Congress. Both Eisenhower and Kennedy enforced school integration rulings by federal courts—Eisenhower in Arkansas in 1957 and Kennedy in Mississippi in 1962 and Alabama in 1963. After Lyndon Johnson became President in 1963, more laws were passed to secure civil rights for all. Two important civil rights laws were passed in 1964 and 1965, providing civil rights protection in public accommodations and voting. President Johnson also nominated civil rights lawyer Thurgood Marshall in 1967 to be the first black member of the United States Supreme Court.

Fidel Castro (1926–)

On April 15, 1959, Fidel Castro arrived at Washington National Airport as a guest of the Press Club. During his visit, he tried to persuade American officials that his new government had good intentions; meanwhile, he was confiscating property owned by major U.S. corporations. President Eisenhower, however, refused to meet with him. After visiting the United States, Castro joined forces with Nikita Khrushchev, the leader of the Soviet Union. This new partnership ultimately led to the Cuban Missile Crisis in 1962.

Martin Luther King, Jr. (1929–1968)

Phyllis Stewart Schlafly (1924–)

Stop ERA

By the end of 1973, it looked as if the Equal Rights Amendment (ERA) would inevitably become part of the Constitution. Congress had passed the proposed amendment in 1972 by overwhelming margins, and thirty states had already ratified the proposed amendment. Only eight more were needed.

One person, however, would not give up. Phyllis Schlafly, an author and activist, organized the "Stop the ERA" grassroots campaign. Mrs. Schlafly was able to educate much of the public that if the ERA became part of the Constitution, it might contribute to changes to American society, including the possible conscription of women into the military and government payment for abortions. By the time Phyllis Schlafly was done, the ERA was defeated, still needing three states when time ran out for ratification.

At the same time that the federal government was moving to improve civil rights for African-Americans, blacks were also acting on their own. Various people became active in the civil rights movement. Some like Malcolm X were black nationalists who advocated separation from white Americans. Many, however, advocated nonviolent resistance to racial segregation so that blacks could participate in an integrated society. The most prominent civil rights leader of the time was Dr. Martin Luther King, Jr. Dr. King was a black Baptist minister who served churches in Alabama and Georgia. He was a founding member of the Southern Christian Leadership Conference and was active in nonviolent demonstrations and marches throughout various parts of the South, Washington, D.C., and Chicago. James Earl Ray, however, assassinated Dr. King on March 29, 1968. A national holiday was declared in his honor in 1986.

Another change that occurred in America was the growth of the modern feminist movement. President Kennedy helped to prepare for the new feminist movement when he established the Presidential Commission on the Status of Women in 1961. Its purpose was to address issues of concern about the status of women, particularly in the workplace and with regard to women's legal rights. A number of the members of the commission went on, however, to found the National Organization of Women. In 1972, Congress passed the Equal Rights Amendment (ERA) and sent it to the states for ratification. Although initially it seemed likely to be added to the Constitution, it was never approved by a sufficient number of states. While the ERA debate was going on, another began about abortion when the United States Supreme Court legalized abortion nationally with its *Roe v. Wade* decision in 1973. With this decision and other similar ones, the Court—without clear reference to past constitutional history—overruled laws by many states banning or restricting abortion. Abortion continues to be legal in the United States with few restrictions, resulting in the deaths of millions of unborn children. Most, although not all, feminists have sup-

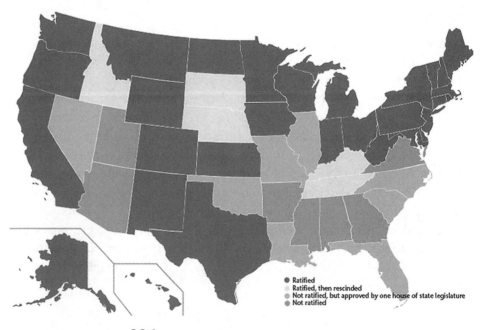

● Ratified
  Ratified, then rescinded
● Not ratified, but approved by one house of state legislature
● Not ratified

ported legalized abortion in order for women to have complete control over their bodies, even in pregnancy.

Lyndon Johnson Becomes President. On November 22, 1963, President Kennedy was murdered by Lee Harvey Oswald. No one knows for sure why he killed the President because he was killed soon afterward himself, but it is interesting to note that he had lived in the Soviet Union for a short period of time during the 1950s and had tried to get into Cuba after Castro had come to power. Vice President Lyndon B. Johnson became President after the death of President Kennedy.

Lyndon Johnson served as President of the United States from late 1963 until early 1969. During his time as President, the role of the federal government expanded greatly. Through his Great Society and War on Poverty programs, he attempted to solve many of the problems of the poor through extensive gov-ernment spending. He also sought to support and defend the civil rights of Americans through the activities of the federal government. This was a period of difficulty between the races, and riots broke out in several American cities. Tensions were particularly high after Dr. Martin Luther King, Jr., was killed in 1968, with riots occurring in over 100 cities. While many of these needs were real and some of these programs were helpful, they also greatly extended the influence of the government in the life of the nation and made the federal government's budget problems worse.

Lyndon Baines Johnson
(1908–1973)

On November 22, 1963, two hours after President Kennedy was shot, Lyndon Johnson was sworn in as President on *Air Force One* (the President's airplane) at Love Field Airport in Dallas.

While President Johnson was trying to deal with problems at home, he also had problems around the world as well. The United States intervened in the Dominican Republic in 1964 when radicals threatened the stability of that country. In 1967, war broke out among Israel, Egypt, Syria, and Jordan. War was threatened in Korea in 1968 when North Korea captured the USS *Pueblo*, a United States Navy ship. Also in 1968, the Soviet Union and its allies invaded Czechoslovakia to stop a reform movement within that country. However, his greatest foreign problem was in Vietnam.

In 1968, North Korea captured an American intelligence ship, the USS *Pueblo*, and held its crew hostage for a time, until a committee of American patriots, led by Chicago-area clergyman Paul Lindstrom (1939–2002), pressured authorities into securing their release on December 23, 1968 (*release shown above*).

The Vietnam War. The United States had been involved in Vietnam since the end of World War II. In 1945, America sent a modest amount of weapons and other supplies to a group of Vietnamese nationalists, led by Ho Chi Minh, who were fighting the Japanese occupiers of this French colony. After the war ended, America came to realize the communistic nature of the leaders of this movement and began to support the French in their fight against this communist-led nationalist group. Despite much American aid, the French had to grant independence to Vietnam in 1954. Two countries emerged: a Communist North Vietnam and a non-communist South Vietnam.

Australia and New Zealand also sent ground troops to Vietnam, hoping to protect their national security and to stop the further spread of communism in the region of Southeast Asia.

Air Combat assault missions were executed by using helicopters over Southeast Asia.

Communist rebels in South Vietnam, supported by the Communist government in North Vietnam, continued their fight to take over all of Vietnam. President Eisenhower sent supplies and some advisors to help the South Vietnamese people defend themselves. When John Kennedy became President, he sent even more help to South Vietnam.

The nation's new President, Lyndon B. Johnson, decided to send large numbers of American combat soldiers to Vietnam during 1964 and 1965. At the start of this conflict, many Americans were in favor of sending troops to Vietnam. However, as the 1960s unfolded, the war became bigger and bloodier. The United States military found it difficult to win a guerrilla war against South Vietnamese Communist fighters and North Vietnamese soldiers. In addition, the United States was afraid of starting another world war and so limited attacks against North Vietnam. In 1968, Communist forces launched a massive offensive called the Tet Offensive. Although the Americans and South Vietnamese were initially surprised, they eventually defeated the Communist attack, killing many of the Communist troops.

Opposition to the Vietnam War already existed in the United States, but with the surprise of the Tet Offensive, many more of the American people began to march in the streets and demand that the United States pull the soldiers out of Vietnam. The American people became divided on this issue, and the country no longer had the will to support the Vietnam War in a unified way. Thousands of American soldiers were being killed every day, but it seemed as if the government was unable or unwilling to win this conflict. Many people engaged in anti-war protests, and a few even participated in terrorist activities against the government of the United States.

This was a sad time in American history. The enemies of freedom had managed to damage the noble spirit of America. Many people in the United States began to doubt their government leaders and questioned if their great country should stop trying to save the world from communism. By 1972, President Richard M. Nixon realized that it was foolish to keep soldiers in Vietnam if America did not have the will to win; therefore, a ceasefire was signed with the Communists. The final American armed forces were removed from Vietnam in 1973, and many American prisoners of war came home. The Vietnam War finally ended in 1975 as the Communist forces took over the nation of South Vietnam. It took many years for the American people to regain the spirit of patriotism that they lost during the Vietnam War.

Richard Nixon Is Elected President. President Johnson decided not to run for reelection in 1968, and Richard Nixon defeated George Wallace and Hubert Humphrey to become the next President. President Nixon began the process of withdrawing American forces from Vietnam and sought to find an honorable peace to end the war. While he was President, a wonderful event took place in 1971 that helped young adults to become more involved with American government. An amendment to the United States Constitution was passed by the Congress and ratified by the states. This is the Twenty-sixth Amendment, which says that anyone who is a citizen of the United States eighteen years old or older can vote in all of the country's elections. Before this amendment, citizens had to be at least twenty-one years old before they could vote. It is a great privilege and duty to help vote good and godly people into public office. All patriotic Americans who are old enough to vote should be responsible enough to vote as often as possible.

Richard Milhous Nixon (1913–1994)

In 1972, shortly before the close of the Vietnam War, President Richard Nixon was reelected as the nation's President. Nixon was under constant pressure from the American people to pull the soldiers out of Vietnam. Violent protests were common during the early 1970s, as Americans demanded an end to the war. Other citizens were marching in the streets to protest the fact that black Americans were not being given fair treatment. Adding to this confusion, the United States was going through an economic recession. The war between Israel, Egypt, and Syria in 1973, and the resulting oil embargo by many Arab countries against nations that had supported Israel, made the economic problems worse.

President Nixon became involved in a cover-up of what became known as the Watergate Affair. In 1972, a few Nixon staff members burglarized the Democratic party headquarters in Washington, D.C. This led to a long and ugly investigation of Richard Nixon and his administration in 1973 and 1974. It was determined that Mr. Nixon had lied to the American people regarding the actions of his staff. Finally, on August 19, 1974, Nixon decided to resign as President of the United States. Vice President Gerald Ford took over the office of President after Richard Nixon's resignation and became America's thirty-eighth President.

Gerald Rudolph Ford, Jr.
(1913–2006)

America's Space Program. During this era of history, American inventors and scientists developed many new products and services. They also improved on many earlier inventions. Color television sets became commonplace in many homes during the 1970s. Computers, calculators, stereos, and supersonic jets were just a few of the high-technology items that were invented during the middle of the twentieth century.

One of the greatest successes of American scientists was the space program. During the 1950s, scientists in America and other nations began to experiment with rockets that could travel into outer space. The Soviets launched two satellites into orbit around the earth during 1957, which they called *Sputnik I* and *Sputnik II*. This event encouraged the United

States to speed up its own space program. The United States government had already selected Werner Von Braun, a former German scientist, to organize America's space and rocket programs. By 1958, the United States had also launched a satellite into space.

President Kennedy built upon President Eisenhower's beginning efforts toward space exploration. In a speech before Congress in 1961, he committed the United States to a goal of landing men on the moon by the end of the 1960s. In the early 1960s, the United States began to send men into space. In 1961, Alan Shepard, Jr., became the first American to go into space. John Glenn became the first American to orbit the earth on February 20, 1962. The United States also sent its first communications satellites into space in 1962.

Perhaps the brightest and best achievement of the United States in the late 1960s was the successful landing of a man on the moon. In 1969, millions of Americans watched astronauts Neil Armstrong and Edwin Aldrin walk on the moon for the first time. No other nation has ever been able to send men to the moon and return them safely to earth.

America's space program has continued to grow over the years. In 1981, the United States developed a special reusable spacecraft known as the space shuttle. This craft can carry several astronauts into outer space and return to earth in much the same manner as a regular airplane. Therefore, the space shuttle can be used over and over again.

Apollo 15 astronauts used the Rover to explore the moon's surface in 1971. Astronaut James Irwin stands by the flag. Irwin, a devout Christian, formed the High Flight Foundation and became an evangelical lecturer after retiring from NASA.

America Enters a Period of Decline. When Gerald Ford became President of the United States on August 9, 1974, he became the first unelected President in United States history. He was originally appointed Vice President after Richard Nixon's first Vice President, Spiro Agnew, had to resign from office due to crimes unrelated to the Watergate Affair. Therefore, Gerald Ford was not elected as either Vice President or President. President Ford had a difficult time as President and was only able to complete the time of Richard Nixon's second term of office. The economy continued to do poorly, and the foreign situation was difficult. Communists took over the countries of South Vietnam, Cambodia, and Laos and made inroads in Africa after the collapse of the Portuguese empire in Africa. Communists also took over the country of Ethiopia in 1974 when army officers overthrew the government of the Ethiopian emperor. President Ford gave Richard Nixon a pardon for any crimes he may have committed during the Watergate Affair, but many people believed that Nixon should not have been given this pardon.

In 1976, the American people elected a new President. James (Jimmy) E. Carter defeated President Ford and became the nation's thirty-ninth President. Jimmy Carter, a former governor of Georgia, was the first person from the deep South to be elected President since 1848. Many people were initially attracted to President Carter because of his religious background as a member of a Baptist church in his home town; he seemed to be personally honest and have a nice family. He expressed a great concern for civil rights in America and human rights around the world. However, over time, his popularity declined. The economy continued to do poorly, and there were several difficult foreign problems. He was unable to move the nation in a positive, forward direction.

Executive Office of the President of the United States

James Earl "Jimmy" Carter Jr.
(1924–)

America's image as a world power suffered greatly during the late 1970s. Many nations around the world lost respect for the United States. Communist influence continued to grow in the world, particularly in Africa and Central America. The Soviet Union invaded the country of Afghanistan with a large number of troops in late 1979 to support the Communist government of that country in its fight against anti-communist Afghans.

An Islamic revolution in the oil-rich nation of Iran occurred in 1978, causing a further spike in oil prices and making the economic problems worse. Then, on November 4, 1979, the Iran Hostage Crisis unfolded when a group of fifty-two American diplomats in the United States embassy in Iran were kidnapped by radical Muslim students. President Carter, however, provided poor leadership during this crisis.

President Carter was very active in relations with different countries. Some of his activity was considered very helpful, while other things were more controversial. He signed a nuclear arms agreement with the Soviet Union, although it was never ratified by the Senate because of the Soviet invasion of Afghanistan. He established nor-

Department of Defense

The hostages endured 444 days of captivity until Reagan secured their release in 1981. They are shown disembarking *Freedom One.*

mal relations with the Communist government on Mainland China while breaking relations with the Nationalist Chinese government on the island of Taiwan. The United States signed a treaty with the nation of Panama, in which the United States agreed to return control of the Panama Canal Zone to the Panamanians in 1999. Carter's most popular and positive foreign work was his help in getting the nations of Israel and Egypt to sign a peace treaty in 1979.

The 1970s were a difficult time for the United States. Communism made significant gains around the world, and America was humiliated in Vietnam. The constitutional crisis of the Watergate Affair brought the government institutions into question. The economy did very poorly, worsened by large increases in oil prices. The country sank to new lows during the Carter years.

Summary. A new generation of leaders came to power in America with the election of John F. Kennedy as President of the United States in 1960, bringing change to the nation. Civil rights and voting rights were improved for African-Americans and young people. The United States was able to successfully send astronauts to the moon and back. At the same time, the role of the federal government grew significantly. Political violence increased with the murders of President Kennedy and Dr. Martin Luther King, an increase in the number of large-scale protests, and the many riots that took place within America's cities.

John F. Kennedy stopped the flow of nuclear missiles into Cuba during 1962. He was murdered in late 1963, and Vice President Johnson took over as President. President Johnson decided to vastly increase the number of American soldiers in South Vietnam during the mid-1960s to help South Vietnam defend itself against Communist rebels and soldiers from North Vietnam. The American people could not unite behind this war effort, and the United States Army left Vietnam in 1973. Communist forces took over South Vietnam in 1975. America was humbled by scandals and troubles during the 1970s. President Carter tried very hard to help America, but was unable to motivate the American people.

John F. Kennedy

Comprehension Questions

1. Who was elected as the thirty-fifth President of the United States?
2. Who took over as dictator of Cuba in 1959?
3. Why did America enter the Vietnam War?
4. During what year did the Vietnam War end?
5. When did American astronauts first land on the moon?
6. What was the reason for the Twenty-sixth Amendment of the United States Constitution?
7. Why did President Nixon have to resign from office?
8. How did the Islamic revolution in Iran in 1978 affect the United States?

Chapter 39
Ronald Reagan (1911–2004)

By the end of the 1970s, the spirit of America was low. The economy was suffering; the Communists seemed to be expanding; and the United States was humiliated by the Iran Hostage Crisis and, again, by the failed attempt to rescue its diplomats. President Carter seemed unable to improve the situation. The American people began to look for a new President in 1980. The nation decided to elect a President who could motivate the American people to return to the values that made the country great. The people chose Ronald Reagan as their new President.

Ronald Reagan's Early Years. Ronald Reagan grew up in a variety of small towns in Illinois, graduating from Dixon High School. As a young person, he was baptized as a member of a Disciples of Christ congregation. He graduated from Eureka College—a Disciples of Christ college—in 1932, studying economics and sociology. After graduating from college, he moved to Iowa and became a radio sports broadcaster at various stations.

In 1937, Ronald Reagan became an actor. Reagan was never considered one of the top actors of his time, but he had several positive reviews of his movies. His movie career lasted until 1964. He appeared in over fifty movies during his career. During the 1950s and early 1960s, Reagan also worked in television. Reagan was also active in the Screen Actors Guild, which represented movie—and, later, television—performers in their dealings with the studios. He served several years as president of the guild.

During World War II, Ronald Reagan served in the Army. He enlisted in the Army reserves as early as 1937 and was appointed a second lieutenant. He was called to active duty in early 1942, although he was never sent overseas due to his nearsightedness. He spent most of his time in the Army helping to create publicity and training films for the military. He left the Army as a captain in December 1945.

Interest in Politics. Ronald Reagan was originally an admirer of Franklin D. Roosevelt and a supporter of Roosevelt's New Deal programs. However, by the early 1950s, Reagan became more interested in limited government, especially after becoming a spokesman for General Electric. Ronald Reagan became a supporter of Dwight Eisenhower in the 1952 and 1956 elections and Richard M. Nixon in the 1960 election. In 1964, Reagan supported Barry Goldwater for President against Lyndon B. Johnson. Although Goldwater lost badly to Lyndon Johnson, Reagan's speech in favor of Goldwater attracted support in his home state of California.

In 1966, Ronald Reagan was elected governor of the state of California on conservative themes. He took a tough stance against the protest movement

Ronald Reagan Presidential Library

This is a photo of Ronald Reagan as a teenager in Dixon, Illinois.

U.S. Federal Government

Reagan became the host of *General Electric Theater* from 1954 to 1962.

of the period. Reagan opposed the expansion of welfare in California. He also advocated a reduction of business regulations. One of Reagan's most controversial actions occurred in 1967, when he signed a bill making abortions far more easy to obtain in California. Reagan later came to regret signing this bill and became strongly opposed to abortion, including writing the pro-life book *Abortion and the Conscience of the Nation* in 1983.

Ronald Reagan served one more term as governor, winning reelection in 1970. In 1976, Reagan ran for the Republican nomination for President against President Gerald Ford, but narrowly lost the nomination. President Ford went on to lose the general election to Jimmy Carter. Reagan ran for President again in 1980. This time he won the election, defeating President Carter and independent candidate John Anderson.

The Spirit of America Revives. Ronald Reagan told the American people that they should not look to big government to save them; they were told to look to God for help and strength. In his inaugural address, President Reagan affirmed his commitment to limited constitutional government. "Our government," he said, "has no special power except that granted it by the people. It is time to check and reverse the growth of government which shows signs of having grown beyond the consent of the governed." Further, "It is my intention to curb the size and influence of the federal establishment and to demand recognition of the distinction between the powers granted to the federal government and those reserved to the state or to the people. All of us need to be reminded that the federal government did not create the states; the states created the federal government." In just a few short years, the people of America began to wake up and realize that they had to change their thinking. President Reagan helped to remind people that it was love of God, hard work, and a compassion toward their fellow citizens that made America great.

President Reagan's time in office was not easy. Early in his time in office, President Reagan was shot and almost killed on March 30, 1981. However, God preserved him and he recovered to full health. He also had to deal with a strike by the air traffic controllers a few months later. He gave the controllers forty-eight hours to report to work, and those who did not would lose their jobs. President Reagan showed he meant what he said when he fired over 11,000 striking controllers.

The economy was very bad for the first couple of years of his administration. Unemployment rose to its highest level since the Great Depression. President Reagan, working with Congress, cut income tax rates significantly in an effort to make the economy begin to grow again. After 1982, America's economic system began to improve, eventually creating 16 million new jobs by the end of President Reagan's time in office. Some economists have argued that President Reagan's tax cuts even contributed to the economic growth of the 1990s. Unfortunately, however, President Reagan was unable to control federal budget deficits (i.e., spending more money than is taken in), which tended to grow during his years in office.

Ronald Wilson Reagan (1911–2004)

Executive Office of the President of the United States

U.S. Federal Government

On March 30, 1981, President Reagan and three others were shot and wounded by John Hinckley, Jr.

President Reagan established a foreign policy of "peace through strength." The country's military was strengthened during the 1980s as new threats to the nation began to develop. The threat of Middle Eastern terrorism increased. The United States, along with other countries, sent peacekeeping forces to help the Middle Eastern nation of Lebanon overcome a deadly civil war. Over 200 Marines, however, were killed in 1983 by Islamic terrorists, and America was forced to leave the nation the next year without accomplishing much good. The United States and Libya clashed during much of the 1980s. In 1986, after a series of terrorist attacks in Europe linked to Libya, American Navy and Air Force planes attacked Libyan targets.

U.S. Marine Corps

On April 18, 1983, a suicide bomber killed sixty-three at the U.S. Embassy in West Beirut, Lebanon. On October 23, 1983, a suicide bombing (*as shown above*) targeted the headquarters of the U.S. and French forces in Beirut, which killed 241 American and fifty-eight French servicemen.

The United States supported those fighting against Communists, especially in Central America and in Afghanistan. The American armed forces invaded the island of Grenada in 1983 to free it from an oppressive Communist government and to protect American students who were attending medical school there. American military forces in Europe were strengthened as part of an effort to improve NATO's defenses against possible threats from the Soviet Union. President Reagan's confrontations of communism were not simply military, however. On June 12, 1987, he challenged Soviet leader Mikhail Gorbachev in a speech at the Berlin Wall when Reagan said: "Mr. Gorbachev, open this gate! Mr. Gorbachev, tear down this wall!"

By the time President Reagan left office in 1989, he had left the United States a far stronger country than when he had taken office. A stronger economy and a stronger military helped the United States regain respect around the world. The Communists in the former Soviet Union and the Soviet Bloc countries of Eastern Europe began to take steps toward a less repressive style of government and move away from their Cold War actions.

Executive Office of the President of the United States

"Mr. Gorbachev, open this gate! Mr. Gorbachev, tear down this wall!"

After leaving office, President Reagan returned to his home in California, but he did not have an easy retirement. In 1994, he announced in a letter to the nation that he had been diagnosed with Alzheimer's Disease. Ronald Reagan died in 2004.

The Last World War II President. In 1988, the American people elected George H. W. Bush, who had been President Reagan's Vice President, to be their nation's forty-first President. President Bush would be the last President of the World War II generation. George Bush was born into a prominent family in Connecticut and entered the Navy in 1942 after graduating from high school. He became the youngest aviator in Navy history at the age of eighteen. He served in the Pacific, flying over fifty combat missions and earning a variety of medals. He was even shot down once by the Japanese.

After World War II, George H. W. Bush went to Yale University and moved to Texas after graduation to get into the oil industry, where he did quite well. He was elected to Congress in 1966 and served for two terms—a total of four years. In the 1970s he served as an ambassador to the United Nations, envoy to China, and director of the Central Intelligence Agency.

George H. W. Bush decided to run for President during the 1980 presidential campaign. He ran against Ronald Reagan in the Republican primary campaign. Bush did well initially but lost to Ronald Reagan. Bush's political career did not end there, however, because Ronald Reagan asked Bush to be his vice-presidental candidate. During the eight years of President Reagan's administration, George H. W. Bush served loyally and effectively as Vice President. George H. W. Bush ran again for President in 1988, defeating Michael Dukakis in the general election. George H. W. Bush became the first sitting Vice President to be elected President since 1836.

President Bush struggled during his four years in office, having to deal with difficult economic and foreign problems. He sought to address the growing budget deficits by approving a tax increase proposed by Congress, even though this violated his "no new taxes" campaign pledge during the 1988 campaign. Soon afterwards, the United States' economy worsened, entering a mild recession.

Executive Office of the President of the United States

George Herbert Walker Bush
(1924–)

U.S. Federal Government

On November 22, 1990, George H. W. Bush and General H. Norman Schwarzkopf, Jr., inspected troops in Saudi Arabia.

President Bush sent American soldiers to fight on two different occasions. The United States intervened in Panamanian affairs in 1989 and liberated that country from a military dictator. Soon afterwards, President Bush sent troops to Saudi Arabia after Iraq conquered the neighboring country of Kuwait in August 1990. Hundreds of thousands of American and allied troops came into the Middle East to prepare to liberate Kuwait. This conflict is often called the Gulf War and was one of the shortest wars in American history. Americans and others helped the country of Kuwait to regain its freedom from the bloody occupation of the Iraqi army in 1991. Toward the end of his administration in December 1992, President Bush sent American forces to Somalia as part of a United Nations effort to bring humanitarian aid and security to the country. Somalia was so disorderly, however, that the effort was ultimately a failure.

In spite of many difficult problems, there were successes during President Bush's administration. Communism continued its decline in much of the world. The Soviet military was forced to leave Afghanistan in 1989. Then from 1989 to 1990, Communist governments in Eastern Europe and Mongolia collapsed, bringing an end to the Cold War. This led to the reunification of Germany in 1990 and the dissolution of the Soviet Union into

Dr. Jerry Falwell (1933–2007)

The Rise of the Religious Right

In 1976, *Newsweek* magazine declared it to be the Year of the Evangelical. It was responding to a census in which over 50 million Americans identified themselves as being "born again," and the two presidential candidates that year, Gerald Ford and Jimmy Carter, both presented themselves as evangelicals. Recognizing this potentially powerful force, Baptist minister Jerry Falwell formed the Moral Majority in order to unite the conservative (or traditional) Christians politically to battle the evils he saw in American society. These evils included abortion, communism, bad public schools, and excessive violence. Thus, he thought America needed to be reminded of its identity as God's chosen nation. The Moral Majority succeeded in registering over three million voters, most of whom voted for Ronald Reagan, helping in ushering in a high point in conservative political power and influence. Even though the Moral Majority disbanded in 1989, its influence has been felt as recently as the two previous elections in which evangelicals overwhelmingly supported George W. Bush's campaigns to be President.

several countries in 1991. Other Communist governments also fell during this time, including those in Nicaragua, Ethiopia, and Afghanistan. In addition, the Communist rebels of El Salvador had to give up the fight so they could participate in elections.

In 1992, President Bush decided to seek reelection as President, running against Governor William Clinton of Arkansas and independent candidate and businessman Ross Perot. However, in spite of a successful foreign policy, George H. W. Bush lost the election to Governor Clinton because of the country's economic problems.

Summary. The spirit of America revived during the 1980s, as first Ronald Reagan and then George H. W. Bush successfully improved America's defenses and helped to bring about the demise of communism in the Soviet Union, Eastern Europe, and much of the developing world. However, America's conflicts in the Middle East began during this period.

Comprehension Questions

1. What was Ronald Reagan's career before being elected governor of California?

2. Whom did Ronald Reagan defeat during the 1980 presidential election?

3. How did President Reagan respond to striking air traffic controllers?

4. What did President Reagan do to improve the American economy early in his administration?

5. What was the name of President Reagan's foreign policy?

6. List two of the positions held by George H. W. Bush during the 1970s.

7. What did President Bush do in an effort to control budget deficits?

8. How did the Cold War end?

Chapter 40
In Recent Years (1993–2008)

William Jefferson "Bill" Clinton
(1946–)

Bill Clinton was born in Hope, Arkansas, as William Jefferson Blythe, III. His father, William Jefferson Blythe, Jr., was a traveling salesman who died in a car accident three months before Bill was born. During his early years, he was known as Billy and did not adopt his stepfather's surname until the age of fourteen.

Just as in the 1961 election, the 1992 election brought a new generation to political power. The time of the World War II generation was ending, and it was time for the next generation. Known as "baby boomers" because of the large number of children born between 1945 and 1964 (76 million in the United States), the children of the World War II generation were ready to take over.

William Jefferson Clinton. William Jefferson Clinton was the first baby boomer President. Generally known as Bill Clinton, he was born in 1946 and was the third youngest President; only Theodore Roosevelt and John F. Kennedy were younger than Bill Clinton at the time they became President.

Bill Clinton grew up in Arkansas, where he gained an interest in government and politics after meeting President Kennedy while on a trip to Washington, D.C. While attending college, he became an opponent of the Vietnam War and participated in anti-war protests. He never served in the American armed forces, and so was the first President since Franklin Roosevelt who was never in the military.

Bill Clinton's first major experience in politics was helping with Senator George McGovern's effort in 1972 to defeat President Nixon as part of an anti-war effort. Although Senator McGovern lost to President Nixon, Bill Clinton gained valuable political experience from the effort.

Bill Clinton finished his law degree studies at Yale University in 1973 and returned to Arkansas. He taught law at the University of Arkansas for a few years and then was elected as the attorney general of Arkansas in 1976. Two years later, he was elected governor, a position he held for twelve out of the next fourteen years.

In 1992, Bill Clinton ran for President of the United States. After winning his party's nomination, he ran against President George H. W. Bush—who wanted to serve a second term as President—and independent candidate Ross Perot. Clinton won the election and was elected as the forty-second President of the United States. Many Americans voted for Mr. Clinton because they were dissatisfied with the sluggish American economy and wanted a change in leadership.

The Clinton Presidency. President Clinton served in office for eight years, winning his reelection campaign in 1996. He ended his time with a high approval level. The economy did very well during most of his time in office, although some weaknesses appeared at the very end of his administration. The good economy enabled President Clinton to run the first *balanced federal budget* (spending equal to the taxes collected), and even a *budget surplus* (collected more taxes than were spent), since 1969.

President Clinton's time in office was not without its difficulties. He had campaigned in 1992 as a **moderate**—neither **liberal** nor **conservative**. Yet, soon after he came to office, he attempted to enlarge the activities of the federal government, especially in the area of healthcare. He successfully increased taxes, but he failed to get Congress to pass a national healthcare plan developed by his wife Hillary Rodham Clinton. On the other hand, President Clinton did encourage freer trade within North America by successfully supporting the passage of the North American Free Trade Agreement (NAFTA) between the United States, Mexico, and Canada.

A more conservative political party gained control over Congress as a result of the 1994 election. Neither the new Congress or President Clinton were able to get their own way, and they eventually had to work together on occasion. The results of this election, therefore, caused President Clinton to take less liberal positions. One of the major reforms eventually agreed to by both Congress and the President was welfare reform, which emphasized work and limited federal payments to the poor. When President Clinton signed the welfare reform bill into law in 1996, he said that this fulfilled his campaign promise to "end welfare as we know it." In the same year, President Clinton also signed the Defense of Marriage Act supporting biblical marriage relationships nation-wide.

While President Clinton had a generally successful administration, he had several scandals during his time in office. Mr. Clinton was faced with several controversies regarding misconduct stemming from old business dealings, former women friends, security problems in the White House, questionable campaign fund raising, and questionable presidential pardons.

President Clinton brought shame and disgrace upon the office of President during 1998 when he committed immoral acts with Monica Lewinsky, a young woman who worked at the White House. To make matters worse, Mr. Clinton chose to lie directly to the American people and in a federal court regarding his actions, as he tried to hide his sin.

President Clinton, however, decided not to resign his office. As a result of his attempted cover-up by lying to the federal court, the House of Representatives voted on December 19, 1998, to impeach (i.e., charge with a crime) the President. The Senate of the United States, however, refused to convict him. As a result, President Clinton was able to stay in office until his second term was completed. This entire scandal and impeachment declaration, however, greatly tarnished the legacy of William J. Clinton.

President Clinton's time in office was generally peaceful, but there were foreign problems to handle. He began by withdrawing the American forces from Somalia, which is part of the Horn of Africa across the Red Sea from the Arabian Peninsula, after the killing of several soldiers.

Are You a Liberal or a Conservative?

In American politics, political leaders and voters who support them are usually divided into three groups: *conservatives*, *liberals*, and *moderates*. **Liberals** tend to believe in active government involvement in people's lives and the economy; **conservatives**, however, usually hold to limited government, free-market capitalism (the buying and selling of goods by private individuals or corporations to gain a profit), and traditional moral values; **moderates** normally fall somewhere in between, or hold to a mixture of these two positions.

UNITED STATES OF AMERICA

CANADA

MEXICO

The North American Free Trade Agreement (NAFTA) includes the United States, Canada, and Mexico.

239

The Bosnian War lasted from 1992 to 1995, ending with the Dayton (Ohio) Peace Agreement, which was signed on November 21, 1995. The final peace agreement was signed in Paris on December 14, 1995, as shown above.

Standing, from left to right: Felipe Gonzalez (Spain), Bill Clinton (USA), Jacques Chirac (France), Helmut Kohl (Germany), John Major (UK), and Viktor Chernomyrdin (Russia).

Seated from left to right: Slobodan Milošević (former Yugoslavia [1992–2003], later Serbia and Montenegro [2003–2006], now two separate countries), Franjo Tudman (Croatia), and Alija Izetbegovic (Bosnia and Herzegovina).

America's conflict with Iraq continued during the Clinton administration. In June 1993, the United States launched air attacks against Iraq because of violations of the agreement ending the Gulf War and because of a plot to kill former President George H. W. Bush. Later, in October 1998, Congress passed and President Clinton signed into law the Iraq Liberation Act, which advocated removing Saddam Hussein from power in Iraq. Two months later, the United States launched a four-day bombing campaign against Iraq.

The conflict with Islamic terrorists increased during the Clinton administration as they launched a series of attacks against American interests. Terrorists unsuccessfully tried to blow up the World Trade Center in New York City in 1993. Nineteen American servicemen were killed in an attack in Saudi Arabia in 1995. Three years later, terrorists bombed the American embassies in Kenya and Tanzania in East Africa. Finally, in 2000, terrorists attacked an American warship near Yemen, killing several sailors. America's response to these attacks was ineffectual, launching minor air attacks against possible terrorist camps in Sudan and Afghanistan.

President Clinton sent troops as part of NATO into conflicts in Europe in the 1990s. American soldiers were sent to Bosnia and Kosovo—both part of the old Yugoslavia in Eastern Europe—to stop what was called "ethnic cleansing." These "peacekeeping" missions were designed to keep small conflicts from developing into big wars. Eventually, these wars were ended in uneasy peace in each case. United States peacekeeping troops also went to Haiti in 1994.

Shortly before the end of President Clinton's time in office, he attempted to bring peace to the Arab-Israel Conflict. The negotiations between Israeli Prime Minister Barak and Palestinian leader Yassir Arafat were unsuccessful, however, and the conflict between Israelis and Palestinians increased.

George W. Bush. George W. Bush was elected President in 2000. He was raised in Texas and, after earning college degrees from Yale University and Harvard University, returned to Texas and, like his father, entered the oil industry. He later became part owner of the Texas Rangers baseball team. He served as a fighter pilot in the Texas Air National Guard but never served on active duty. George W. Bush served as governor of Texas for six years, winning election in 1994 and reelection in 1998.

In 2000, George W. Bush defeated Vice President Albert Gore in a very close election, becoming the forty-third President of the United States. The election was so close that it took a few weeks after the election was over before a large number of votes could be recounted and the winner officially announced. The vote in the state of Florida—which was the key state; whoever won Florida would win the election—was extremely close and greatly disputed. It eventually took the United States Supreme Court to settle the Florida vote and, in effect, the election. Although Vice President Gore had won more popular votes than George Bush, Mr. Bush won more electoral votes and thus the election—the first time this has happened since the election of 1888.

George W. Bush is actually the son of George H. W. Bush, who was the forty-first President. When George W. Bush was elected, he became only the

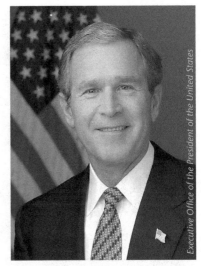

George Walker Bush (1946–)

What Is the Electoral College?

The Framers of the Constitution believed that the establishment of an intermediate body to select the President would "... be much less apt to [shake up] the community ... than the choice of one who was himself to be the final object of the public wishes." The members of the Constitutional Convention decided to leave it to electors who are specially chosen by the people for the task; as Hamilton put it, "... the executive should be independent for his continuance in office of all, but the people themselves." Hamilton believed that this method would ensure the election of highly qualified Presidents.

This plan of indirect election of the President by the people is found in Article II, Section 1, Clause 2 and the Twelfth Amendment of the Constitution, giving the details for the selection of the President by what is known as the Electoral College. The Electoral College consists of 538 electors—535 for the fifty states and three for the District of Columbia. As you can see from the accompanying example of Oregon, each state's electoral vote total equals the number of senators and representatives it has in Congress.

Senators   Electors

=

Representatives

=

TOTAL OF 7 ELECTORS
OREGON

In the vast majority of cases, there has been little controversy regarding the Electoral College; the person who won the popular vote also won the electoral vote. There have been a few occasions, however, when that was not the case. Two elections, 1800 and 1824, required the House of Representatives to select the President, with the popular vote winner in 1824, Andrew Jackson, losing in the House to John Quincy Adams. In the election of 1876, Samuel Tilden won a slight majority of the popular vote, but Rutherford B. Hayes very narrowly won the electoral vote after the disputed sets of electors for four states were awarded to him. Another example of when the Electoral College failed to elect the candidate with the most popular votes was in 1888, when Grover Cleveland won the popular vote by 110,476 votes but Benjamin Harrison comfortably gained a majority of the electoral vote. After 1888, there had not been a serious likelihood that this situation would arise again, until the 2000 election, when Vice President Al Gore narrowly won the popular vote, while Governor George W. Bush narrowly won the electoral vote, after a recount of the election results in Florida. Consequently, Bush became the forty-third President of the United States.

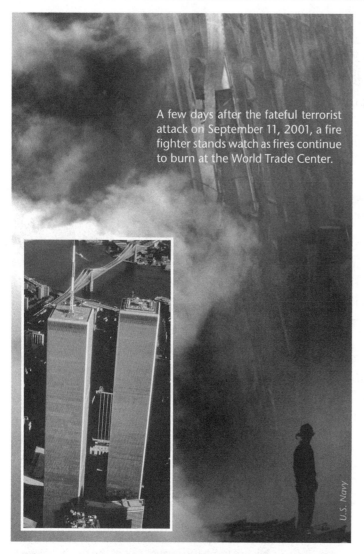

A few days after the fateful terrorist attack on September 11, 2001, a fire fighter stands watch as fires continue to burn at the World Trade Center.

U.S. Navy

NASA

second person to have been elected President after his father held that office. John Quincy Adams, the sixth President of the United States, was the son of John Adams, the second President.

President Bush had many challenges during his two terms in office. He had to deal with terrorist attacks, two wars, economic troubles, and natural disasters. The American economy had weakened towards the end of the Clinton administration and got even worse in the first two years of the Bush administration, especially as a result of the terrorist attack on September 11, 2001. Early in his time in office, President Bush pushed tax cuts through Congress, which helped the economy recover. The economy grew rapidly from 2003 until 2007, when trouble in the housing market and financial system caused the economy to slow down significantly. The economy also suffered from rapid increases in the price of oil and gasoline.

President Bush defeated Massachusetts senator John Kerry in the presidential campaign of 2004. President Bush advocated continued commitment to fighting the wars in Iraq and Afghanistan, reforming the Social Security program, vigilance against terrorism in the United States and around the world, and the establishment of a temporary immigrant worker program. However, President Bush was unable to pass changes to the Social Security program or the immigration system after his reelection.

Hurricane Katrina hit the United States and the Caribbean in August 2005, causing large numbers of deaths and heavy property damage. It killed over 1,800 people, caused significant flooding in the city of New Orleans, and heavily damaged the coastal area of Mississippi. Hundreds of thousands of people left their homes before the storm hit. Many, however, were unable to leave in time and had to suffer during the storm and afterwards until they could be rescued. All levels of government were later criticized for poor planning and an inadequate response to the hurricane.

Hurricane Katrina was one of the most powerful storms to strike the United States. This Category 5 storm covered much of the Gulf of Mexico, producing winds of 160 miles per hour (257 kilometers per hour) with stronger gusts.

War on Terror. On September 11, 2001, President Bush and all Americans were shocked and angered by an attack upon two major U.S. cities by radical Islamic terrorists who were part of the al Qaeda organization led by Osama bin Laden. Al Qaeda terrorists had earlier attacked American targets in Africa and the Middle East. Now they were going after the United States directly.

These attackers hijacked four American airliners and managed to fly two of them into the World Trade Center in New York City and one into the Pentagon building in Washington, D.C. The goal of the fourth plane was the United States Capitol building, but it crashed in rural Pennsylvania after the passengers and crew tried to recapture the airplane. Over 3,000 people were killed in these tactics. This was the worst single act of terrorism in U.S. history.

Osama bin Laden (1957–)

Shortly after the attack, many American allies provided help to the United States, including NATO and Australia. On September 20, President Bush declared a war on terror: "Our war on terror begins with al Qaeda, but it does not end there. It will not end until every terrorist group of global reach has been found, stopped and defeated." American armed forces, along with those from other countries friendly to the United States, began to attack terrorist strongholds in Afghanistan in October 2001, overthrowing its pro-terrorist government. While the pro-terrorist government in Afghanistan was overthrown and al Qaeda's bases were destroyed, a guerrilla war continues in Afghanistan against the new Afghan government, American troops, and allied forces.

President Bush warned the American people that the military effort against terrorist strongholds would be long, hard, and costly. One positive result of the September 11 attack was that the people of the U.S. began to unite and support each other. The reality of terrorism simply underscores the truth of Scripture regarding the total depravity of man, as well as man's need for salvation through the Prince of Peace.

Soldiers of 10th Mountain Division of the U.S. Army are shown boarding a Chinook helicopter. They are returning to Kandahar Army Air Field after searching for Taliban (radical Islamic) fighters and illegal weapons caches in Zabol Province, Afghanistan.

While the war was being fought in Afghanistan, the United States government determined to improve its national defenses. Soon after the September 11 terrorist attack, Congress passed and President Bush signed the USA Patriot Act, which expanded the government's power to combat terrorism. In addition, in massive government reorganization in 2003, a new Department of Homeland Security was created to improve the coordination of security and emergency services by the federal government.

Above, President George W. Bush is shown honoring U.S. Service personel during a visit to Al Asad Air Base, Iraq, on September 3, 2007.

President Bush began his presidency with approval ratings near 50%. Following the September 11, 2001, attacks, Bush's approval ratings jumped up to 80–90% for several months after the attacks. Since December 2004, however, Bush's approval rating stayed below 50%. By the fall of 2008, he only garnered a 28% approval rating.

As the struggle against terrorism grew, President Bush asked Congress to approve the use of military force against Iraq in October of 2002. After months of failed negotiations through the United Nations, George W. Bush sent U.S. and allied troops into Iraq to remove the pro-terrorist Iraqi leader, Saddam Hussein, to destroy any weapons of mass destruction that could kill large numbers of people, and to wipe out training camps that could be used by terrorist groups. This military action, called "Operation Iraqi Freedom" lasted from March 19 to May 1, 2003.

The United States military forces succeeded in removing Saddam Hussein from power and freed the oppressed people of Iraq; however, U.S. forces have had a difficult task of rebuilding the nation and establishing a new stable government. President Bush and other government leaders acknowledge that it will take several years to transform Iraq into a peaceful nation capable of governing itself. For a time, it seemed as if the anti-American terrorists operating in Iraq might win, but a new strategy of sending more troops to Iraq that began in 2007—along with the Iraqi people's growing distrust of the al Qaeda terrorists operating in their country—has done much to improve security within Iraq.

While the war in Afghanistan has generally had wide support from among the people of the United States, the war in Iraq has been more controversial. The debate over the Iraq War became an issue in the 2004 presidential election. Many people opposed intervening in Iraq because Iraq was not directly involved in the September 11 attack. In addition, the failure to find stockpiles of weapons of mass destruction made others doubt the reasons for the war. Finally, the fact that the United States seemed to be losing the war for a time made it less popular.

A New President. In 2008, the Americans elected a new President. The presidential campaign was not a typical election. President George W. Bush was unpopular with much of the American public because of the difficulties with the war in Iraq and serious economic problems. Therefore, no one was running for President as a supporter of Mr. Bush.

The presidential campaign was one of firsts. For the first time in American history, both an African-American and a woman were serious contenders for their party's presidential nomination. Senator Barack Obama of Illinois, considered to be one of the most liberal members of the United States Senate, won the Democratic party's presidential nomination after defeating Senator Hillary Clinton of New York, who is the wife of former President Clinton.

The Republican party, on the other hand, nominated Senator John McCain of Arizona, who would have been the oldest President if elected. He was the only Vietnam War veteran and former prisoner of war to win a major party's nomination for President. Senator McCain selected Governor Sarah Palin to be his vice presidential candidate. Governor Palin was the first person from Alaska to run for a national office and was only the second woman to be a major party vice presidential candidate.

On November 4, 2008, the American people elected Senator Barack H. Obama to be the forty-fourth President of the United States. For the first time in American history, a black man has been elected to lead the United States. This election shows how far the United States has progressed from the days of slavery and legal discrimination. Most African-American citizens are understandably elated with the election of Mr. Obama as President. On the other hand, his liberal record as a senator caused many to be concerned about the policies he would support as President. His first two years in office confirmed this, especially with the passage of health care reform and various economic stimulus policies. The mid-term election of 2010 also showed that Americans were not pleased with these policies.

Current Problems and Biblical Solutions. Now that America has begun the new millennium, we can see many problems. We have many problems in our cities and between the various races in America. Riots in Los Angeles and other cities in the 1990s are clear examples of these problems. Many people are concerned about the environment and the problems of pollution. How big an issue is global warming, how is global warming caused, and what, if anything, should be done about it? One of the greatest current problems of our nation is how to deal with international terrorist groups.

A constant problem is keeping control of government spending. It has never been as much of a problem as it is today. The federal government's main role under the United States Constitution is to protect the American people. The federal government was never supposed to be spending great

Saddam Hussein
(1937–2006)

Saddam Hussein was found guilty of crimes against humanity and sentenced to death by hanging. He was executed on December 30, 2006.

Barack Hussein Obama II (1961–)

President Barack Obama defeated John McCain in the presidential election of 2008 with 365 electoral votes to McCain's 173, becoming the first African American to be elected President of the United States. In his victory speech, delivered before hundreds of thousands of supporters in Chicago's Grant Park, Obama declared that "change has come to America."

245

sums of money to provide for the social needs of the American people. Nevertheless, since the 1930s, the role and power of the federal government in our society has been greatly expanded. This situation has become so bad since the 1950s that the government is now spending billions of dollars that it does not own, trying to meet the needs of various groups of people. Although Congress balanced the budget each year from 1998 to 2001, by the end of 2003 the American government still faced a seven trillion dollar debt. Since then budget deficits have grown, and the national debt is now well over nine trillion dollars!

The federal government must get out of the business of social welfare before America is destroyed financially. The job of providing for the needs of the poor and needy should be done primarily by families, churches, and private charitable organizations like the Salvation Army. Christians must lead the American people by actions and statements to see their duty to serve the poor and the needy.

Democrats for Life demonstrate at the March for Life in Washington, D.C., in 2006.

These problems, however, reflect an even deeper problem. A movement began to try to remove God from America and destroy the nation's Christian heritage. The United States Supreme Court ruled in 1962 that it was illegal for children to pray in the public schools. The Bible could no longer be taught in the public schools, and the Ten Commandments could not be read in the classroom. In addition, in 1973, the Supreme Court ruled in the case known as *Roe vs. Wade* that it was no longer illegal for a mother to kill her unborn child. This ungodly ruling has encouraged the women of America to murder their own unborn babies in violation of God's Law that says "Thou shalt not kill." As recently as 2003, over 800,000 babies were legally aborted in America; and, in some years, there were more than one million abortions.

When the courts and government leaders permitted God and the Bible to be removed from society, they opened the way for many evil forces to gain power in the land. America in the twenty-first century is staggering under

a heavy load of sin. The country is losing its greatness because it is losing its moral goodness. The nation's only hope is to turn away from lawlessness and immorality, and return to God and His Word. It is true that righteousness exalts a nation and that blessed is the nation whose God is the Lord.

What can you do now to help America overcome these problems? To begin with, you can study God's Word, the Bible, so that you can learn about how you and our society should live. You can also study

American history to learn about the principles of our country. As you have learned from this book, not everything that has happened in this country has been good, but there is much we could learn that should be applied to the United States today. The people who started the United States had definite ideas about running their government. They thought the people should make decisions about what kind of government they live under. For over 200 years, our government has operated according to the principles of these men. People in the United States have benefited from their kind of government. They have enjoyed a better life because every individual has had the opportunity to improve his way of life through education and hard work. Let all Americans, young and old, work and pray to the end that our nation may continue to be one nation, under God, with liberty and justice for all.

You should also pray for our President and others in authority over us that God would give them wisdom to lead our country out of the difficult military and economic problems that it is currently facing. In I Timothy 2:1–2, the Apostle Paul urged Timothy to pray "… [f]or kings, and all who are in authority in order that we may lead a quiet and peaceable life in all godliness and honesty."

Part of our prayers should also be for God to bring revival in America and that leaders like George Whitefield, James McGready, and J. Gresham Machen would rise up to be used by God to call many Americans to Himself. Finally, you can pray that God would raise up Christians like John Witherspoon, who would try to faithfully apply the Scripture to problems in the United States.

As you grow up, you should try more and more faithfully to apply the Word of God to all of your life. Follow the Word of God when it states in I Corinthians 10:31: "Whether therefore, ye eat, or drink, or whatsoever ye do, do all to the glory of God." Only as more and more people faithfully serve God with their whole lives can America truly become great.

Statue of Liberty

**An Excerpt from Witherspoon's sermon,
"The Dominion of Providence over the Passions of Men," May 1776**

… I would take the opportunity on this occasion, and from this subject, to press every hearer to a sincere concern for his own soul's salvation…. Can you have a clearer view of the sinfulness of your nature, than when the rod of the oppressor is lifted up, and when you see men putting on the habit of the warrior, and collecting on every hand the weapons of hostility and instruments of death? I do not blame your ardour in preparing for the resolute defense of your temporal rights; but consider, I beseech you, the truly infinite importance of the salvation of your souls. Is it of much moment whether you and your children shall be rich or poor, at liberty or in bonds? Is it of much moment whether this beautiful country shall increase in fruitfulness from year to year, being cultivated by active industry, and possessed by independent freemen, or the scanty produce of the neglected fields shall be eaten up by hungry publicans, while the timid owner trembles at the tax-gatherer's approach? And is it of less moment, my brethren, whether you shall be the heirs of glory or the heirs of hell? Is your state on earth for a few fleeting years of so much moment? And is it of less moment what shall be your state through endless ages! Have you assembled together willingly to hear what shall be said on public affairs, and to join in imploring the blessing of God on the counsels and arms of the United Colonies, and can you be unconcerned what shall become of you for ever, when all the monuments of human greatness shall be laid in ashes, for "the earth itself, and all the works that are therein shall be burnt up."

Summary. A new political generation has come to power—one that was not part of World War II—with the election of Bill Clinton. This generation does not have to deal with the dangers of the Cold War but, instead, must resist a new threat, that of Islamic extremism. Although the attacks of Islamic terrorists began as early as the Reagan administration, these terrorists became particularly active during the time of President Clinton and launched the worst terrorist attack in American history on September 11, 2001. Although these terrorists are not all from the same group, they all share a hatred of the United States.

Not all of the challenges of this time are new, however. This new generation still has to deal with economic ups and downs and foreign problems. The federal government still needs to learn how to spend less money so we can stop adding to the national debt, a particularly difficult lesson to learn during times of economic difficulties. Unborn children are still being killed through abortion.

The United States has never been a perfect country. There has always been a need for Christian citizens and churches to proclaim the Word of God and live out the principles of Scripture as witnesses to those around them. This time is no different. Christian churches need to get busy and give those around them the spiritual and physical help they need in fulfillment of the Great Commission of our Lord Jesus Christ. Nevertheless, we must claim by faith that God is not finished using our nation. We must also act upon the words printed so clearly on the Liberty Bell: "Proclaim liberty throughout all the land unto all the inhabitants thereof" (Leviticus 25:10). Remember that God is in control, regardless of what is going on around us.

Comprehension Questions

1. Name the first baby boomer President.
2. Name a plan supported by President Clinton that failed to be passed by Congress.
3. Which President was impeached by the House of Representatives?
4. Name three places where American troops were sent on peacekeeping missions by President Clinton.
5. Who was elected President of the United States in 2000?
6. Name the hurricane that heavily damaged New Orleans and Mississippi.
7. On what date did the United States receive the worst terrorist attack in its history?
8. Why was the Department of Homeland Security created?
9. What Bible verse is printed on our nation's Liberty Bell?

APPENDIX ONE:
The History of Our Presidents

No.	Name	Born/Died	Years in Office	Home State
1	George Washington	1732–1799	1789–1797	VA
2	John Adams	1735–1826	1797–1801	MA
3	Thomas Jefferson	1743–1826	1801–1809	VA
4	James Madison	1751–1836	1809–1817	VA
5	James Monroe	1758–1831	1817–1825	VA
6	John Quincy Adams	1767–1848	1825–1829	MA
7	Andrew Jackson	1767–1845	1829–1837	TN
8	Martin Van Buren	1782–1862	1837–1841	NY
9	William Henry Harrison	1773–1841	1841	OH
10	John Tyler	1790–1862	1841–1845	VA
11	James K. Polk	1795–1849	1845–1849	TN
12	Zachary Taylor	1784–1850	1849–1850	LA
13	Millard Fillmore	1800–1874	1850–1853	NY
14	Franklin Pierce	1804–1869	1853–1857	NH
15	James Buchanan	1791–1868	1857–1861	PA
16	Abraham Lincoln	1809–1865	1861–1865	IL
17	Andrew Johnson	1808–1875	1865–1869	TN
18	Ulysses S. Grant	1822–1885	1869–1877	IL
19	Rutherford B. Hayes	1822–1893	1877–1881	OH
20	James A. Garfield	1831–1881	1881	OH
21	Chester A. Arthur	1830–1886	1881–1885	NY
22	Grover Cleveland	1837–1908	1885–1889	NY
23	Benjamin Harrison	1833–1901	1889–1893	IN
24	Grover Cleveland	1837–1908	1893–1897	NY
25	William McKinley	1843–1901	1897–1901	OH

No	Name	Born/Died	Years in Office	Home State
26	Theodore Roosevelt	1858–1919	1901–1909	NY
27	William Howard Taft	1857–1930	1909–1913	OH
28	Woodrow Wilson	1856–1924	1913–1921	NJ
29	Warren G. Harding	1865–1923	1921–1923	OH
30	Calvin Coolidge	1872–1933	1923–1929	MA
31	Herbert Hoover	1874–1964	1929–1933	CA
32	Franklin D. Roosevelt	1882–1945	1933–1945	NY
33	Harry S. Truman	1884–1972	1945–1953	MO
34	Dwight D. Eisenhower	1890–1969	1953–1961	NY
35	John F. Kennedy	1917–1963	1961–1963	MA
36	Lyndon B. Johnson	1908–1973	1963–1969	TX
37	Richard M. Nixon	1913–1994	1969–1974	NY
38	Gerald R. Ford	1913–2006	1974–1977	MI
39	James E. Carter	1924–	1977–1981	GA
40	Ronald W. Reagan	1911–2004	1981–1989	CA
41	George H. W. Bush	1924–	1989–1993	TX
42	William J.Clinton	1946–	1993–2001	AR
43	George W. Bush	1946–	2001–2009	TX
44	Barack H. Obama	1961–	2009–	IL

APPENDIX TWO:
Important Facts on Our Fifty States and Territories
—STATES—

Name	Capital	Abbreviation	Date of Admission to Union	Number in Order of Admission
Alabama	Montgomery	AL	1819	22
Alaska	Juneau	AK	1959	49
Arizona	Phoenix	AZ	1912	48
Arkansas	Little Rock	AR	1836	25
California	Sacramento	CA	1850	31
Colorado	Denver	CO	1876	38
Connecticut	Hartford	CT	1788	5
Delaware	Dover	DE	1787	1
Florida	Tallahassee	FL	1845	27
Georgia	Atlanta	GA	1788	4
Hawaii	Honolulu	HI	1959	50
Idaho	Boise	ID	1890	43
Illinois	Springfield	IL	1818	21
Indiana	Indianapolis	IN	1816	19
Iowa	Des Moines	IA	1846	29
Kansas	Topeka	KS	1861	34
Kentucky	Frankfort	KY	1792	15
Louisiana	Baton Rouge	LA	1812	18
Maine	Augusta	ME	1820	23
Maryland	Annapolis	MD	1788	7
Massachusetts	Boston	MA	1788	6
Michigan	Lansing	MI	1837	26
Minnesota	St. Paul	MN	1858	32

Name	Capital	Abbreviation	Date of Admission to Union	Number in Order of Admission
Mississippi	Jackson	MS	1817	20
Missouri	Jefferson City	MO	1821	24
Montana	Helena	MT	1889	41
Nebraska	Lincoln	NE	1867	37
Nevada	Carson City	NV	1864	36
New Hampshire	Concord	NH	1788	9
New Jersey	Trenton	NJ	1787	3
New Mexico	Santa Fe	NM	1912	47
New York	Albany	NY	1788	11
North Carolina	Raleigh	NC	1789	12
North Dakota	Bismarck	ND	1889	39
Ohio	Columbus	OH	1803	17
Oklahoma	Oklahoma City	OK	1907	46
Oregon	Salem	OR	1859	33
Pennsylvania	Harrisburg	PA	1787	2
Rhode Island	Providence	RI	1790	13
South Carolina	Columbia	SC	1788	8
South Dakota	Pierre	SD	1889	40
Tennessee	Nashville	TN	1796	16
Texas	Austin	TX	1845	28
Utah	Salt Lake City	UT	1896	45
Vermont	Montpelier	VT	1791	14
Virginia	Richmond	VA	1788	10
Washington	Olympia	WA	1889	42
West Virginia	Charleston	WV	1863	35
Wisconsin	Madison	WI	1848	30
Wyoming	Cheyenne	WY	1890	44

—TERRITORIES—

Name	Capital	Abbreviation	Established or Acquired
American Samoa	Pago Pago	AS	1899
District of Columbia	Washington	DC	1791
Guam	Tamuning	GU	1898
Puerto Rico	San Juan	PR	1898
Virgin Islands	Christiansted	VI	1917

Index

A

abolitionist movement 168
abortion 226–227, 234, 237, 246, 248
Abortion and the Conscience of the Nation
  by Ronald Reagan 234
Act for the Propagation of the Gospel amongst the Indians 50
activist, conservative
  Phyllis Stewart Schlafly 226
Adams, Ansel 202
Adams, John 79, 95, 109, 242
Adams, John Quincy v, 241, 242
Adams, Samuel 110
Aesop's Fables 159
Afghanistan 231, 236–237, 240, 242–244
Africa 6–7, 151, 187, 231, 243
  East 217, 240
  French North 218
  North 216–217
African-Americans
  Barack H. Obama 245–246
  Booker T. Washington 170
  George Washington Carver 170–171
  rights improved for 225–226, 232
African slaves 24
Agnew, Spiro 231
Aguinaldo, General Emilio (Philippines) 183
Air Force
  United States 210, 228, 235
Air Force One
  the President's airplane 227
Air National Guard
  Texas 241
airplanes 192, 201
  invention of 173–174
Airport
  Love Field 227
  Tempelhof 214
  Washington National 225
Alabama 131, 141–142, 144, 152–153, 164, 170, 225–226
Alabama River 142
Alamance River 120
Alamo, Fort 153
Al Asad Air Base 244
Alaska 152, 156, 185, 223
Albania 205, 221

Albany, New York 133
Alderman, John 53
Aldrin, Edwin 230
Alexis de Tocqueville 115
Allegheny Mountains 85, 96, 99, 131
Allegheny River 86, 97
Allen, Charles 162
Allen, Ethan 119
Allied Forces 183
  Western 214
alligators 60
Al Qaeda terrorists 243–245
alternating current
  Nikola Tesla 183
Alzheimer's Disease 235
Amendments
  First 48
  Tenth 110
  Twelfth 241
  Twenty-sixth 229
  Twenty-seventh 111
America, origin of name 15
American Communist party 209
American Red Cross Society 181–182
American River 154, 156
Amish 57
Amsterdam 27
Anderson, John 234
Angel of Marye's Heights 168
Anglicans 20, 79
Annapolis, Maryland 44, 87, 105
anti-war protests 228–229, 238
Anzio, Italy 219
Apollo 15, spacecraft 230
approval ratings
  George W. Bush 244
Arab-Israel Conflict 241
Arab countries 229
Arabian Peninsula 239
Arbella, ship
  flagship of Winthrop Fleet 39
Arctic
  islands 27
Arizona 245
Arizona, battleship 217
Arkansas 166, 208, 225, 237–238
Armistice Day 195
Armstrong, Hannah
  wife of Jack Armstrong 162
Armstrong, Jack 161

Armstrong, Neil 230
Armstrong, William "Duff"
  son of Jack Armstrong 162
Army
  British 79, 91, 112, 122, 142, 216
  U.S. 12th 218
  United States 88–89, 92, 122, 142, 170, 184, 190, 205, 209–211, 213, 216, 220, 233, 243
Army Corps of Engineers 208
Arnold, Benedict 92, 119
"arsenal for democracy"
  United States as 205
Articles of Association (1774) 79
Articles of Confederation 79, 104–105, 107
Asbury, Francis 80, 113, 115–116
Asia 6, 10, 12, 13, 15, 29, 151, 186, 217, 221
  Southeast 7
Assistant Secretary of the Navy
  Theodore Roosevelt as 179–180
Associated Electrical Industries 173
astronauts
  Alan Shepard, Jr. 230
  Edwin Aldrin 230
  James Irwin 230
  John Glenn 230
  Neil Armstrong 230
Atlantic Ocean 4, 6–8, 11–12, 13, 28, 36, 86, 99, 148, 150–151, 156, 169, 172, 179–181, 184, 188, 217
  Lindbergh's flight over 201
  Sea of Darkness 8, 10–11
atomic bomb 213
Attorney-General
  Bill Clinton as (AR) 238
  heads the Department of Justice 107
Australia 6, 211, 228, 243
Austria 203, 205
Austria-Hungary 188
automobile 200
  "Horseless Carriage" 174
  invention of 173–174
Axis powers 205–206

B

Backus, Isaac 76
Bacon's Rebellion 24
Badlands
  Theodore Roosevelt as hunter in 177
Balboa, Vasco de 16–17, 184, 188
Baltimore, Lord 41–45
Baltimore, Maryland 44, 149–150
Bank of the United States 111
banks closed (1930s) 201
Baptists 79, 104
  Calvinistic 76
  Dr. Martin Luther King, Jr. 226
  Jimmy Carter 231
  Philadelphia Baptist Association 76
  Rev. Jerry Falwell 237
Barak, Prime Minister Ehud 241
Barcelona, Spain 10
Baron of Baltimore
  First (George Calvert) 41
  Second (Cecilius Calvert) 42
  Third (Charles Calvert) 43–44
  Fourth (Benedict Calvert) 45
  Fifth (Charles Calvert) 44
  Sixth (Frederick Calvert) 45
Barton, Clara 181
Bassett, Richard 80
Bataan Peninsula 210
Battle
  of Alamance 120
  of Britain 216
  of Bunker Hill 88
  of Cowpens 139–140
  of El Alamein, First 217
  of El Alamein, Second 217
  of Fallen Timbers 123
  of Gettysburg 167
  of Hobkirk's Hill 140–141
  of Horseshoe Bend 142
  of Kings Mountain 121
  of Manila Bay 179
  of Midway 212
  of New Orleans 143–144, 177
  of Santiago 180–181
  of Saratoga 122
  of Springfield 77
  of Stalingrad 217
  of the Bulge 218–219
  of Thiepval Ridge 193
  of Tippecanoe 135–137

Bay of Pigs, Cuba 225
beans 136
Beardstown, Illinois 162
Beirut, Lebanon 235
Belgium 188, 194–195, 205, 216, 218
Bell, Alexander Graham 171–172
Benjamin, Judah P. 165
Berkeley, Sir William 24
Berlin, Germany 220–221
Berlin Blockade/Airlift 214
Berlin Wall 224
    Reagan challenged Gorbachev at 235
Bermuda
    Indian slaves sold to 53
Bethesda Home for Boys 59, 63–65
Bible
    Abraham Lincoln and 159
    and missionary work 198–199
    and public schools 246
    Andrew Jackson and 141
    and science 196–197
    cf. Numbers 23:23 149
    George Washington Carver and the 171
    James McGready and 112–113
    Jefferson's rejection of miracles in 112
    Miles Standish's 39
    Pilgrims and 35
    proclamation of 248
    Quakers and 55
    study of 246
    Washington swore on 94
    Witherspoon taught from 77
Bill of Rights 110–111, 222
bin Laden, Osama 243
Black Hawk War of 1832 161
Black Sea 206
"Black Tuesday"
    October 29, 1929 201
Blake, Eli and Philos
    nephews of Eli Whitney 126
Blue Ridge Mountains 84, 128
boats
    diving boat 132
    paddle wheel scow 131
Bolsheviks 203
Bonaparte, Napoleon 103, 129, 132
"Bonus Army"
    World War I veterans 209
Book of Wonders, The
    by Marco Polo 12
Boone, Daniel 97, 100–103, 119–120

Boone, Jemima
    daughter of Daniel 102
Boone, Nathan
    youngest son of Daniel 103
Boonesborough, Kentucky 97, 101, 103
Booth, John Wilkes 167
"born again"
    presidential candidates claim to be 237
Bosnia and Herzegovina 188, 240
Bosnian War 240
Boston, England 39
Boston, Massachusetts 39, 40, 46, 70, 71, 75, 87–90, 121–122, 146, 150–152, 171–172, 179
Boston Harbor 122
Boston Tea Party 87
Boulder Dam. *See* Hoover Dam
Bowie, Colonel James "Jim" 153
Bowman, Captain Joseph 99
Braddock, General 86
Bradford, Governor William 36–38
Bradley, General Omar 219
branches of government 105
Brazil 15, 172, 187
Brewster, Elder William 37
bridges
    iron 132
Bridgewater lads
    under Captain Church 53
Bristol, England 13–15
Britain 17, 19, 45, 74, 76, 79, 81, 97, 110, 119, 153, 173, 188, 200, 205–206, 210, 214, 218, 240
    Battle of 216
Brookfield, Massachusetts 51
Brooklyn, armored cruiser 180
budget deficits, federal 234, 236, 246
buffalo 144
Buffalo, New York 147, 183
Bulgaria 216
Bunker Hill 61, 88
Burlington, New Jersey 70
Burma (now Myanmar) 213
Bush, George H. W. 224, 235–240
Bush, George W. 237, 241–245
business regulations
    reduction of 234
Butler, General Benjamin 181

C

Cabinet
    of the President 106
Cabot, John 13–15, 18, 46
Cabot, Sebastian 13
Caldwell, Rev. James 77
California 154–157, 184, 206, 233, 233–235
Callaway, Elizabeth and Frances
    friends of Jemima Boone 102
calm revivalists
    Asahel Nettleton 114–115
    Dwight L. Moody 174
Calvert, Benedict
    son of Charles (first) 45
Calvert, Cecilius (Cecil)
    eldest son of George 42–44
Calvert, Charles
    son of Cecilius 43–44
Calvert, Charles (second)
    son of Benedict
        grandson of Charles (first) 44
Calvert, Frederick
    son of Charles (second)
        grandson of Benedict 45
Calvert, George
    First Baron of Baltimore 41–45
Cambodia 206, 231
Cambridge, Massachusetts 89, 146
Camden, South Carolina 140
campaign fund raising
    questionable 239
camp meetings 112–116
Canada 4, 29, 80, 85–86, 89, 137, 214, 218, 221, 239
Canal Zone. *See* Panama Canal
Canary Islands 8
canoes 21, 31, 42
Canonchet, Chief
    grandson of Canonicus 52–53
Canonicus, Chief 38
Canton, Ohio 183
Cape Bonavista, Newfoundland 13
Cape Breton Island 13
Cape Cod 36, 49
Cape Horn 151, 185
Cape of Good Hope 151
capitalism
    free-market 239
Capitol building, U.S. 243
Captain's Hill
    Standish homestead 39
Caribbean 242

Carpenters' Hall, Philadelphia 105
Carroll, Daniel 80
Carter, James E. "Jimmy" 231–232, 234
cartoons
    "Willie and Joe" 219
Carver, George Washington 170–171
Carver, John 36–37
Castro, Fidel 225–226, 227
Category 5 storm
    Hurricane Katrina 242
Caterpillar Tractor Company 193
Catholics 57, 80, 224
    at Fort Kaskaskia 98
    Benedict Calvert renounced faith 45
    English 43
    James II of England 44
    Lord Baltimore converts to 41
    Marie Antonia, French 42
    missionaries 17
Cayuse Indians 152
Centennial Exposition 172, 174
Central America 11, 15, 231
Central Intelligence Agency 225
    George H. W. Bush as director of 236
Cervera, Admiral Pascual (Spain) 179–181
Chagres River 185
Charles I of England 41, 45, 51
Charles II of England
    son of Charles I 51, 55–56
Charleston, South Carolina 60, 87, 91–92, 141, 166
Charlestown, Massachusetts 88, 147
Charlottesville, Virginia 128
Chernomyrdin, Viktor (Russia) 240
Cherokee Indians 121
Chesapeake Bay 20, 27, 44
Chicago 8, 145, 150, 164, 169–170, 174, 226–227
Chief Justice
    of the Supreme Court 106
Chief of Staff of the Army
    Douglas MacArthur 209
    Dwight D. Eisenhower 220–221
China 27–28, 31, 150–151, 179, 182, 203, 205, 210, 213–214, 217, 236
    Mainland 221, 232

Chinook helicopter 243
Chirac, Jacques (France) 240
Christian heritage
of the United States 246
Christianity 10, 174
core beliefs of 197
Evangelical 199
Christianity and Liberalism
by J. Gresham Machen 197,
199
Christians
communist oppression of
204
George Washington Carver
170–171
James Irwin, astronaut 230
church
membership 115
revivals in the 112
Church, Captain Benjamin
52–53
Bridgewater lads under 53
church attendance
Williams against requirement
47
Churchill, Winston 206, 217,
220
Church of England 35, 41,
43, 45, 47, 79
Anglican Church 20
Church of Scotland 77
Church of the Holy Sepulchre
24
Cincinnati, Ohio 122, 146
circuit-riding preachers 113
Civilian Conservation Corps
202
civil rights 231–232
expansion of 225–227
Civil War
English 51
Lebanese 235
Russian 203
Spanish 204
Civil War, American. *See* War
Between the States
Claiborne, Ferdinand L. 142
Clark, George Rogers 96–99,
121
Clark, William 152
Clinton, Hillary Rodham 239,
245
Clinton, William J. "Bill"
237–241, 245, 248
coal 55, 169
Cold War 214, 220–221, 223,
248
College of New Jersey 77–78,
104
Coloma, California 154–157
Colombia 200

Colonial National Historic
Park 25
Columbia, ship 151–152
Columbian Exposition.
See World's Columbian
Exposition
Columbian Exposition, Chi-
cago 8
Columbia River 152, 157
Columbia University 220
Columbus, Christopher 4,
6–12, 13, 15, 177, 182
Commonwealth of Nations
195
communism 225, 228, 232,
236–237
Communist party 203
threat of 220–223
Communists
Afghanistan 235, 237
Cambodia 231
Central America 235
China 214
Eastern Europe 214, 236
El Salvador 237
Ethiopia 237
Grenada 235
Laos 231
Mongolia 236
Nicaragua 237
North Korea 214
North Vietnam 227–228,
232
Russia 203–204, 235
South Vietnam 231
Soviet Bloc countries 235
Third World 237
computers 172, 229
Concord, Massachusetts 88
Confederate States of America
164, 166–167
Congregationalists 79
Congress
Continental 76, 79, 88, 90,
94, 96, 104–105, 129
First Continental 57
law-making power of 106
Congress, United States
109–111, 149, 158,
163, 171, 178, 183,
186, 202, 205, 209,
210, 217, 222, 225,
234, 236, 239, 241,
242, 244
Congressional Medal of
Honor
Alvin York 191
Arthur MacArthur 208
Douglas MacArthur 211
Connecticut 40, 50, 62, 76,
115, 119, 126, 235

Connecticut (*cont.*)
ratification of Constitution
108
Connecticut River 51
conservatives
Christians 237
political 233, 237, 239
Constitutional Convention
79–80, 241
Virginia 111
Constitution of the United
States 48, 79, 105–
111, 119, 123, 226,
229, 245
Framers of 241
Constitution of Vermont 119
Continental Army 89, 91
Continental Congress 57,
76, 79, 88, 94, 96,
104–105, 129
Coolidge, Calvin 171,
200–202
corn 21–22, 100, 135
Indian 36
Cornwallis, Lord Charles
90–93
Corregidor, Philippines 211
cotton 60, 125–126, 128, 164
cotton gin 125–126
Court of Inquiry
investigation of USS *Maine*
explosion 178
Cowpens, Battle of 139–140
Cranham, England 61
creation 196
Creek Indians 141–142, 152
Creek War 141–143
crimes against humanity
Saddam Hussein found
guilty of 245
criticism
of George Whitefield 64
of Second Great Awakening
113–114
Croatia 240
Crockett, David 153
Cuba 10, 177–184, 187,
224–225, 227, 232
Cuban Missile Crisis 224–225
Culebra Hills, Panama 185
Cumberland Gap 101
Cumberland River 121
Custis, Martha
wife of George Washington
85
Czechoslovakia 205, 221,
227
Czolgosz, Leon
assassin of President McKin-
ley 183

D

D-Day
launching of 218
Dallas, Texas 227
Dare, Virginia 18
Darien, Connecticut 76
Darwin, Charles 196, 199
Davis, Jefferson 164–166
Dayton (Ohio) Peace Agree-
ment 240
Dayton, Ohio 173
Declaration of Independence
75–76, 78–79, 90–91,
129–130, 172
Declaration of Rights 109
Deerfield, Massachusetts 51
Defense of Marriage Act 239
deficits. *See* budget deficits
de Grasse, François Joseph
Paul 93
Delaware 43, 80, 166
ratification of Constitution
108
Delaware Bay 27
Delaware River 55, 70–71,
90–91
Democracy in America, book
115
Democratic party 229, 245
Connecticut 126
Democrats for Life 246
Denmark 3–4, 205, 216
Denny, Ebenezer 122
Denver, Colorado 150, 216
Department
of Homeland Security 243
of Justice 107
de Soto, Hernando 16–17
Detroit, Michigan 96, 99, 141
Dewey, Commodore George
179, 181
dictatorships 203–205, 207
Disciples of Christ 233
Discovery, ship 29
discrimination
legal 245
racial 222
diving boat 132
Dixon, Illinois 233
Dixon, Jeremiah 43
Dixon High School
Reagan's alma mater 233
Docherty, Rev. George M.
222
Dominican Republic 10, 186,
227
"Dominion of Providence
over the Passions of
Men" 78
Dos Rios, Cuba 177

Doud, Mamie Geneva
  wife of Dwight D. Eisen-
    hower 216
Douglas C-54 Skymaster 214
drugs 7
"dugouts," underground
    192, 194
Dukakis, Michael 236
Dunkers 80
Dutch East Indies 217
Dutch Settlement 30–31
Duxbury, Massachusetts 39
Dwight, Timothy 126

E

Earl of Granville 81
Earthquake of 1811, Great
    133
East Africa 217, 240
Eastern Europe 207, 214, 216,
    220–221, 235–237, 240
East Germany 223–224
East Indies 210
  Dutch 217
Ebenezer, Georgia 60
economy
  American 201–202, 207,
    231–239, 242, 245
  economic reform 177
  Italian, 1930s 204
  Japanese 214
  national 95
Edison & Swan United Electric
    Light Company 173
Edison, Thomas A. 172–174
Edwards, Henrietta
  daughter of Pierpont
    Edwards
    granddaughter of Jonathan
      Edwards 126
Edwards, Jonathan 126
Edwards, Pierpont
  son of Jonathan Edwards 126
Egypt 217, 227, 229, 232
Eisenhower, Dwight D.
    216–225, 233
Eisenhower Interstate System
    222
El Alamein, Egypt 217
Electoral College
  described 241
  electoral votes 241
  unanimously elected George
    Washington 95
electricity 73–75, 148, 150,
    171–173
electric light
  invention of 173–174
electric railroad car 173
Eliot, John 50

Elizabeth I of England 18–19
Ellsworth, Annie G. 149
El Salvador 237
Emancipation Proclamation
    167
embassy, U.S. 231, 235
emotional response
  in camp meetings 113–114
England 3–4, 7, 13–15, 18,
    20, 23, 30–31, 37, 39,
    41, 50, 56–57, 59–61,
    73–75, 79–81, 86–87,
    90, 94–95, 132, 137,
    143–145, 146, 165,
    189–190, 193–195
English Civil Wars 24
environmental issues
  global warming 245
  pollution 245
Episcopalians 79
  James Madison 104
Equal Rights Amendment
    226
Ericsson, Leif 3–4
Erie Canal 147–148
Ethiopia 205, 217, 231, 237
"ethnic cleansing" 240
Eureka College 233
Europe 6–7, 13, 28, 45, 56,
    58, 74, 81, 129, 181,
    183, 188, 190–191,
    204–207, 210, 217,
    220–221, 223–224,
    235, 240
  Eastern 207, 214, 216, 220–
    221, 235–237, 240
  Western 214, 221
Europe Day 220
Evangelical Christianity 199
  Year of the Evangelical 237
Evans, Captain Robley Dungli-
    son 180
evolution, theory of 196, 199
executive branch 105–107

F

Fairfax, Colonel William 83,
    94
Fallen Timbers, Battle of 123
Falwell, Jerry 237
FAX machine 172
Federal-Aid Highway Act 222
federal budget
  balanced, surplus 239
  deficits 234, 246
Federal Bureau of Investiga-
    tion 206
federal government 105
Federal Hall 95
Federalist, The 108

feminist movement 226
Ferdinand
  king of Spain 7, 10–11
Ferdinand, Franz (Austro-
    Hungarian) 188
Ferguson, Senator Homer S.
    (MI) 222
Filipino armed forces 210–
    211
Finney, Charles 114
fireside chats
  Franklin D. Roosevelt's 201,
    205
First Amendment 48
fishing industry 41
Fitzsimmons, Thomas 80
five-year economic plans
  Joseph Stalin's 204
Flag Day 222
flamethrowers 192
flat-bottomed boat 131
Florida 16–17, 59–60,
    144–145, 164, 177,
    178, 225, 241
  Spaniards of 60
  West, taken from Spain 111
Florida Territory
  purchased by U.S. 144
  Spanish controlled 142
flying machine. *See* airplane:
    invention of
Flying Squadron
  Commodore Schley's 179
Ford, Gerald 229, 231, 234,
    237
Ford, Henry 174
Forefathers' Day 36
foreign policy 200
Forest Service
  United States 186
Fort Alamo 153
Fort Amsterdam 30–31
Fort Detroit 99
Fort Kaskaskia 97, 99
Fort Mims 141
Fort Myer, Virginia 173
Fort Nashborough 121
Fort Necessity 86
Fort Sumter 166
Fort Ticonderoga 119
Fort Vincennes 98–99
Fort Watauga 121
42nd Infantry Division 208
Fosdick, Harry Emerson
    196–197, 199
442nd Regimental Combat
    Team 206
France 3–4, 14, 41, 74–75,
    91, 92, 95, 103, 122,
    129, 132, 148, 188,
    190–191, 193–195,

    200, 205–206, 208,
    210, 214–216, 218,
    240
Franco, Francisco (Spain) 204
Franco-Prussian War 181
Frankfort, Kentucky 103
Franklin, Benjamin 63, 69–75,
    82, 89, 91, 112, 122,
    129, 147
  the "Water-American" 72
Franklin, James
  brother of Benjamin 70
Fredericksburg, Virginia 168
free-market capitalism 239
freedom
  of religion 48, 110
  of speech 110
  of the press 110
freedom fighters
  Cuban (1870s) 177
Freedom One, aircraft 231
free will 114
French and Indian War 85, 119
French Republic 190
French Tunisia 217
Fulton, Robert 131–134
fundamentalists
  Christian 196–197
fund raising
  campaign 239
furs 151

G

Gabaldon, Guy 209
Gadsden Purchase 156
Gage, General Thomas
    88–89
gasoline
  price increases 242
Gatun Locks 185
General Assembly
  of Rhode Island 109
General Electric Company
    173
General Electric Theater
  Reagan as host of 233
General of the Army
  Douglas MacArthur 220
  Dwight D. Eisenhower 220
Genesis (creation) 196
Genoa, Italy 6–7
George I of England 45
George II of England 59, 77
George III of England 86–87,
    90
Georgia 59, 62, 74, 87, 125,
    142, 164–165, 226,
    231
  ratification of Constitution
    108

Germany 81, 188–195, 203–207, 210, 216–217, 219–220, 240
    reunification of 236
Gettysburg, Battle of 167
Gettysburg, Pennsylvania 167, 222–223
Gilbert du Motier. *See* Lafayette
Glenn, John 230
glider 173
global warming 245
Gloucester, gunboat 181
God 112–114, 141, 149, 171, 196, 204, 234, 237, 246
    freedom to worship 35, 43, 45, 48
    in control of history 248
    Law of 246
Goethals, Colonel George W. 184–186, 188
Goffe, Colonel William 51
gold 10, 154–157, 169
    and Panama Railway 184
Goldwater, Barry 233
Gonzalez, Felipe (Spain) 240
Gorbachev, Mikhail (Russia) 235
Gore, Albert 241
gospel of Jesus Christ 113
government
    federal 105
    limited 239
    state 105
governor
    Bill Clinton as (AR) 238
    George W. Bush as (TX) 241
    Ronald Reagan as (CA) 233
    Sam Houston as (TN & TX) 142
    Sarah Palin as (AK) 245
Grant, General Ulysses S. 167
Granville, Earl of 81
Gray, Captain Robert 151–152, 157
Great Awakening 62, 72
Great Britain. *See* Britain
Great Commission 81, 199, 248
Great Depression 200–203, 207, 209, 234
Great Lakes 134
Great Society
    Lyndon Johnson's 227
Great War, the. *See* World War I
Great White Fleet
    Theodore Roosevelt's 186
Great Wolf of North Carolina. *See* Tryon, William
Greece 216, 221

Greene, Catharine Littlefield 125
Greene, General Nathanael 92, 125, 140
Greenland 4, 29
Green Mountain Boys 119
Grenada 235
Groton, Massachusetts 51
Guam 177, 181–183, 206
Gulf of Mexico 242
Gulf War 236, 240

H

Hadley, Massachusetts 51
Haiti 240
Haiti, Republic of 10
Half Moon, ship 27–29
Halsey, Admiral William "Bull" 211
Hamilton, Alexander 79, 95, 105, 107–109, 241
Hamilton, Colonel Henry 96–97, 98
Hampton Institute 170
Hanks, John 160, 163
Harding, Warren Gamaliel 200
Harrison, William Henry 135–137
    as Hero of Tippecanoe 137
Hart, John 79
Harvard College 50
Harvard University 241
Harvester. *See* reapers
Havana, Cuba 178–179, 182
Hawaii
    became 50th state (1959) 182, 223
Hawaiian Islands
    annexed by U.S. (1898) 182
    442nd Regimental Combat Team from 206
    Pearl Harbor 210, 217
Hayes, Rutherford B. 241
healthcare 239
helicopters
    Chinook 243
    Vietnam War 228
Helluland 4
Henriette Marie 42, 45
Henry, Patrick 25, 79, 97, 99, 107, 128
Henry VII of England 7, 13–14
Hernando de Soto 16–17
"Hero of Manila"
    Commodore Dewey as 179
Hessians 77
high-technology 229
High Flight Foundation
    James Irwin, astronaut 230

Highlands, New York 28–29
Highway Act, Federal-Aid 222
Hinckley, Jr., John
    would-be assassin of Reagan 234
Hindenburg Line (World War I) 194
Hispaniola 10
History of the United States, book 159
Hitler, Adolf 204, 219
Hobkirk's Hill, Battle of 140–141
Hobson, Lieutenant Richmond P. 180–181
Ho Chi Minh 227
Hocking, William Ernest 198
Holland. *See* Netherlands
Holt, Benjamin 193
"Holy Ground"
    Red Stick Indians' 142
Holy Spirit 113
Homeland Security 243
home ownership 200
Hong Kong 179, 206
Hoover, Herbert 201–202
Hoover Dam 202
Hopewell, ship 27
Horn of Africa 239
Hornsby & Sons
    U.K. engine manufacturer 193
"Horseless Carriage". *See* automobile
Horseshoe Bend, Battle of 142
hostages
    Americans held as (Iran) 231
House of Representatives 106, 109, 222, 224, 239
    selection of President 241
Houston, Sam 142, 152–157
Houston, Texas 153
Howe, Elias 146–147, 150
Howe, General William 89
howitzer (short cannon) 193
Hudson, Captain Henry 27–32
Hudson Bay 30
Hudson River 35, 92, 133–134
    also Grande River 27–29
Hudson Strait 29
human rights
    religious freedom 48
Humphrey, Hubert 229
Hungary 203, 216, 223
Huntsville, Texas 154–155
Hurricane Katrina 242

Hussein, Saddam 240, 244–245
Hussey, Obed 146, 150

I

Iceland 3–4, 6
Idaho 152, 157
Illinois 96–97, 99, 131, 160–165, 167, 193, 233, 245
immigration
    of Japanese 200
    system, changes to 242
Immigration Act of 1924 200
impeachment of
    U.S. President 239
income tax
    Reagan cut rates 234
India 213
Indiana 96, 112–113, 131, 135–137, 158–159
Indianapolis, Indiana 99
Indiana Territory 136
Indian Rock 122
Indians 84–85, 89, 100–103, 161
    American 10, 16, 17, 21
    Cayuse 152
    Cherokee 121
    Creek 141–142, 152
    help Williams escape 47
    Mohegan 53
    Narragansett 52–53
    near Marietta, Ohio 122–123
    Nez Perce 152
    Nipmuck 50
    Nonantum 50
    Praying 50
    Quaker treatment of 56
    Seminole 144
    Shawnee 135
    Wampanoag 37, 49
    William "Red Eagle" Weatherford 141
    Williams, missionary to 46
Indies 6–7, 12, 20, 27, 31
Indochina 206
Industrial Revolution 196, 199
inner light
    of the Quakers 55
International Committee of the Red Cross 181
Invasion of Normandy 218
Iowa 233
Iowa, battleship 180
Iowa State Agricultural College 171
Iran 231
Iran Hostage Crisis 231, 233

Iraq 236, 240, 242–244
Iraq Liberation Act 240
Iraq War 244
Ireland 3–4
Irish-Scotch Presbyterian
    Rebellion 77
iron 55, 169
"Iron Needle-woman".
    See sewing machines
Irwin, James 230
Isabella
    queen of Spain 7, 10–11
"I shall return"
    MacArthur's motto for the
        Filipinos 211
Islamic terrorists 235, 240, 248
    Al Qaeda 243
Israel 227, 229, 232
Isthmus
    of Panama 184
Italy 6–7, 13, 195, 200,
    204–207, 217, 219
Iwo Jima, Japan 213
Izetbegovic, Alija (Bosnia and
    Herzegovina) 240

J

Jackson, Andrew 138–144,
    153, 241
Jackson, General Thomas
    "Stonewall" 167
James I of England
    and James VI of Scotland
        19–20, 35
James II of England 44
James River 20
Jamestown 19, 20–26, 27
Japan 8, 15, 186, 200,
    204–208, 210–217
    occupation of Philippines
        183
Japanese-Americans
    Guy Gabaldon and 209
    treatment of (WWII) 206
Jasper, Sergeant William 92
Jay, John 107–108
Jefferson, Thomas 95, 110,
    112, 128–130, 138,
    153, 187
    as Pen of the Revolution 129
Jehovah Witness 216
Jenkins' Ear, War of 61
Jesus Christ 113, 196–199,
    248
Jews 57
Johnnycake 43, 100
Johnson, Lyndon B. 225,
    227–228, 232–233
Johnston, Sir Guy 96
"Join, or Die" motto 74

Jordan 227
judicial branch 105–106

K

Kandahar Army Air Field 243
Kansas 216
Kaskaskia, Illinois 96–97, 99
Katrina, Hurricane 242
Kennedy, John F. 186, 223,
    224–230, 232, 238
Kentucky 96–97, 99–103,
    113, 119–121, 123, 131,
    158, 166
Kentucky River 101–103
Kenya 240
Kerry, John 242
Key, Francis Scott 127
Key West, Florida 178
Khrushchev, Nikita (Soviet
    Union) 225
King, Dr. Martin Luther
    226–227, 232
King Philip's War 50–53
Kings Mountain
    Battle of 121
Kirkland, Sergeant Richard
    as The Angel of Marye's
        Heights 168
Knoxville, Tennessee 121
Kohl, Helmut (Germany) 240
Korea 208, 213–215, 220,
    227
Korean War 211, 214–215
    truce (under Eisenhower)
        223
Kosovo 240
Kuwait 236

L

L'Anse aux Meadows 4
Lady Washington, ship 151
Lafayette, Marquis de 92–93,
    95
Lake Champlain 119
Lake Erie 85
Lake Michigan 145, 170
Laos 206, 231
Latin America 225
laws
    Watauga Association 120
League of Nations 200
Lebanon 235
Lee, General Charles 82
Lee, General Robert E. 167
Legion of the United States
    123
legislative branch 105–106
Lenin, Vladimir Ilyich 203
Leonardo da Vinci

Carver as "Black Leonardo"
    170
Leviticus 25:10 248
Lewinsky, Monica 239
Lewis, Meriwether 152
Lewis and Clark Expedition
    Jefferson promoted 130
Lexington, Massachusetts 88
Leyden, Netherlands 35, 73
Leyden jar 73
Leyte Island, Philippines 211
liberal politics 245
liberal religionists
    man-centered 196–197,
        199
liberals
    political 239
Liberty Bell 248
Liberty Bonds 190
Libya 217, 235
Life of Washington 159
limited government 239
    Reagan as advocate for
        233–234
Lincoln, Abraham 158–168,
    181, 187
Lincoln, Mary Ann Todd
    wife of Abraham 163
Lincoln, Robert Todd
    son of Abraham 163
Lincoln, Thomas
    father of Abraham Lincoln
        158–159
Lindbergh, Charles 201
Lindstrom, Rev. Paul 227
Lisbon, Portugal 6–7
Lithuania 205
Little Rock, Arkansas 208
Livingston, Robert R. 107,
    129, 132–133
Logan County, Kentucky 113
log cabins 20, 36, 69, 100,
    153
    Abraham Lincoln 158–160
London 19, 24, 27, 42, 57,
    71–72, 87, 146, 200,
    220
    prisons of 59
Long Parliament 50
Los Angeles 128, 209, 245
"Lost Battalion," rescued 206
Louisiana 128, 153, 164
Louisiana Purchase 103, 110,
    129–130, 153, 156
Louisiana Territory 129, 131,
    158
Louisville, Kentucky 99
Love Field Airport 227
Loyalists 77, 79–81, 96
Luke 18:14 71
Lusitania, ocean liner 189

Lutherans 57, 81
Luxembourg 216

M

MacArthur, Arthur 208
MacArthur, Douglas 208–
    216, 220
Machen, J. Gresham 196–
    199, 247
machine guns 192–194
Machinery Palace
    at Panama-Pacific Interna-
        tional Exposition (1915)
        189
Madison, James 78, 104–111
    as Father of the Constitution
        104–105, 111
Maine 40, 50, 53, 59, 62, 87,
    146
Maine, battleship 178
Major, John 240
malaria 184
Malaya 206
Malcolm X 226
Mallory, Stephen 165
Manhattan Island 27, 30–31
Manhattan Project 205
Manila, Philippines 178–179,
    181, 211
Manila Bay, Battle of 179
Manomet Hill 36
Mao Tse-tung (China) 221
March for Life, 2006 246
Marconi Corporation 173
Marco Polo 12
Marie Antoinette 122
Marietta, Ohio 122
Marines
    United States 209, 211,
        215, 220, 235
Markland 4
marriage
    biblical 239
Marshall, George 221
Marshall, James Wilson
    154–155
Marshall, John 107
Marshall, Justice Thurgood
    225
Marshall Plan 221
Martí, José 177
Marye's Heights, Virginia 168
Mary II of England 44
Maryland 42–45, 55, 80, 166
    ratification of Constitution
        108
Mason, Charles 43
Mason-Dixon Line 43
Mason County, Illinois 162

Massachusetts 40, 46–51,
    53, 61, 62, 74, 76,
    108–110, 122, 124,
    126, 146–147, 224, 242
  General Court of 50
  ratification of Constitution
    108
Massachusetts Bay Colony
    39–40, 47
Massacre at Fort Mims 141
Massasoit, Chief 37–38, 47,
    49
Mather, Rev. Moses 76–77
Matthew, ship 13–14
Mauldin, Bill
  cartoonist 219
Mayflower, ship 36, 121
  second (1630) 39
Mayflower Compact 36
McCain, John 245
McCormick, Cyrus H.
    145–146, 150
McGovern, George 238
McGready, James 112–116,
    247
McKinley, William 177–179,
    183, 186–187
Medal of Honor
  Douglas MacArthur 208
  Japanese-American soldiers
    206
Mediterranean 206, 217
  Sea 4, 6, 13
meetinghouse
  Friends' 57
  Hadley, Massachusetts 51
  in the Waxhaws region 139
  Pilgrim 38
  Quaker 71
Memminger, Christopher
    165
Menéndez de Avilés, Pedro
    17
Menlo Park, New Jersey 173
Mennonites 57, 80, 216
Merrimac, steamship
  used as a collier 180
Merritt, General Wesley 179,
    181
Metacomet (King Philip)
  son of Massasoit 49
Methodists 79–80, 113
  in the camp meetings 113
  Welsh (Calvinistic) 59
Mexican-American Marine
    209
Mexican-American War
  campaigns of 157
Mexico 153–157, 177, 208,
    239
  Gulf of 17

Miami River 122
Michigan 96, 131, 172, 222
Middle East 236–237, 243
Middletown, Connecticut 62
Midway, Battle of 212
Miles, General Nelson Apple-
    ton 181
militia
  Georgia 142
  Mississippi Territory 142
  of the Northern states 166
  Reynolds's 161
  Tennessee 121, 142
  Vermont 119
Miller, Nancy 160
Milošević, Slobodan (Serbia
    and Montenegro) 240
Minnesota 186
Minuit, Peter 30
miracles of the Bible 197
missiles, nuclear 225, 232
missionaries
  opportunities opened for
    182
  work of 198–199
Mississippi 225, 242
Mississippi, State of 131, 142,
    164, 167
Mississippi River 16, 86, 99,
    103, 128–130, 131,
    133–134, 143–145,
    152, 156, 160,
    166–167, 169, 177
Mississippi Territory 142
Missouri 103, 166, 170
Missouri, battleship 213
Missouri River 134
Missouri Territory 103
moderates, political 239
Mohegan Indians 53
Mongolia 203, 236
Montana 103, 152
Montenegro 188, 240
Montgomery, Bernard
  Field Marshal 217
  General 219
Monticello 128–129
Montpelier, Virginia 104
Moody, Dwight Lyman 174
Moody Bible Institute 174
moon (earth's) 230, 232
Moral Majority 237
moral values
  traditional 239
Moravians 80–81
Morgan, Brigadier General-
    Daniel 92
Morse, Samuel F. B. 147–150,
    171
mortise lock 126
Moscow 217, 219

mosquitoes
  malaria carrying 184–185
Mother of Presidents.
    See Virginia
motion pictures
  invention of 173–174
Motor Torpedo Boat (PT-109)
    224
Moultrie, Colonel William
    91–92
mountains
  Mount Rushmore 187
  Pacific coast ranges 185
Mount Hope, Rhode Island
    47
Mount Vernon 83, 94–95
movie production 200
Muslim terrorists
  Iranian 231
Mussolini, Benito 204, 219

N

NAFTA 239
Nagasaki, Japan 213
Naples, Italy 13
Narragansett Bay 49, 51, 52
Narragansett Indians 38,
    52–53
NASA 223, 230
Nashborough, Fort 121
Nashville, Tennessee 121, 141
National Aeronautics and
    Space Administration.
    See NASA
national anthem
  of the United States 127
national debt 246, 248
nationalists
  black (Malcolm X) 226
  Chinese 203, 214, 232
  Serbian 188
  Spanish 204
National Organization of
    Women 226
National Park Service 202
National Socialist (Nazi)
    party. *See* Nazi party
Native Americans 4, 29
  and the Pilgrims 37–39
  King Philip's alliance 53
  languages of 46
  Moravian missionaries to 81
  of New England 49
  Quakers and the 56–57
NATO 214, 221, 223, 235,
    240, 243
natural resources
  conservation of 186
Navajo code talkers 211

naval blockade
  Cuban Missile Crisis 225
Navy
  Japanese 212
  United States 179, 180,
    186, 187, 202,
    205–206, 209, 212,
    220, 224, 227, 235
Navy & Marine Corps Medal
  John F. Kennedy 224
Navy Cross
  Guy Gabaldon 209
Nazi party 204, 220
Netherlands 30, 35, 205, 216
Nettleton, Asahel
  calm revivalist 114
New Deal programs 201–
    202, 205, 233
New England 36, 39–40, 42,
    49, 53–54, 59, 87, 121
Newfoundland 13–14, 41
New Guinea 211
New Hampshire 40, 119, 181
  ratification of Constitution
    108
New Haven, Connecticut 126
New Jersey 56, 70, 74, 79,
    90–91, 173
  ratification of Constitution
    108
New Mexico 156
New Netherland 27, 30–31
New Orleans 128–130, 133,
    143–145, 160–161, 242
  Battle of 143–144
New Salem, Illinois 161, 163
newspapers 82, 189
  Pennsylvania Gazette 69, 72
Newsweek, magazine 237
New World 4, 9–10, 12,
    13–15, 103, 182
New Year's Day 182
New York City 30–31, 70,
    87, 90–91, 93–95,
    109, 128, 133–134,
    146–147, 150, 172,
    179, 183–184, 196,
    220, 240, 243
New York Convention 107
New York State 21, 91, 96,
    105, 107–109, 119,
    146–147, 183, 201–
    202, 216, 245
  legislature of 202
  ratification of Constitution
    108
New York Times 171
New Zealand 228
Nez Perce Indians 152
Niagara, New York 96
Niagara Falls 183

Nicaragua 237
Nicholas II of Russia 203
Niña 8
Nipmuck Indians 50
Nixon, Richard M. 228, 233, 238
Nobel Peace Prize
  Theodore Roosevelt 186
"No Man's Land" 192
Nonantum Indians 50
nonviolent resistance 226
Normandy, France 218
Norsemen 3–4
North Africa 216–217
  French 218
North America 4, 6, 13–15, 16–17, 18, 29, 56, 59, 74, 151, 156, 239
  Indian tribes of 21
North American Free Trade Agreement. *See* NAFTA
North and South
  America divided 164–167
North Atlantic Treaty Organization. *See* NATO
North Carolina 18, 59–60, 81, 92, 100, 103, 107, 120, 138–139, 166
  ratification of Constitution 109
Northeast Passage 27
North Korea 208, 214–215, 220–221, 227–228
North Pole 27
North Pole, discovery of 187
North Vietnam 227, 232
Northwest Passage 29
Northwest Territory 121, 123, 158
Norway 3–4, 205, 216
Notes of Debates in the Federal Convention of 1787 111
Nova Scotia 13–14
nuclear weapons 225
nurses
  Red Cross 182, 191

O

Oakman, Congressman Charles (MI) 222
Obama, Barack H. 245
observation balloons 192
Oglethorpe, Captain James 59–61
Ohio 99, 121–123, 131, 136, 173, 183–184
Ohio River 85–86, 97, 121–123, 133, 160

oil
  embargo 229
  industry 236, 241
  price increases 231–232, 242
Okinawa, Japan 213
Old World 18
Omaha Beach (WWI) 218
Operation Iraqi Freedom 244
Oregon 152, 157, 206, 241
Oregon, battleship 179, 184
Oregon Territory 152–153, 157
orphanage
  Bethesda Home for Boys 63–64
Orthodox Presbyterian Church 198–199
Osama bin Laden 243
Oswald, Lee Harvey
  assassin of President Kennedy 227
Ottoman Empire 188
Oxford, England 74

P

Pacific Ocean 6, 16–17, 20, 22, 27–28, 144, 151–152, 156, 169, 172, 177–178, 184, 188, 212–213, 216–217, 224, 235
pacifism 56, 80
paddle wheels 131–132
Palace of Fine Arts
  at Panama-Pacific International Exposition (1915) 188
Palin, Sarah 245
palisade (fence) 38
Palisades 133
Palisades, New York 28
Palos, Spain 7–8, 10
Pan-American Exposition (1901) 183–184
Panama 216, 232, 236
  Isthmus of 16
  Railway 184
  Republic of 184
Panama-Pacific International Exposition (1915) 188
Panama Canal 184–189
  opening of (1914) 186
  return control of (1999) 232
pardons, presidential 239
Paris 190, 240
Parker, Captain John 88
Parker, Samuel 152
Parliament 74
  Long 50

pastors
  Second Great Awakening 112
Patent Office, United States 146, 149
Patriot Act, USA 243
Patriots 80
Patton, General George S. 219
Patuxet 36
Paul, Apostle 247
Peace Corps 225
"peacekeeping" missions 240
peanuts 171
Pearl Harbor (Hawaiian Islands) 206, 210, 217
Peary, Commander Robert E. 187
Peggy Stewart, ship 87
peninsula
  of Korea 214
Penn, Admiral William
  father of William Penn 55
Penn, William 55–58, 69, 80
Pennsylvania 43–45, 55–58, 74, 77, 80, 90–91, 96–97, 100, 121, 131, 134, 167, 222–223, 243
  ratification of Constitution 108
Pennsylvania Gazette 69, 72
Pensacola, Florida 17
Pentagon 243
Peoria, Illinois 193
Perot, Ross 237–238
perpetual Union of the States
  Abraham Lincoln on 166
persecution
  of Quakers 56
Pershing, General John "Black Jack" 190, 194–195, 200, 216
Petrograd, Russia 203
Philadelphia, Pennsylvania 56, 69–75, 82, 87–88, 91, 94, 105, 132, 172, 174
Philadelphia Baptist Association 76
Philip, King
  a.k.a. Metacomet, son of Massasoit 49–54
Philippine-American War 183
Philippine Republic, First 183
Philippines 177–179, 181–183, 206, 208–211, 216–217
phonograph
  invention of 172, 174

"Pied Piper of Saipan".
  See Guy Gabaldon
Pilgrim's Progress 159
Pilgrims 35–40, 41, 121
Pinta 8
Pittsburgh, Pennsylvania 97, 121, 133
plantations 126, 128, 164, 170
  sugar and tobacco 178
Pledge of Allegiance 222
Plymouth, Massachusetts 36, 46, 49
Plymouth Colony 36–40, 41, 50–51
  Swansea settlement 51
Plymouth Rock 36
Pocahontas 22–23
poison gas 192
Poland 205, 207, 210, 216, 223
politics
  conservative 233, 237, 239
  liberal 239, 245
  moderate 239
pollution 245
Ponce de León 16–17
Port Conway, Virginia 104
Portland, Maine 146
Portsmouth, New Hampshire 181
Portugal 6–7, 14
Portuguese 231
post offices 190
potatoes 18–19
Potomac River 41–42, 83, 173
Powhatan, Chief 22
Powhatan Confederacy 22
Praying Indians 50
  John Alderman 53
  John Sassamon 50
preaching
  outdoors 64
  Whitefield's style of 63
prejudice 171
Presbyterians 196–199, 222
  James McGready 113
  John Witherspoon 76–79
  Orthodox Presbyterian Church 198–199
  Presbyterian Church USA 198–199
  Synod of New York and Philadelphia 76
Presidential Commission on the Status of Women (1961) 226
Presidential Unit Citations
  Japanese-American soldiers 206

President of the Confederate States of America
Jefferson Davis as 164
President of the Republic of Texas
Sam Houston as 153, 157
President of the United States
George Washington as (1st) 82, 94–95, 109, 121–123
John Adams as (2nd) 242
Thomas Jefferson as (3rd) 110, 128–130
James Madison as (4th) 110–111
John Quincy Adams as (6th) 241, 242
Andrew Jackson as (7th) 144–145, 153, 241
William Henry Harrison as (9th) 137
Abraham Lincoln as (16th) 163–168, 181
Rutherford B. Hayes as (19th) 241
Benjamin Harrison as (23rd) 241
William McKinley as (25th) 177–179, 183, 186–187
Theodore Roosevelt as (26th) 170–171, 177, 183–187, 201, 238
Howard Taft as (27th) 187
Woodrow Wilson as (28th) 185, 188–191, 202
Warren G. Harding as (29th) 200, 202
Calvin Coolidge as (30th) 171, 200–201
Herbert Hoover as (31st) 201–202
Franklin D. Roosevelt as (32nd) 95, 171, 201–207, 210, 213, 219, 222, 233, 238
Harry S. Truman as (33rd) 213, 215, 221–222, 224–225
Dwight D. Eisenhower as (34th) 221–225, 230, 233
John F. Kennedy as (35th) 186, 223, 224–230, 232, 238
Lyndon B. Johnson as (36th) 223, 225, 227–228, 232–233
Richard M. Nixon as (37th) 228–229, 233, 238
Gerald Ford as (38th) 229, 231, 234, 237
James E. "Jimmy" Carter as (39th) 231–232, 234, 237
Ronald Reagan as (40th) 233–237, 248
George H. W. Bush as (41st) 224, 235–240
William J. "Bill" Clinton as (42nd) 238–241, 245, 248
George W. Bush as (43rd) 237, 241–245
Barack H. Obama as (44th) 245
Electoral College's selection of 241
impeachment of 239
office of 106
Press Club 225
Prince of Peace 243
Princeton Theological Seminary 196–199
Princeton University 77, 104
printing press 189
prisoners of war
Lt. Hobson and his men 180
Protestants 41–44, 80
French 57
German 60
protest movement, 1960s 233
Proverbs 22:29 69
Providence, Rhode Island 47
public library
first in Philadelphia 73, 75
public schools
prayer in 246
quality of 237
Pueblo, technical research ship 227
Puerto Rico 177, 181–183
pumpkins 135
Puritans 43, 46–47, 79
Purple Heart 208
Japanese-American soldiers 206
Purple Heart Battalion 206
Putnam, Rufus 121–122

Q

Quakers 55–58, 69, 71, 80

R

racial
discrimination 222
reconciliation 171
radio broadcasting 200
railroads 131, 169, 172
electric railroad car 173
Panama Railway 184
South's rail system 164
steam 144–145
Raleigh, Sir Walter 18–19
Randolph, Edmund 107
ratification
of the Constitution 107–110
Ray, James Earl
assassin of Dr. King 226
Re-Thinking Missions
by William Ernest Hocking 198
Read, Deborah
wife of Benjamin Franklin 71
Reagan, John H. 165
Reagan, Ronald 233–237, 248
assassination attempt on 234
reapers
McCormick 145–146, 150
"record player". *See* phonograph
Red Cross 181–182, 191. *See also* American Red Cross Society
International Committee of 181
Red River, Kentucky 113
Red Sea 239
"Red Stick" Creek Indians 141–142
refined revivalist. *See* Moody, Dwight Lyman
religious liberty 46–48, 55, 76, 80
Religious Right
rise of 237
religious toleration 44–45, 55
law 43
Remembrance Day 195
repentance
in the camp meetings 113
Republican party 234, 236, 245
Republic of Panama 184
Republic of Texas 153
resurrection of Christ 197, 199
Revere, Paul 88
revivals 247
calm 114–115, 174
First Great Awakening 62–65, 72, 77
Second Great Awakening 112–116
Reynolds's militia 161
Rhode Island 38, 40, 46–48, 50, 53, 92, 105, 107, 125, 151, 157
ratification of Constitution 109
Richmond, Virginia 128, 167
Ridgeway, General Matthew 208, 213
right
to a speedy trial by jury 110
to bear arms 110
to vote restricted 44
Roanoke Island, North Carolina 18
Roberts, David 193
Robertson, James 120–121
Robinson Crusoe 159
Rocky Mountains 129
Roe v. Wade decision (1973) 226
Roman Catholic. *See* Catholics
Rommel, Field Marshal Erwin Johannes Eugen 217
Roosevelt, Franklin D. 95, 171, 200–207, 210, 213, 219, 233
Roosevelt, Theodore 170, 177–187, 201, 238
"Rough Riders"
Colonel Roosevelt's 180
Rumania 216
Russia 156, 186, 188, 203, 207, 210, 214
Russian Civil War 203

S

Sacramento, California 154
Sacramento River 154
Saipan, Northern Mariana Islands 209
Salem, Massachusetts 46
Salvation Army 246
Lassies 191
Samoset 37
Sampson, Rear Admiral William T. 179–180
Samuel de Champlain 36
San Antonio, Texas 153, 216
San Domingo 11
San Francisco 156, 172, 179, 184, 188
San Juan Heights 180
Sankey, Ira 174
San Salvador 10
Santa Maria 8
Santiago, Cuba 179–181
Battle of 180–181
Santo Domingo 182
Sarajevo, Bosnia 188
Saratoga, New York 91, 122
Sassamon, John 50
satellites
communications 230
Sputnik I and *Sputnik II* 229
Saudi Arabia 236, 240
Savannah, Georgia 59, 61, 69, 125, 165
Savannah River 59

scandals
    Clinton administration 239
Schlafly, Phyllis Stewart 226
Schley, Commodore Winfield
    Scott 179–181
Schwarzkopf, Jr., General H.
    Norman 236
science
    and the Bible 196–199
Scotland 77
Scottish
    "Red Eagle," half 141
scow, paddle wheel 131
Screen Actors Guild
    Reagan as president of 233
Scrooby, England 35
Second Great Awakening
    112–116
Secretary of
    Agriculture 107
    Commerce 107
    Defense 107
    Education 107
    Energy 107
    Health and Human Services
        107
    Housing and Urban Devel-
        opment 107
    Interior 107
    Labor 107
    State 107
        George Marshall as 221
        James Madison as 110
    the Treasury 107
    Transportation 107
    Veterans Affairs 107
segregation 170
Seminole Indians 144
Senate 80, 106–107, 109,
        149, 179, 224, 239, 245
Seoul, Korea 215
September 11 attack 242–
        243, 244, 248
Serbia 188, 240
Serbian nationalists 188
Sevier, John 120–121
sewing machine 146–147
Shafter, General William Rufus
        180
Shawnee Indians 135–137
Shepard, Jr., Alan 230
Sherman, Roger 79
ships
    Santa Maria, Pinta, and
        Niña 8
    Viking 3–5
Sicily, Italy 217–218
Sigsbee, Capt. Charles D. 178
silk 7, 60
silver 169
Sims, Admiral William
        Sowden 189

Skymaster, Douglas C-54 214
slavery 44, 163, 167, 170–
        171, 245
    communist rule as 204
    freedom granted to slaves
        168
    Jefferson's slaves 128
    John Smith 20
    slave states 165–167
smallpox 140–141
Smith, Captain John 20–26,
        27, 36
    Father of Virginia 22–23
Social Security 242
Society of Friends 55
Solomon Islands 224
Somalia 236, 239
Song of Hiawatha, The 21
Sons of Liberty 31
South America 6, 11, 15, 21,
        151, 177, 179, 184–185
South Carolina 59–60, 62,
        91–92, 92, 121, 138–
        140, 164, 166, 168
    ratification of Constitution
        108
South Dakota 187
Southeast Asia 7, 210, 228
Southern Christian Leadership
        Conference 226
South Korea 208, 214–215,
        223
    invasion of 221
South Vietnam 227–228,
        231–232
Soviet Union 203–207, 210,
        213–214, 216–221,
        223, 227, 231,
        235–237
    dissolution of 236–237
space program (U.S.)
        229–230
space shuttle 230
Spain 7, 10–12, 14, 16–17,
        103, 111, 144–145,
        177–184, 204, 240
Spaniards 59–60
Spanish-American War
        178–184, 190, 208
Spanish Civil War 204
Spanish Louisiana 103
Spencer County, Indiana 158
Spice Islands 13
spices 7
Spirit of St. Louis, plane 201
Springfield, Illinois 161, 163
Springfield, Massachusetts 51
Sputnik I and *II*
    Russian satellites 223, 229
Squanto 37–38

St. Andrews, Scotland 74
St. Augustine, Florida 17, 61
St. Charles, Missouri 103
St. John's Church
    Richmond, Virginia 128
St. Lawrence
    Gulf of 14
St. Louis 98
St. Louis, Missouri 130, 131,
        150
St. Mary's, Maryland 42, 44
St. Mary's University
    of San Antonio, Texas 216
St. Petersburg, Russia 203
Stalin, Joseph 203–204, 206,
        221, 223
Stalingrad, Battle of 217
Stalingrad, Russia 219
stamps
    Thrift Stamps 190
    War Savings Stamps 190
Standish, Captain Miles
        35–40, 41
Star-Spangled Banner, The
        126–127
Stars and Stripes
    official newspaper of the
        U.S. Armed Forces 219
Stars and Stripes, U.S. flag
        94, 99, 182
states' rights 105
    Jefferson Davis on 166
states, addition of new 119
Statue of Liberty 31
Status of Women (1961)
    Presidential Commission on
        226
steamboats
    invention of 132–134
    paddle wheels push 173
steam shovels 185, 189
Stephens, Alexander 165
stereos 229
stock market
    Crash of 1929 201
Stowe, Harriet Beecher 168
Stuart, General J.E.B. 167
submarines
    German 189, 191, 206, 217
    Japanese 217
    United States 213
Sudan 240
sugar 178
Sullivan, General John 96
Sumter, Fort 166
Supreme Allied Commander
    Douglas MacArthur 213
    Dwight D. Eisenhower
        (Europe) 218
    Dwight D. Eisenhower
        (NATO) 221

Supreme Commander of UN
    Forces
    General Douglas MacArthur
        as 214
Supreme Court 106, 202,
        225–226, 241, 246
Sutter, Captain Johann Augus-
        tus 154–157
    Sutter's Fort 154
    Sutter's Mill 154–155, 157
Swan, Sir Joseph W. 173
Swansea, Massachusetts 51
Sweden 3–4
sweet potatoes 171
Switzerland 154, 194
Syria 227, 229

T

Taft, Howard 187
Taiwan (Republic of China)
        214, 221, 232
Taliban fighters 243
tanks 193, 209
    British Mark I 193
Tanzania 240
tariff laws 111
Tarleton, Sir Banastre
    known as "Butcher Tarleton"
        138–139
tax collectors 120
tea 87, 151
tear gas 209
Tecumseh, Chief 135–137,
        141
telegraph 172, 183
    invention of 148–150
telephone 150
    invention of 171–172, 174
    lines 131
    wireless 172
television
    color 229
    Ronald Reagan worked in
        233
Teller Resolution 183
Tempelhof Airport 214
Ten Commandments
    and public schools 246
Tennessee 100–101, 103,
        120–121, 123, 131,
        141–142, 144, 152–
        153, 157, 166, 191
Tenskwatawa, called the
        "Prophet"
    brother of Tecumseh
        135–137
Tenth Amendment 110
10th Mountain Division 243
Ten Years' War
    between Spain and Cuba 177

territorial expansion
 Japanese, 1930s and 1940s 204
terrorism
 international 245
 Middle Eastern 235
 on American soil 242–243, 248
terrorist activities 228
 attacks on the United States 242–243
 Islamic 235, 240
 September 11, 2001 242
Tesla, Nikola 183
Tet Offensive
 Vietnam War 228
Texas 142, 153–157, 164, 208, 216, 236, 241
Texas Rangers, baseball 241
Texas War for Independence 153
Thames River 72
Thanksgiving
 First, at Plymouth 37–38
Theological Institute of Connecticut 115
Thiepval Ridge, France 193
Thirteenth Amendment 167
Thrift Stamps 190
Ticonderoga, Fort 119
Tilden, Samuel 241
Time magazine 170
I Timothy 2:1-2 247
Tippecanoe, Battle of 135–137
Tippecanoe River 135–137
tobacco 18–19, 21, 44, 102, 178
Todd, Dolley Payne 110
Tojo, Hideki (Japan) 204–205
Toombs, Robert 165
torpedo 132
total depravity of man 243
tractors
 "Caterpillar Tractor" 193
traditional moral values 239
traitor
 Benedict Arnold as 92
Travis, Colonel William Barret 153
trench warfare 192–194
Trenton, New Jersey 90–91
Trinity Church, New York City 134
Truman, Harry S. 213, 215, 221, 224–225
Tryon, William 120
Tsar Nicholas II of Russia 203
Tudman, Franjo 240
Tunisia
 French 217

turkeys 14, 18, 37
Turks 20
Tuskegee Institute 170–171
 Agriculture Department 171
Twelfth Amendment 241
Twenty-seventh Amendment 111
Twenty-sixth Amendment 229

U

Uncle Tom's Cabin 168
"under God"
 added to Pledge of Allegiance 222
unemployment 234
 during Great Depression 201–202
Union. *See* Chapter 30, Abraham Lincoln
Union of Soviet Socialist Republics. *See* Soviet Union
United Kingdom. *See* Britain
United Nations 207, 214–215, 220, 236, 244
United States 11, 15, 17, 19, 24, 31, 78, 82, 90–91, 94–95, 109, 113, 119, 121, 129, 131, 134, 137, 142, 144, 150, 153–156, 172–174, 181, 186, 188–190, 200, 208, 210, 214, 216–219, 221, 224–225, 239–240, 247–248
 Christian heritage of 246
 independence from England 57
 peace treaty with England 61
United States Constitution. *See* Constitution of the United States
United States Military Academy 208–209, 216
University of Arkansas 238
University of New York 148
University of Oxford 74
University of Pennsylvania 73
University of St. Andrews 74
University of Virginia 111

V

Vail, Alfred Lewis 148–150
Valladolid, Spain 182
Valley Forge, Pennsylvania 91
Valley of Virginia 84
values
 traditional moral 239
Vancouver Island 151

Vandalia, Illinois 163
Venezuela 186
Venice, Italy 7, 13, 14
Vera Cruz Expedition 208
Vermont 40, 119, 121, 123
Vermont Republic 119
Vespucci, Amerigo 15
veterans
 of War for Independence 121
 World War I 209
Veterans Day 195
veto
 power of 106
Vice President of the Confederate States
 Alexander Stephens as 165
Vice President of the United States
 Albert Gore as 241
 Calvin Coolidge as 200
 George H. W. Bush as 236
 Gerald Ford as 229, 231
 John Adams as 109
 Lyndon B. Johnson as 227, 232
 office of 106–107
 Spiro Agnew as 231
 Theodore Roosevelt as 183
Vicksburg, Mississippi 167
Vietnam 206, 224, 227–229, 232
Vietnam War 211, 227–229, 238, 245
Vigo, Francis 98
Vikings 3–4
Vincennes, Indiana 96, 98–99
Vinland 4
violence 237
virgin birth of Christ 197, 199
Virginia 20–26, 27, 36, 41, 43–45, 59, 79, 82, 85–86, 92–93, 97, 99, 104–105, 107–111, 119, 145, 166–168, 170
 Colony 18–26
 Mother of Presidents 25
 ratification of Constitution 108
Virginia Convention of 1776 104
Von Braun, Werner 230

W

Wabash River 98
Wahunsenacawh. *See* Powhatan, Chief
Wainwright, Commander Richard 181

Waldseemüller, Martin 15
Walker, LeRoy Pope 165
Wallace, George 229
Wampanoag Indians 37, 49–51
Wamsutta, Chief
 son of Massasoit 49
War Between the States 153–154, 166–168, 170, 174, 190, 208
War for American Independence 25–26, 31, 40, 48, 57, 60–61, 65, 74–76, 79–81, 82, 94, 96–97, 109, 112, 115, 119, 121–122, 124–126, 128, 140, 151, 156, 165
War for Independence, Texas 153
War of 1812 110–111, 137
War of Jenkins' Ear 61
War on Poverty
 Lyndon Johnson's 227
War on Terror 243–244
War Savings Stamps 190
"War to End All Wars".
 See World War I
Washington, Booker T. 170
Washington, Colonel William 139–140
Washington, D.C. 137, 149, 173, 185, 190, 195, 200, 209, 226, 229, 238, 241–242, 243
Washington, George 25, 26, 31, 74, 79, 82–96, 105, 109–110, 121–122, 123, 128, 140, 187
 as Father of His Country 109
Washington, Lawrence
 eldest brother of George 83
Washington National Airport 225
Washington State 152, 157, 206
Watauga, Fort 121
Watauga Association laws 120
Watauga River 120–121
Watergate Affair 229, 231–232
Watson, Thomas Augustus 172
Watts, Isaac
 hymnals 77
Waxhaws region 138
Wayne, General Anthony 123, 136
weapons of mass destruction 244–245

Weatherford, William "Red Eagle" 141
welfare 202, 234, 246
Wesley, John and Charles 80–81
West Beirut, Lebanon 235
West Berlin, Germany 214, 224
Westboro, Massachusetts 124, 126
Western Allies 214
Western Europe 214, 221
Western Front
  World War I 192–193
West Indies 10, 13, 16, 21, 93, 177
Westminster Theological Seminary 197, 199
West Point 92. *See* United States Military Academy
West Virginia 43
West Virginia, battleship 210
Weymouth, Massachusetts 38
wheat 145, 150
Wheeler, General Joseph 180–181
Whiskey Rebellion 95

Whitefield, George 59, 62–65, 72–73, 77, 247
White House
  President Wilson opened Panama Canal from 185
  security problems 239
Whitman, Marcus 152
Whitney, Eli 124–127
Whitneyville, Connecticut 126
wigwams 21, 51, 52, 56, 135, 153
  King Philip's 49
  Massasoit's 47
  Tecumseh and Creek 141
Wilderness Road 101, 103
Wild West 116
William III, Prince of Orange 44
Williams, Roger 46–48
Williamsburg, Virginia 24
"Willie and Joe"
  cartoon characters 219
Wilson, Woodrow 185, 188–191, 202
Windsor Castle 42, 57
Winthrop, Governor John 39–40, 46, 47
Wisconsin 131

Witherspoon, John 76–79, 81, 247
Word of God. *See* Bible
Works Progress Administration 202
World's Columbian Exposition 169–170
World's Fair
  Centennial Exposition (1876) 172
  Pan-American Exposition (1901) 183
  Panama-Pacific International Exposition (1915) 188–189
  World's Columbian Exposition (1893) 169–170
World Trade Center 240–242
World War I 186, 188–195, 200, 203, 208–209, 215
World War II 183, 186, 188, 202–203, 205–209, 214–215, 224–225, 227, 233, 235–236, 238, 248
  Douglas MacArthur 210–211
  Dwight D. Eisenhower 216–220

Wright, Orville and Wilbur 173, 192, 201
Wyoming 103, 152

Y

Yale College 124, 126, 148
Yale University 236, 238, 241
Yalta, Ukraine 206
Yalta Conference 206
Year of the Evangelical 237
yellow fever 184
Yellowstone River 103
Yemen 240
York, Alvin 191
Yorktown, Virginia 76, 92–93
Yugoslavia 216, 221, 240

Z

Zabol Province, Afghanistan 243
Zeppelins (German) 192
Zhukov, Marshal Georgy (Soviet Union) 219
Zinzendorf, Count Nicholas Ludwig von 81